OUT OF BOUNDS

OUT OF BOUNDS

WHEN PARENTS CROSS THE LINE IN THE PLAYER-COACH RELATIONSHIP AND OTHER BASKETBALL EXPERIENCES

DARREN AULT

THE PAPER HOUSE
PUBLISHING

Published by The Paper House
www.thepaperhousebooks.com

Printed in the USA

CONTENTS

REFLECTION

"It is not the critic who counts; not the man who points out how the strong man stumbles, or where the doer of deeds could have done them better. The credit belongs to the man who is actually in the arena, whose face is marred by dust and sweat and blood; who strives valiantly; who errs, who comes short again and again, because there is no effort without error and shortcoming; but who does actually strive to do the deeds; who knows great enthusiasms, the great devotions; who spends himself in a worthy cause; who at the best knows in the end the triumph of high achievement, and who at the worst, if he fails, at least fails while daring greatly, so that his place shall never be with those cold and timid souls who neither know victory nor defeat."

Theodore Roosevelt

IN APPRECIATION

Being a coach at any level requires a strong commitment of time and effort. Those elements are not unique to the coach but often involve the family and require much personal sacrifice. To that end, I owe a tremendous gratitude to my wife, who has been extremely patient and supportive since I started coaching basketball in 1989. I finished coaching 33 years later. My wife would often jest about my being married to basketball, and I understand why. However, her patience and willingness to give me the grace to pursue my passion were truly a gift and something I am eternally grateful for. I am also grateful for the opportunity to coach all three of my children. Our relationship on the court was solid, which enhanced our relationship at home and in life.

As I extend my gratitude to my family, I also feel compelled to apologize. I am sorry for the times when they were fans of the game, watching one of my teams play, but having to listen to the few parents who sat in the stands and berated me, my style of coaching, or the players who were trying to function as a team on the floor. Too many times, my wife and children had to listen as other "adults" took the opportunity to verbally and very publicly flog me or my players. It should be noted that these incidents were much more the exception rather than the rule. I should also point out that some of these incidents turned out just fine in the end. However, it is the sad reality that some people feel free to say and do whatever they want, no matter how unfair or inappropriate. Those indiscretions served as the foundation for this book.

I also want to acknowledge all the great coaches I have worked with and for. As an assistant coach at the Naval Academy Prep School, St. John Vianney High School, the Middletown Hotshots, and the JSE Elites. I learned from some great basketball minds, excellent coaches, and even better people. As the head coach at Holy Family School, Mater Dei High School, the Jersey Shore Wildcats, the Middletown Hotshots, the JSE Elite, and Holmdel High School, I had the pleasure of working with great assistant coaches who were all very capable of leading on their own. I learned as much from them as they ever did from me. It was a pleasure to serve alongside each of you.

Finally, I want to thank all the parents I have encountered over my coaching career. For the vast majority, I have enjoyed wonderful experiences in the relationship we shared. I sincerely hope I was able to support your efforts in raising your son or daughter through the game of basketball and the coach-player relationship. I am honored and humbled that many of my relationships with players still thrive today. I am also thankful, albeit unhappy, for the negative encounters with a few misguided parents. At worst, they indicated the darker side of human nature. At best, they were learning experiences that I have grown from.

"To play the game is good, to win the game is great, to love the game is greatest of all."

Plaque that was hung in the lobby of the Philadelphia Palestra.

ONE
START WITH THE END IN MIND

JANUARY 11, 2022, I was in my fourth year as the head coach at Holmdel High School in New Jersey, my 33rd year of coaching overall. We were heading into our eighth game of the season on a bit of a roll with a three-game win streak, having recently beaten a division rival and a top 10 team in the Shore Conference. The team was heading in the right direction, and there was a lot of positive energy going into tonight's game against perennial powerhouse Red Bank Catholic, ranked third in the Shore Conference, the power conference for high school girls basketball in New Jersey, and 9th in the state. We were always ramped up to play RBC because they were one of the measuring sticks for program success. Beat them, and you put one in the books for program memories.

What helped make this game so promising was the momentum we had built going into it and the fact that we were still living high off our victory over RBC the year before. Back in our gym a year later, we faced a bigger, stronger team fueled with a vengeance. RBC always had multiple future Division I players in their lineup. This year was no different; it showcased a 6' 1" swing that had committed to Tennessee and a 6' 5" center bound for Boston College. Both players were in their senior year and had the bitter taste of defeat lingering from the previous season.

My team was excellent and on a mission to break into the local and state rankings. We had two senior captains who "grew up" in my program, having been with me since their freshman year. Touting a DI recruit of our own, we had a 6' swing committed to Colgate. My other captain was a 6' 1" center by default but had tremendous abilities still being developed as an outside shooter, with a quick first step should a defender overplay the shot. She was committed to Emory, maturing in talent and confidence with every game. Rounding out a talented starting five: a junior forward who was a terrific player with tremendous passion for the game, a scorer's mentality, and a sweet outside shot, a talented junior point guard with a smaller frame but the heart of a lion, and a raw but very talented sophomore who was fast and fearless.

As great as I felt about my team and the development of our program, I knew we would be up against it in this game. Nobody gave us a chance the previous year, but we pulled it off. Expectations were different for us this year, but most people still felt RBC was the better team and were motivated to exact revenge. I knew this was a pivotal moment in our early season. We had overcome some early hiccups and were playing much better. Our three-game win streak felt good. More importantly, the team chemistry felt great in the locker room and on the court. We were starting to click, so this game was significant in terms of keeping the ball rolling. I watched a lot of film during the week in preparation for the rematch with RBC, including our game from last year. I was looking for what worked, areas where we would need to adjust, tendencies in our opponent, and weaknesses to attack. I started to realize that there was a consistent pattern in the way their big played defense. She was a traditional center . . . a strong-bodied paint protector who was still learning post-footwork and improving with every game. She was a handful for us and a tough matchup. Any action we had going downhill toward the basket would be a challenge due to her paint presence.

As I watched film, it became more and more apparent that her ability, or willingness to defend, did not extend past the foul line. She often matched up to the opponent's big or the least offensively threatening player, allowing minimal defensive movement. The limited range of her defense would be our point of attack.

Looking at last year's game and studying the matchups, I assumed that RBC's center would be matched up to my center, based on the hunch that my opponent would see her as the "slowest" and "least threatening" from an offensive standpoint, allowing his big to prowl the paint and mid-range areas. I knew that would be a mistake, as my player had started to come into her own this year. Our offenses had more movement and good, unselfish screen action. Inspired by a constantly improving offensive game, outside and inside, my center had taken great strides in maturity, confidence, and leadership. She also had a knack for playing her best against larger, more physically dominating opponents. In practices and film sessions leading up to the big game, we had several conversations around the defensive tendencies, our offensive movement, and where and when to strike. One of our screening series, run out of the UCLA offense, often brought my big to the three-point arc, where she could be very effective. We were going to work toward pulling RBC's center out and either giving us a good look from outside or opening driving lines for attack.

As the teams warmed up, there was a large crowd and a nervous energy in the gym. Our fans were ready to pull off another surprise win against the mighty Caseys. RBC players and fans were anxious to prove last year was a fluke and how bad this bigger, stronger RBC team would beat Holmdel. The same people were also nervous because Holmdel had been steadily improving every year and had finished in the Top 10 of the Shore Conference the previous year, bolstered by the fact that we had beaten RBC last season.

The teams went through normal warm-ups. Both teams looked sharp and confident. In our last huddle, before letting the players take the floor, I reminded the team of our keynotes from the scout and the hard work they had put into preparing for this game and reassured them of the power in our team. I then looked directly at my center and reminded her that she has always had great success defensively against more prominent players. Now was her time to let it rip offensively. Work hard through our offensive sequences and, when curling off outside screens, be shot-ready and pull the trigger. I reminded her that RBC's big will not follow her beyond the foul line. As she looked back at me, there was nothing but fire, grit, and determination in her eyes. As a senior captain, she was ready to lead in word and action. Her teammates were excited, confident, and eager to play well. We were ready for tip-off.

The game couldn't have started any better. My team played the scout beautifully on both ends of the court. On one of our early offensive possessions, my center curled off a series of screens, bringing her to a shot-ready position outside the 3-point arc. As expected, RBC's big was the matchup, and she stopped short of a closeout to the spot. It was an easy pull off the incoming pass and a splash for three. The Holmdel fans erupted as my team sprinted back to defend the home basket. Our early defense was stingy and created a quick offensive opportunity. In an eerily similar sequence, my big hits for another 3-point shot, then added another on the next possession. In the blink of an eye, she had gone 3-for-3 from beyond the arc, and our team was on a roll. Early momentum favored us, prompting a quick timeout from the RBC bench.

Our team sprinted to the bench with palpable exuberance, that feeling of watching a plan come together. The demeanor during the timeout was one of focused intensity. All eyes and ears were on me as we discussed anticipated adjustments from the other team. I congratulated my center on having the hot hand and encouraged her to continue attacking. I expected their big would be forced to close out more aggressively, bringing her out of her defensive comfort zone and opening driving lanes. My instructions were simply to give a shot fake, rip past the lunging defender, attack the basket, and finish. Our final encouragement to the team before breaking the huddle was to "stay connected to the vine." This was a phrase I pulled from reading Jay Wright's book *Attitude*. Coach Wright was sharing a team moment when Father Rob, the team chaplain, quoted a parable from the Bible. "Jesus used a parable about how leaves are strong when connected to the vine, but when they break off and get loose, they fly in the wind and lose their strength." I adopted the phrase "stay connected to the vine" before the season and had often referred to it as our team mantra. In the moment of this game, with all our early success, the phrase served as a reminder to keep working together as a team and to find our strength by staying connected to the vine.

We broke the huddle and picked up right where we left off. Our defense was swarming. Our offense was confident and aggressive. We were not backing down from this powerhouse opponent. After a couple of exchanges, my team worked the ball through our offense, continuing to execute with patience and precision. As the ball swung from side to side, my center began to work her way out to the perimeter through another series of screens and cuts. RBC's big began to move more aggressively, fighting through screens and trying to position for defense of the arc. As my player received the ball in a shot-ready position, the 6' 5" defender closed out high and hard in an effort to alter her shot. Instead, a beautifully executed ball fake sent the closing defender up, and my center ripped by left to attack the basket, finishing and adding to an already incredible 1st quarter performance. As the buzzer rang to close out the quarter, we were up 19-15 and saw a lot of frustration going to the opponent's bench. My senior captain finished the quarter with 11 points and was playing tremendous defense on the big for RBC.

The teams battled to a 30-29 halftime score, with RBC on top. We had sustained a high level of play on both ends of the court, frustrating our opponents with a tough defense and getting contributions from everybody. The team was fired up and focused during our halftime locker room visit. I didn't have to say much. We ran through some anticipated adjustments from RBC, the captains offered motivation to their teammates, and we headed back out to the court on an absolute mission.

The back-and-forth contest continued throughout the third quarter. When it ended, we came to the bench with a two-point deficit. My team continued to execute well against RBC's center. Her minutes were challenged because of the speed and movement of my team. The coach had to work subs to keep up with our tenacity and provide a countermeasure to our offensive successes. On our defensive side of the floor, my center was adding to an already amazing game, further frustrating the RBC center and minimizing any offensive opportunities.

If my defender was caught exposed, the rotating help provided support perfectly. The final box score would show us effective, holding the Boston College recruit to just four points. Eventually, the depth of weapons on the RBC roster began to impact the game. The center for RBC had two younger sisters who played on the team. While not as physically powerful and younger in the game, they were both very talented players. One of them provided an offensive spark and a more complicated match-up for us, as she had a good mixture of size, strength, and speed. While her older sister was stymied offensively, she contributed 16 points to the game and filled the void. The Tennessee recruit hit for a deep three to give RBC a seven point lead late in the fourth quarter. We got to a point in the game where the clock was no longer our friend, and RBC was all too willing to slow down offensively to eat up time. I called a timeout and instructed my team to be aggressive, going after steals and fouling intentionally when playing the ball. Obviously, the play here is to target less effective free-throw shooters, stop the clock, hope for misses, and gain extra possessions. Our problem was that RBC was very effective from the line. In fact, both teams shot very well from the free-throw line that night, netting 38 out of 43 attempts. Unfortunately for us, during our late fourth-quarter efforts, RBC went 12 for 12 from the line and didn't give us the wiggle room we were looking for. We ended up losing a hard-fought game by 9 points.

I headed to the locker room, frustrated that we had lost, but that feeling was quickly surpassed by my pride in how my team played. With the momentum we brought into the game, it was essential for us to play well against a dominant opponent. The girls did that and much more. The bond between the girls and the team chemistry was forged that night. I knew we had something special in this team when preparing for the season, and I felt it come together in the RBC game, even in the loss. The mood was somber as I entered the locker room to address the girls in our post-game. I didn't want that to be the way we left the gym or negatively impact what I saw as the noticeable improvements in our team play. I acknowledged the loss, and the feelings around it, but quickly pivoted to the positive aspects and the lessons offered in defeat. We played very well. The girls executed the scout to near perfection. Even in a loss, we made a statement to the rest of the conference and the state that Holmdel was a force to be reckoned with. I encouraged the girls to rest up and be ready for practice tomorrow. Our focus now needed to move to our two upcoming games, the next against Raritan, a lesser division opponent but one we couldn't afford to take lightly. That game needed to be a demonstration of our continued growth. More importantly, we played Ewing on Saturday, another Top 20 team in the state. I told the girls we would continue to build together and, "When we beat Ewing on Saturday, we will break into the Top 20 in New Jersey." The girls erupted with cheer. We gathered in the center of the locker room, where I encouraged them again to stay connected to the vine. As was our custom, we huddled up, joined hands, and ended with "Together."

Those proved to be my last words to the girls and the last words I would ever utter as a coach. The next day, Holmdel High School suspended me indefinitely.

TWO
BEGINNINGS

I ADMIT I was spoiled by my introductory years as a basketball coach in 1989, working as an assistant at the Naval Academy Preparatory School (NAPS) in Newport, RI. Most of the "boys" on the team were 18-20 years old and were just a few years younger than I was at the ripe old age of 23 during my first season as the assistant coach. However, age was never an issue because I had already graduated from the US Naval Academy, and they were working hard to get there. I was an Ensign in the Navy, and they had just enlisted to begin their enrollment in school. The established hierarchy made me older and more experienced than the reality of our age. I had the distinct pleasure of being an assistant coach at NAPS for four years. Working with the young men in fine-tuning their goals and ambitions on and off the court was an absolute pleasure.

I was spoiled because we were handed a group of hard-working, self-motivated individuals every year. One year, we had as many as 10 recruits for the Naval Academy. The following year, we only had three. No matter what, all of the players were good people first. I had the opportunity to learn a lot about these young men and help mold and shape them in preparation for the challenges that were waiting for them in Annapolis. It was a pure player-coach relationship, and we learned much from each other. There was never any interference, only support from the parents. Heaven!

The coaching staff had ample opportunity to interact with parents as they attended games throughout the Northeast. All those interactions were polite and supportive. There was genuine respect between the parent and the coach. Their demeanor at games was pleasant. Their expectations were tempered by the joy of getting to watch their sons play a game, affording the players an escape from the everyday rigors of prep school. We shared handshakes, hugs, joys, and frustrations with parents throughout the season. The common bond was their son and the knowledge that the coaching staff was working toward a shared goal of helping them become better men.

The mission of the Naval Academy is to develop midshipmen morally, mentally, and physically and to imbue them with the highest ideals of duty, honor, and loyalty so that they can become graduate leaders who are dedicated to a career in naval service. Those words shaped our approach when it came to coaching as well. Yes, we were strict with the team, but we were fair. The young men embraced our instruction and worked hard to be better players and better people. Parents watched and admired the growth and development of their sons.

When I took my first job as the head coach of the boys' varsity team at Holy Family School in Hazlet, New Jersey, in 1994, I brought a similar mission. I knew I wasn't dealing with 18–20-year-old, academy-bound young men anymore. The players were now boys, 12-14 years old. However, the opportunity to help shape their moral, mental, and physical aspects remained.

THREE
THERE BY THE GRACE OF GOD

A CATHOLIC GRAMMAR school is an interesting place to work as a Methodist. Loaded with some differences in the practice of our common Christian faith, I felt there were enough commonalities where I could be effective in positively influencing the boys on the team. Having heard all about the discipline and structure of Catholic schools, Holy Family didn't seem like that much of a departure from the atmosphere at NAPS. Reverence and respect may not be part of the three R's in education, but they were prevalent in the administration led by a stern but humble Irish priest and a petite but powerful nun. This was the perfect place to continue my development as a coach.

In my first year, I had inherited a team that recorded three wins in the previous season. They were not used to structure in practice and had the run-of-the-mill during games. It was a free-for-all. They weren't used to discipline. They weren't used to working out and running. They weren't used to being accountable to their teammates, let alone their coach. Somehow, the discipline and structure from above weren't getting to the kids. Things were about to change.

At one of my first Athletic Association meetings, the question of gym time was being discussed. Trying to cut gym time between three levels of teams for boys and girls was no easy task. We also had to accommodate the needs of the cheerleading team. As a first-year head coach, I was told that I could have two nights a week, and that was it. I knew I needed more. Four hours a week wasn't enough to increase the skill levels, get through individual drills, and begin teaching the X's and O's of the game in preparation for our season. The board members were a little stunned when I asked for gym time at 7 AM on Saturdays. I believe their exact words were, "Have fun with the parents on that one."

Surprisingly, I didn't have any pushback from parents on the early morning practices. They seemed to embrace the idea. In their minds, I think this was some way of getting back at their boys for anything bad done during the week. On more than one occasion, I saw parents laughing as they pulled away from the gym, leaving their sleepy-eyed, bedhead kid with me for two hours of basketball practice. Looking back on it, I'm not sure if they were laughing at their son or me. Either way, I set off on my mission of helping prepare these boys for basketball and trying to shape game lessons into life lessons.

FOUR
THE FIRST CUT IS THE DEEPEST

THE FIRST CHALLENGE of every season was the decision on cuts. Who would make the roster, and whose hopes would be dashed? Sensitive to the fact that cuts were a delicate matter, I decided the best way to address the situation was to talk to all the boys individually on the last day of tryouts. I hoped that seeing all the boys one by one would allow for some level of anonymity and give me the chance to share areas of improvement for each of them, whether they made the team or not. This particular method worked very well, for the most part.

In my 12 years at Holy Family, I had three circumstances of player and parent interaction that provided some unique insight into individual make up. Every year, I conducted a thorough and intense three day tryout to help me determine who would be right for the team. I was especially diligent in my review of seventh graders because I coached a two-year program and certainly wanted the opportunity to shape younger players who demonstrated potential. In the first year of my tenure, an eighth grader was trying out for the team. I wasn't sure to what level he played the previous year. In watching him progress through the various drills used in tryouts and in watching him struggle with some of the basic initial plays, it was apparent that he wasn't at the same level as his peers, even the seventh graders. It was even more obvious that this young man would not go on to play in high school. With those factors in mind, my assistant coach and I decided to let him go. After our one-on-one discussion and sharing the staff's thoughts on areas for improvement, the young man and I shook hands and went our separate ways. Honestly, I was impressed with how he took the news and how he conducted himself. Decisions on cuts usually stuck with me for a couple of days until we could get into our first "real" practice of the season. Once that came and went, I didn't give much thought to my decision. In this case, I didn't think about it at all until one month later.

With a month of practice now behind us, we were in the final stages of preparation for our season opener. I'll never forget the strange feeling when, standing at the center of the gym conducting a full-court drill, a strange man walks through the doors and right toward me. He appeared lost and disregarded the kids running the drill around him. As he approached me, I asked if I could help him. He introduced himself, but his last name didn't register until he told me I had cut his son from the team. Not wanting our discussion to interfere with the practice, I blew the whistle and sent the boys on a water break. Once the floor was clear, I gave the father my undivided attention. He was angry and confused but remained civil throughout the discussion. When I offered him my assessment of his son's abilities, he offered counterarguments. Finally, wanting to get back to the practice at hand, I asked the father a straightforward question, "Sir, if this is so upsetting to you, where was this concern a month ago when the decision was first made?" With a perplexed look and not another word, the father left the gym. My question bothered me for a while that day. I wasn't trying to be a jerk to the father, but I was curious as to what triggered the will to drive to the school, interrupt a practice by marching through the middle of an active drill, and confront a coach. That was the first "run-in" with a parent and, by all measures, a very mild one.

With a few years under my belt at Holy Family, a competitive program was established, and the school's reputation restored in the league, parents and kids had grown accustomed to the process. Coaches of younger teams would encourage better performance out of their boys, pointing to the need to be at their best to make the seventh and eighth grade team. With the increased success of the program, more boys started to try out for the team. Having more people attend the tryouts was beneficial because the competition level was more intense. Unfortunately, the decision-making process as to who would make the team and who would be cut also became more intense. I filtered through the same scenario, working with my assistant to determine what players would make up the team.

Preparing the cut list for our 1997-98 season, we had a young man, a 7th grader, who was on the fence based on our criteria. I was truly torn because I saw some potential in him, but he had a questionable work ethic. He was very promising when he paired the two. When there was a clear disconnect, he looked completely out of place. We finally came to his name by calling the boys back one at a time. Even as I called his name, my assistant and I were unsure of the decision. The young boy made up our minds for us. After watching ten boys before him hustle back to hear their individual fate, then hustle back to get their stuff and depart for the day, I was shocked at what occurred next. Upon hearing his name called, the boy slowly rose from where he was seated and, even more slowly, walked to the back of the gym where my assistant and I waited. He didn't seem to care if he made the team. As coaches, we expressed our disappointment in his lack of enthusiasm. We further shared our concern over his struggles to connect potential and desire to get better. Then, we shared the truth . . . we were truly unsure of his fate until he walked back to talk to us. We then encouraged him to play township ball and work on certain game components. We also encouraged him to try out again as an eighth grader. I wasn't well prepared for what would come next.

The boy's mother was the cheerleading coach at the school and a spirited person, to say the least. She and I were friendly, often chatting at the monthly Athletic Association meetings. We would share details about home games, where the cheerleaders would come out to support the basketball teams and assist each other in coordinating the parental work schedule for home games, shared by parents of both teams. After making cuts, the next Athletic Association meeting wasn't too far around the corner. This was my first introduction to how far out of bounds parents are willing to go. I was also reminded of the saying, "You can take the girl out of the city, but you can't take the city out of the girl."

At every meeting, coaches would take turns talking about their respective teams, explaining current team status, and making any requests for uniforms, tournament entries, or fundraisers. When it came time for cheerleading news, the coach, Mom, took advantage of the time to launch an all-out verbal offensive toward me. There wasn't even a question raised in private conversation, but given the audience, all sorts of colorful expletives were thrown my way. What could have been discussed more discretely and courteously became a very heated public display. The question at the heart of her argument wasn't what her son could have done differently to make the team or what could he do to prepare for next year, but rather why, as a coach at the school, wasn't her son an automatic choice for the team. Sadly, her concern wasn't really about her son but more about why she wasn't given the proper "due" as a coach. Eventually, things calmed down on the subject. I didn't make any adjustments to the roster but stuck to my guns, reaffirming that her son had a few things to work on and that I encouraged him to try out again as an eighth grader. The mother and I learned to coexist despite the verbal barbs and hateful stares directed at me. The team went on that year to post a 24-0 record in the league and won the first league championship in school history. I don't offer that to point out how good the team was without the boy. I look at it in the opposite manner. If the boy had just demonstrated the last nod of enthusiasm and desire, he would have been an active part in a very exciting season.

The following year, the young man showed up on the first day of tryouts. This time, there was an obvious attitude change. He had played recreational basketball and worked at various components of his game. Another year of physical and mental maturity helped him realize his potential as a player. Working hard, he made the team as an eighth grader and was an instrumental component to a team that made another deep run into the league playoffs. We didn't win the championship that year, but we had a gritty team of boys who worked hard to overcome what they appeared to lack in basketball skills, making up for that with heart and desire. We lost in the semi-final round by four points, placing us in the game for third place against our archrivals, St. Ann, a team that had beaten us three times during the course of the regular season. Winning that game felt like a championship, coming back from 18 points down at halftime. At the heart of the comeback was a young man who didn't make the team as a seventh grader. He didn't quit on himself and took the opportunity to get better. To his credit, he did more than get better. He was a significant contributor to the team's success.

Stories on cuts don't all take the same shape and form. In fact, another young man had a very similar experience to the previous boy in seventh grade. The difference here is that this boy was all heart and even more hustle. Unfortunately, compared to his peers, he didn't have a ton of basketball experience and associated skills.

Notably behind the other players, cutting him was the obvious choice, but it was one of the most difficult to execute. Unlike the previous boy, when his name was called, he sprinted to the back of the gym, eager to hear his fate. As I talked to him, he figured out where the conversation was headed but didn't drop his head or waiver in confidence. He was very receptive to advice about how to get better. In short, he would do anything to be on the team, and that was apparent. Seeing this, I asked him if he would stay on as our manager. To set the proper expectations, I carefully detailed that he was more than welcome to participate in practice and work on his skills but that he would not be able to suit up for games. The offer was welcomed with the joy of a child opening their favorite toy on Christmas Day. Even better, the other kids on the team welcomed him with open arms and embraced his participation at practice. He worked hard in every practice and showed up at every game, eager to perform his duties as manager. At the end of the season, I encouraged the boy to continue working hard through the summer and to be ready to go for tryouts.

Summer came and went very quickly, and it wasn't long before we were on the eve of tryouts again. I didn't doubt for a moment that the young man who served as the team manager the year before would be a part of the tryouts as an eighth grader. I was unsure whether he took to heart my words of advice in preparing for this season. It didn't take long to notice a bigger, faster, stronger young man. It was also clear that he had worked on the individual skills required to improve his game. Even more impressive was his ability to retain the plays from the previous year, even with limited participation in practice. I think every coach looks for what I call "light bulb" moments. It is the instance when you can see that a player gets it and has embraced the coaching offered, putting principles into action. This was one of those moments. The boy made the team and, like his predecessor who had been cut, made significant contributions to the team. The entire experience was also a "light bulb" moment for me.

Well, after his eighth grade season, I would often see this player, a young man now, at Mass on Sunday. Whenever we saw each other, he would come up to me, shake my hand, and give me a big hug. We would spend the next few minutes talking about high school, his new passion for sports, soccer and tennis, and life in general. As he aged, our conversations grew deeper about life and pursuing every opportunity with the same vigor as his seventh and eighth grade years. He went on to play soccer and tennis in college and ultimately became a coach. As he shared his successes as a coach and his progress in life's pursuits, he was always quick to tell me that I showed him the way. Truth be told, the lesson was mine to learn. Every coach has the wonderful opportunity to be a tremendously positive influence in the life of a child or young adult. The especially refreshing part of this opportunity was that the parents allowed our relationship to be a unique experience. They didn't interfere or try to influence my decision to cut him in 7th grade through the administration of the school or the church. Instead, they helped hold their son accountable for what was his ambition. If he wanted this, he would have to work hard for it. It was a wonderful but rare lesson in the world of youth athletics today.

Unfortunately, in the world of sports and coaching, the good stories outside of game results are rarely shared, so the lessons are rarely realized. A couple of years later, still at Holy Family, I experienced a rather difficult challenge at tryouts. The eighth grade class that year was not very talented. They were good kids but didn't really possess even adequate basketball skills. Five eighth graders and a talented, deep group of seventh graders were trying to make the team. Three of the eighth graders had returned from the previous year, but none of them saw much playing time. One of the returning players was the son of a prominent figure in the school, President of the Athletic

Association, and a major contributor to the church coffers. All in all, the father was a good guy, very generous with his time and money. One of the eighth graders trying out was cut from the previous year because of a demonstrated lack of hustle and care. He ended up being cut for the same reason in his eighth grade year. The third eighth grader, whose father was the Vice President of the Athletic Association, didn't play in seventh grade and looked like he had gone a long time since last picking up a basketball. In fact, as an eighth grader, he still dribbled with two hands. I cut him from the team but despite his lack of age-appropriate basketball skills, it wasn't an easy decision. I knew this one carried a certain level of sensitivity with it as his family and my wife's family were practically neighbors and ran in many of the same circles. However, I wanted to continue building the program with integrity. Instead of keeping him on the roster and watching him suffer the indignities brought on by his lack of skill, I offered the young man the manager position. What I thought was the right thing to do to preserve harmony within the school and the community turned out to be the beginning of a holy war.

The father, clearly using his position on the Athletic Association and bolstered by his friendship with the association's President, began an assault to mandate a "no cut" policy. Not wanting to hear anything about his son lacking even the basic skills to play at the level, he set out on a personal crusade. At the next Athletic Association, the Vice President set out to change by-laws written about team size and cuts. He tried to force me to buy more uniforms to allow more people to make the team. As he attempted to clear a path for his son to play, veiled behind an effort to open the teams up to all interested players, all the coaches countered. The coaches elected the Athletic Association members to liaise with parents and school administration. The more his efforts were met with resistance by me and other coaches, the angrier and more offensive he became.

The sense of entitlement created a sticky situation between the child and the father. In his eyes, the position he held as a school board member guaranteed his son a spot on the team.

When the dust settled from all political posturing and a near brawl in the school cafeteria kitchen, the boy accepted the position of team manager. He made a full commitment to that role and was a very big help to the coaches and players throughout the season. With a maturity not shared by his father, the boy understood his skill limitations and embraced his part on the team. With a very inexperienced team, we went on to have a tough season, only posting six wins. As the season ended, embittered by his experience and failed attempt to force his son onto the team, the Vice President went to work trying to win support for his cause and mandate changes to the by-laws. His son had moved on to high school, but the fight continued in the grammar school. Even when voted down again, the malicious efforts continued as he tried to deny recognition and awards for the success of future teams.

The school had a custom of ordering banners for championship teams. The year after his son left the school, the boys' team ran up another 24-0 league record and championship. Repeating the feat naturally led to excitement about another banner to hang on the gym walls. When the request was brought to the Athletic Association, the initial reaction was that they didn't want to spend the money on making a banner. This was nothing more than an opportunity to get back at me. I told the board I would raise the money, but that was countered by a declaration that the board wasn't allowing banners to be hung in the gym anymore after more than 30 banners had been showcased for all sports over the years. The fight continued and the personal vendetta seemed almost fulfilled. Prior to our awards dinner at the end of the year, I had t-shirts made up for the boys, with a replica of the banner that should be hanging on the walls in the gym. The banner boasted the names of each boy on the team and the 24-0 accomplishment. I kept referring to the "banner" season throughout my speech, reflecting on the year. I proudly displayed the shirt to the families at the event and gave a shirt to each boy on the team. The messaging worked. Eventually, we were awarded a banner that was proudly hoisted to the gym walls. The sad part of it all was the demonstration of putting individual desires before the good of the team and the community.

FIVE
THE POWER OF INFLUENCE

I HAVE ALWAYS CHERISHED the opportunity to influence the lives of the young men and women I have coached over a 33-year span. I sincerely hope that I have been a positive influence, helping them learn more about themselves, the importance of virtues like honor and integrity, and the value of teamwork. Parents certainly have the strongest potential to influence the lives of their children. The influence of traits born through family genes aside, parents can influence attitudes through their view of the world, the behaviors they display, and how they interact with other people. People try to wield the power of their influence in many ways and are not above trying to do so to gain desired outcomes, even in grammar school basketball.

Starting the 1996-97 season at Holy Family, I was blessed with a very talented group of seventh grade players. That group grew to be the core of the first 24-0 team referred to earlier. The seventh grade boys had experienced tremendous success in fifth and sixth grade and were expected to have equal success in everything they did by a very proud group of parents. Because of their early successes, an air of entitlement began to spread throughout the group of boys. Who could blame them? They were good athletes, young men with blossoming egos stoked by parents and a community that put a lot of value in their athletic prowess. They were all good kids with a tremendous group work ethic. They knew they were good, but they were willing to work hard to get better. I knew this was going to be a fun team to coach. However, if one father had his way, my coaching career would have been over before the season ever started.

One of the young men on the team was particularly confident, a multi-sport athlete, a good-looking kid, with a million-dollar smile and the personality to match. Basketball wasn't his first sport, but he brought an uncanny athleticism at his age that made him a key element to our team's success. From a coaching standpoint, we were willing to sacrifice a little offense with him on the floor, knowing that he could shut down anybody in the league defensively. He was a great young man who never gave me trouble. We did, however, have a significant conflict.

At the grammar school level, there is a bit of overlap between the Pop Warner football season and the beginning of the school basketball season, not to mention the tug of township basketball. A couple of players on the team played football, but this particular player lived football. It was his first sport and something he went on to play well in high school and college. On the first day of tryouts for the basketball team, I explained my philosophy on conflicting sports seasons to the boys. My feeling was quite simply that the school should come first. Having said that, I didn't expect anybody to give up football, township basketball, or anything else that may create a conflict. Instead, I set down some simple rules for all the kids to follow. The first was that tryouts were not an option. They needed to be at all three tryouts if they wanted a chance to make the team. No problems there. The remaining rules were relatively simple as well.

If both teams have practice simultaneously, I expected the boys to be at our practice. If we had practice and the other team had a game scheduled simultaneously, I expected them to go to their game. If both teams had conflicting game schedules, I expected them to be at our game. The final rule was a very simple courtesy. If they were going to miss any of our events, I expected a phone call before to let me know so I could draw up practice and plan for games accordingly.

After tryouts, we went into our normal three practices per week schedule. The first couple of practices were great. We had a full house of gifted athletes, eager to learn the game and chomping at the bit to prepare for the season ahead. At the end of that practice, my assistant coach and I were pleased with the quality of effort and the potential of the team. When our next scheduled practice started, I noticed we were missing a player. When I asked where he was, one of the other boys shouted out, "Football." Not having heard from the boy that he would be absent, I was a little upset but reminded myself that this was only the second day of practice. When the next practice came, I was prepared to remind the young man of his commitment to the team and the rules around conflicting sports. It was going to be a low-key conversation to establish a clean slate. As boys were filtering in, he was noticeably absent again. Football was the reason given, but from one of his teammates. Now, I had two straight absences and no communication ahead of time. Finally, the 7th-grade student athlete showed up when Saturday morning practice rolled around. Before practice started, I took the opportunity to talk with him about missing practice and communicating with the coach. He acknowledged that he understood the rules, apologized for the violations, said it wouldn't happen again, and then went on to have a great practice. Like I said, he was a great kid. With the conversation behind us and seeing him on the floor in the mix with all his teammates, I again set my sights on preparing for the season.

Unfortunately, the pattern of absences and no phone calls continued. I was baffled. The message in our last conversation was very clear. Something was amiss. After missing three more practices for the same reason, I had another conversation with the boy. This time, the conversation was a little more frank but still very congenial. I added one caveat this time around. If he missed another practice without communicating to me in advance or missed another one of our practices to go to football practice, then I would expect him to turn in his uniform. I wasn't really expecting what came next.

I was sitting at home with my family that night when the phone rang. It was the boy's father. He was well-established in the school and coached the third and fourth grade boys' basketball team. The conversation started in a civil tone as I was asked to explain the team rules to him. The direction of the dialogue changed rather quickly with his next question, "Who the hell do you think you are making up these rules and asking a kid to turn in his jersey?" The delivery was spiked with Jersey City street tones, reflective of the father's early life. Remaining civil in my rebuttal, I simply pointed out that this was not isolated to his son and that all boys were expected to play under the same rules. In fact, other football players on the team rarely missed basketball practice. If and when they did, I received a phone call in advance. I went on to explain that if we were going to indeed be a team, then every individual needed to work with the same focus, the same intensity, and under the same guidelines. The father then proceeded to get louder and pepper in a few expletives while preaching to me about his influence in the school. He had been a coach there for several years and sat on the Athletic Association. I was in my third year as a coach, still relatively new, and not from the area. I didn't "understand" how things worked. I had no business "holding down" the boys with such "ridiculous" expectations. The deeper he went into his rant, the louder he became, and the less patient I became. Eventually, emotions ran high on both sides of the phone, and F-bombs flew. The call ended with a straightforward threat, "I'm going to talk to Sister (the principal) and have you fired."

Although the phone conversation was over, the pursuit of the "injustice" spilled over into the next Athletic Association meeting. The father brought up my rules and requirements as a topic for group discussion. I wasn't worried about presenting my side of the situation and defending my principles. I was concerned about the Board's ability to listen with an unbiased ear. Again, I was relatively new to the community, and the boy's father was involved in the school for a while. Not only that, one of the other Board members also had a son in 7th grade on the team, and their families were very friendly. The icing on the cake was that Sister also sat on the Board as an advisor. I was a little concerned about the discussion but had faith that cooler heads would prevail. The truth is, for all the boys to work together as a team, they all had to have the same conviction and commitment and abide by the same rules.

The meeting wasn't as contentious as I had anticipated. The father and I were able to come to a respectful, albeit tenuous, understanding. My request for open communication about absences was upheld. The player rarely missed any practices from that point, never missed a game, and was often running into the gym a few minutes late for basketball practice because he had just come from football practice. There was a definite change in attitude about commitment to the school basketball team. I was very happy and embraced the change, not because he was a stud athlete, but because of the positive impact on the team performance and chemistry were obvious. We went on to have a successful season with the talented group of seventh graders. The boys matured tremendously as players and as teammates. In their eighth grade season, there weren't any issues around missing practices due to competing sport seasons. I didn't have any parental issues. Our team, our community, was focused on a season of promise. The destiny for greatness alluded to before was fulfilled as the team accomplished the first undefeated season and league championship in school history.

The 24-0 record in the league didn't come easy, as we played some tough rivals and large parish teams to close games. As we fought our way into the championship, we found ourselves face-to-face with a very talented parish team that we had barely beaten before in the regular season. The league scheduled the finals at the local high school gym to provide good theater for the families, fans, and players. Although the court was no bigger than our gym, playing at the high school was still perceived as the "big stage." The nerves were plentiful that day as we warmed up. My son, who was five years old at the time, was very much a part of our team as he often sat behind the bench at games and listened in on team huddles. As we put our hands in at the end of a huddle during a time out, I would frequently see his little hand sneak in to be a part of the unity. The excitement of the championship moment wasn't lost on him. During warmups, he sat one row behind the bench, anxiously watching every drill. His eyes darted to follow every pass, and he rocked back and forth, waiting for the game to begin.

I called the boys over to go through the final pre-game preparation. Drawing on my coaching board to review plays, detailing our approach to press often, defend well, and create easy opportunities, I could sense the nerves in the huddle. The boys were reticent, breathing labored, and I could hear their hearts beating with excitement. I was searching for something to break the tension. At that moment, my son, apparently also seeking relief, threw up all over the back of my manager, who was sitting on the bench, clipboard in hand. We were seconds away from playing for the league championship and now had a mess to deal with. Without flinching, the manager just unzipped his warm-up jacket and handed it to my wife and another mother, who jumped into action to clean up. My son didn't cry or fuss. He resisted even going to the bathroom to freshen up because he didn't want to miss a second of the game. The team laughed at the situation and then seemed to gain their focus.

During the first half, we played some great team defense, but one of the opposing players hit three consecutive baskets late in the 2nd quarter to put the parish team up by three points at the half. All the momentum seemed to be in their favor. After our locker room talk and halftime adjustments, the boys retook the floor to prepare for the second half. With a minute left in the intermission, I pulled the boys to the bench, prepared to make some final adjustments, and offered additional words of encouragement. As the boys sat on the bench, I kneeled in front of them, noticing a new face intently staring at me and listening in on the huddle. It wasn't my son, but the father who wanted to get me fired the year before because I was holding his son to team policy and attendance at practice. He wasn't doing anything wrong, but he seemed to want to be a part of the moment, perhaps replaying something in his past. I focused on the boys and the task at hand. Summarizing the first half quickly, I pointed to our tremendous team defense that had held the opponent to a very low-scoring first half. I told the boys that I wasn't worried about our offensive production. Being down three points at the half, my following words were the trigger, "We have them right where we want them." I could see the father's face light up as if to question if I knew the score, and then he leaned in to listen more closely.

We did have the opponent where we wanted them, and I could see it in their labored breathing and tired legs. The player who popped off three baskets in a row needed to be dealt with, but other than that, our defensive pressure was suffocating. Still, in the half-time huddle, and with his father peering in, I looked to his son and gave him the assignment to lock down the hot hand on the other team. If the opponent had the ball, I wanted my player right in his face, not giving him room to move. If the opponent didn't have the ball, I didn't want him to get it back. If the opponent went to get a hot dog, "I want you to put mustard on it for him." The individual defensive effort was perfect. The team's defense was incredible. The pressure created turnovers, which led to easy baskets, and the other team became increasingly frustrated. We went on to win the championship and fulfill the destiny of those young men.

Another result of that success was the understanding and respect that continued to develop between the one father and me. People in sports say that winning cures everything, but I don't believe it was just the winning that inspired the change. I like to believe that the father realized why I was so intent on the importance of discipline and working towards team chemistry. Nothing I did in the previous year that became a point of contention was done out of malice or with the intention of harming his son. Quite the opposite, as my efforts were to build a bond between young men centered on a common goal. We worked hard together and had a once-in-a-lifetime season, the kind that makes up the "glory days" often referred to in adulthood and memorialized by Bruce Springsteen. To this day, 26 years later, I still have a great relationship with all the boys from that team.

Earlier, I referred to the second 24-0 season experienced at Holy Family. Ironically enough, the younger brother of the stud athlete was on this team. As a seventh grader, he and his peers suffered through a six win season. Although our eighth graders weren't strong that year, there was something special about the seventh graders and about this young man. Like his brother, he was also a multi-sport athlete, with football as his main focus. I was concerned when he made the team that we might have a relapse into the experiences of the past as far as missing practices because of football. There never

30

was an issue. His father, who had seemingly hated me passionately a few years earlier, was gracious. At the end of it all, when I had finished coaching both boys, the father approached me with his hand extended and proudly spoke words I will never forget, "Thank you for making my sons better men." No greater reward could have been offered.

SIX
ROSE-COLORED GLASSES

I THINK one of the more difficult things for a parent when observing your child playing sports or participating in any group event is the ability to avoid viewing through rose-colored glasses. Of course, we all want our children to succeed at something and have fun while doing it. As a child progresses through youth sports into more competitive environments like AAU or high school athletics, the distinction in talent level and skill sets becomes more evident. Simply put, some players are better than others, whether they are more skillful, more mature, or have a better understanding of the game. Young athletes are keenly aware of this and come to a point where they choose to push on to continue to work on their skills, contributing where they can and enjoying the camaraderie with their team, or they decide to find another area of interest. This awareness becomes clouded when parents refuse to recognize that their child may not be as good as other players on the team. Their child can contribute, enjoy relative individual success, and build relationships within the team. However, because the parent refuses to acknowledge the situation, frustration rises and tempers flare.

Mothers and fathers openly express negative opinions about coaches in front of their child, other players, and their families. Instead of working with the coach to determine what can be done to enhance their child's abilities and improve their experience, they find ways to undermine the player-coach relationship and weaken the fiber of the team with disparaging remarks. I have had a few experiences with this scenario. As a father of three children, who often happened to be the coach of the basketball team my children played for, I tried to be sensitive to this type of situation. I wasn't just careful about how I interacted with the kids on the team and their parents. I was also extremely careful about interacting with other coaches my children played for. I didn't ever want there to be a time when people thought I was showing favoritism toward my children or looking for favor from other coaches. When my children struggled in relationships with their coaches or failed to understand the reason behind a decision, I always encouraged them to talk to their coach. When approached by a player on their team, most coaches will be open to constructive dialogue centered on individual improvement. When a coach sees a player working on the things discussed, they see somebody who is interested in getting better, and they will look for ways to get that player more involved. The key as a player is to listen and truly absorb the coaching. If the coach tells players to work on their ball handling, they are setting expectations and defining how they can improve. The player's job is to work on improving the skill. The player should go even further and ask the coach for specific drills to help improve ball handling.

The player-coach engagement gets clouded when parents decide to interject themselves into the relationship instead of letting it develop naturally. During my last five seasons as the boys' coach at the grammar school, seasons 8-12, I also began coaching Varsity Girls' Basketball at Mater Dei High School. There were some fundamental shifts for me, going from grammar school to high school, as well as moving from boys to girls. I took the approach that basketball is basketball; I just needed to adjust to the level and the personalities of my new players. My coaching style and philosophies remained the same. Every preseason, I would address my players and parents together, letting them know my coaching philosophy. One of the aspects I would cover is the athlete's accountability for their intensity at practice, their individual effort and resulting success, and ultimately, their responsibility to the team. I would tell the athletes that if they ever had questions about how to improve, they should come see me. I would be happy to work with them on specific skills and drills. In addition, I would tell the parents to encourage their children to communicate with me and the rest of the coaching staff. If the athlete came home complaining about playing time, I encouraged parents to direct them to the coaches to find out how to improve. For the majority of parents, this open-door policy worked well, and I had many open, productive conversations with players about methods for improvement. Because of the relationship I was able to have with my players, I was often rewarded not only with the player's hard work but also the pleasure of seeing a young athlete become bolstered by additional confidence in themselves as they began to see their game develop.

Unfortunately, a few parents just couldn't see their way to let their child go and help their child grow. This became particularly evident in the later years of coaching in high school. Newer generations of players seemed to have a sense of entitlement, and parents seemed to support that feeling. Instead of supporting the development of the player-coach relationship, parents began to try to interject and influence the bond, and they requested a meeting with me even though their child never approached me or another coach. I would accept the meeting, but I offered one simple rule . . . we can talk about their child and what is needed to improve their game, but we will not talk about any other player. I have had several meetings with parents, and ultimately, they worked out well. One thing I always did was invite disgruntled parents to attend a few practices, encouraging them to come see what I see on a daily basis. Parents seldom took advantage of that offer. There were a handful of meetings that didn't go so well, generally because the parents refused to take off the rose-colored glasses and open their minds to constructive input, ways to help their child.

One such meeting was with the mother and father of a freshman girl who played on the JV team at Mater Dei. We were a small Catholic high school, so we often relied on freshmen and sophomores playing up to higher levels. This young lady enjoyed great success at the grammar school level, mostly due to an unmatched aggressive quality and an intimidating air about her. She was quick to the ball and would outwill and out muscle smaller girls. Because of these qualities, she started for her school team and saw a lot of playing time in games. When she came to high school, I saw a lot of raw talent that could be molded into a very productive player. However, her skill sets weren't as refined as some of her contemporaries. She also had a difficult time remembering the sequence of movements in our half-court offense. After consulting with my staff, we decided that she would play freshmen basketball and play up to the JV team. By state rules, every player was entitled to five quarters of play on game day. As a staff, we looked to take advantage of this to give younger players more game exposure and more opportunity to hone their skills. So, we had some freshmen playing up at the JV level and some playing up at the Varsity level. Based on her success in grammar school, this young lady's parents couldn't understand why their daughter wasn't playing Varsity. Instead of encouraging their daughter to talk to the coaches and find out ways to improve her game, the parents requested a meeting with me.

I started our meeting with the same structure to the conversation, emphasizing that I would be happy to discuss ways to improve their daughter's game, but I would not discuss other players. Both parents and I agreed upon the concept, and I began to outline areas for improvement. When we got to specific skill sets, the father interrupted the tempo of the meeting with an outburst about how good his daughter was in grammar school just a season ago and made an adamant statement about how she was better than the other freshmen on JV and those that were playing Varsity. It wasn't enough that he made the statement, but he started calling out the other freshmen girls and pointing out weaknesses in their game. Upon hearing this, I kindly asked him to stop and reminded him of our agreement that our focus would be on his daughter and ways to improve her game. Honestly, I was just as anxious to see her improve and move up as they were. I began to talk about her uncertainty with offensive sets and referred to her nervous habit of taking the ends of her hair and putting them in her mouth. Right away, the mother recognized this trait in her daughter and stated that she had told her not to do that and encouraged her to be more confident. When I started to describe what extra steps we could take to help her learn the plays better, the father once again interrupted with the assertion that his daughter was better than other players.

At that point, I respectfully ended the meeting and refused to entertain future meeting requests. Of course, the coaching staff continued to work with the player, and she did show definite signs of progress. There was maturity in the player and game that needed to occur, but we were headed in the right direction. Instead of allowing their daughter to develop as a player and young adult, they decided to transfer her to the public school for her sophomore year. Ultimately, the player ran into some of the same issues early on with her new team and coach. I kept tabs on her because I had a sincere interest in her development, knowing how much she enjoyed playing basketball. Recently, I have seen the player, now a young adult, working at the local bank. She greeted me with a warm smile and a resounding, "Hello, Coach." Hearing those words from her despite the trouble she experienced with her parents was a meaningful acknowledgment that she understood our relationship's value. We often cross paths, as I do business in the same bank. It is nice to see how she has matured into a wonderful young adult.

In my last year as the head coach at Mater Dei High School, parental discord seemed to be at an all-time high. There were a few dynamics at work. First, we had a very young Varsity team comprised of 2 seniors, two juniors, three sophomores, and seven talented freshmen. We had a good JV team with a few more sophomores and freshmen who could easily earn varsity time as well. My staff viewed all of this as positive, figuring that practices would be competitive and the girls would very naturally push each other. The second element was the fact that the girls' soccer team won the sectional championship and made a deep run in the state playoffs that fall. The team was late to develop in the season because they were also very young, fueled specifically by the talents of a couple of sophomores and four freshmen who were now on the basketball team. Parents came into the basketball season expecting soccer's success to translate directly to success in basketball, anticipating that their daughters would play a significant role on the basketball court. What they failed to realize is that girls' basketball in the Jersey Shore area is incredibly competitive, and we played a schedule loaded with some of the Shore's best. Finally, there was a cloud hanging over our team because of a particularly arrogant, mean-spirited father of a very talented basketball player, a story that I share later in the book. All these elements combined for a challenging coaching year.

One of the challenges came from a very athletically gifted freshman. She had natural speed, quickness, and strength that served her very well on the soccer field and previously in grammar school basketball. She was quicker and more aggressive than the competition, and, quite frankly, she had a useful mean streak when in competitive situations. As a basketball player, she had raw talent that needed to be molded. If she had committed herself to developing the game skills and not just relying on athleticism, she could have been an outstanding player and would have seen more minutes on the Varsity squad as a freshman. Unfortunately, she didn't embrace the need for personal development and tried to continue outpacing others with her quickness and aggression.

What she didn't realize is that many of the other girls who may have been slower or less aggressive in previous years had started to mature as athletes. The skills they had worked to develop earlier in life to compensate for less natural athleticism were now aiding them with a more rounded maturity in the game. They were becoming better basketball players. In addition to this change, the young lady was having difficulty picking up plays at the varsity level. She tried to compensate for this lack of comprehension with extra aggressive play, sometimes making her appear selfish. I never believed that to be the case. With some specific coaching, which was offered, and focused work on her part, she could have been a rising star on the team and in the Shore Conference. At this point, the school no longer had a program specific to the freshmen. In order to help her develop without pressure, I had her play JV and swing up to Varsity. She didn't take this well at first, especially with two of her peers and soccer teammates, not only full-time varsity but also starters. She considered herself the better athlete and thought that honor should be hers. So did her father.

The tricky part for me in this relationship was trying to be sensitive about a longstanding relationship I enjoyed with this player's extended family. I had the great fortune of coaching two of her cousins previously. The oldest cousin played for me during my first two years at the school. She was a hard-working individual, very coachable, and committed to giving her best to the game and her teammates. Although a starter for me both years, she was never the star. She had a quiet, steady leadership about her that coaches admired and teammates embraced. She was the focal point in one of my favorite coaching moments.

In the days leading up to a game early in the season, we had been working together specifically on free-throw shooting. As a post player, I had anticipated that she would be spending more time at the charity stripe, and we needed to improve that element of her game. In every practice, she put in extra time and worked on the fundamentals of free throw shooting. Understand this wasn't for the glory of individual statistics. She was very genuine in an effort to help her team improve and knew we would all be relying on her success at the line. Game night arrived, and we were playing one of our division rivals. As a coach trying to develop a program, early success in the season was important, especially within the division. We were at a point late in the game when the ball was fed into the post. This was the moment we had been working on for some time. After receiving the feed, the player made a strong move and was fouled in the act of shooting . . . going to the line for two. Visibly nervous and overthinking the moment, she shot long, and the ball hit hard off the back iron. As I encouraged her to relax, shake it off, and get the next one, she prepared for the second shot. Air ball! Wanting to do so much for her team but not being able to deliver had noticeably bothered her. Her body language screamed defeat, so I called a time out. As she walked off the floor toward the bench, I put out my arms to let her know it was alright. She melted into my encouraging hug and cried on my shoulder, feeling as if she had just let me down, let the team down. I gave her a reassuring hug and got her into the huddle to discuss game strategy. We would figure out another way to be successful.

Later in the game, as the clock was winding down and the gym was heating up with excitement, a foul was called on the opposing team.

The coach got into a heated exchange with the referee, which resulted in a technical foul. As a coach, that is a potentially costly error in a close game, providing the opponent with two foul shots and possession of the ball afterwards. Once things settled down, the official asked me who would shoot the free throws. Without hesitation, I sent my post player to the line. She stepped up and drained them both. The confidence that consumed her from that moment was irreplaceable. We won the game and went on to qualify for the state playoffs for the first time in a long time. The work ethic and desire paid off, and my player was nominated for and awarded a $5,000 "Is it in You" Nike scholarship for college. We have enjoyed a meaningful relationship ever since, and she even returned as an assistant coach for one season.

The next family member I coached was another cousin who happened to be playing the year that the older cousin was my assistant. The younger cousin was not a strong basketball player. She was a decent athlete and needed a lot of development in the game. A lot of kids would shy away from a sport if that was the case. Not this young lady. Like her cousin before her, she had a strong will, a great work ethic, and a desire to get better and contribute in any way she could to support the team. She spent a good portion of her first three years in high school playing JV, even as a junior. Again, a lot of other girls would have given up and gone on to indoor track or something else. She just became more determined. By her senior year, she really started to put things together and became a terrific role player. With increasing minutes, she made more contributions and gained even more confidence.

In addition to her basketball skills, she had an amazing voice and sang the National Anthem for all our home games. She excelled in this area, singing passionately and always working on getting better. One home game during her senior campaign, she took her familiar place behind the microphone to give honor to our nation. Early in the anthem, the mike started to crackle and give out. Without hesitation, she lowered the microphone and belted out one of the most beautiful renditions of *The Star-Spangled Banner* I have ever heard. The amazing poise and confidence displayed at such a young age made me, her teammates, her family, and the whole community proud. She would carry that growth throughout the rest of the year.

We had to travel down to Hammonton, NJ, as we advanced in the state playoffs, to take on another parochial school. We had practiced hard for two weeks, preparing for one of the better athletic post players in New Jersey. At 6' 1", she was strong, quick, and could jump through the roof. My tallest player was 5' 8". Although my player had a raw determination and spent much of the year taking on a multitude of six footers, she was giving away a lot to this post player in size and speed.

We worked on overcrowding the paint defensively to take away the flex cut for the 6' 1" opponent. We had her frustrated for the entire first half, and her teammates were struggling as well. As a team, we also practiced the little components of the game that can add to the frustration of a bigger, stronger athlete. We worked tirelessly on boxing out, team rebounding, and taking charges. I figured we would have a better chance of securing the victory if we could get their best player on the bench with some frustration fouls from over the back or a charge.

Late in the third quarter, we continued to execute our game plan successfully. Everybody was playing fundamentally sound basketball and committed to the team effort of taking the big girl out of the game. We were enjoying a 10-point lead and were poised to advance to the next round. At that time in the game, I had a couple of the starters resting, and some of the role players were on the floor, keeping up the mission. One of those role players was my angelic singer. During one exchange, the other team's 6' 1" powerhouse stole the ball and was driving to the basket with the speed and power of a freight train. Without hesitation, my player slid into the driving line and put herself in a terrific position to take the charge. With a thunderous clap and what I thought was an obvious charge call, my girl goes down in a heap. I was applauding her effort when I realized that the official had called a blocking foul. What could have been the dagger to end it all turned out to be a momentum builder for the other team. Although we didn't get the call, I couldn't have been prouder of the grit and determination of my player, playing in what turned out to be her last game ever, throwing herself in front of a much bigger player to take one for the team. That is the kind of player she and her older cousin were . . . committed to giving all for the team.

Imagine my enthusiasm when I knew the younger cousin was coming to school. Watching her grow up in the community and seeing her at a few of my summer camps, I knew the kind of gifts she possessed as an athlete. My hope was that her athleticism, combined with the steel and willingness to learn demonstrated by her cousins, would result in a magnificent high school career. Instead, she came into the season almost expecting to be great but apparently not willing to work as hard. There was a bit of an air of entitlement, which hampered her early progression. After early workouts and introduction to plays, I divided the teams into JV and Varsity, explaining that the positions are earned every day in practice and can change. To send a subtle message and hoping to motivate the gifted athlete, I started her at the JV level. I explained my decision to her, letting her know what fundamental skills I wanted her to work on, as well as her understanding of the offense. I also let her know that I expected her to rise up to the Varsity level in short order. Unfortunately, this didn't provide the motivation I had hoped for. Instead, her parents became vocal about the decision in public and started to put thoughts into her head that I was treating her unfairly.

After several attempts to coach her up and provide encouragement, to which she would show signs of growth, she wasn't demonstrating the consistency I was hoping for. Her father asked me for a meeting to discuss her playing time. I let him know that I would not discuss playing time or other players, but I would be happy to talk to him about what his daughter needed to do to reach her potential, something I absolutely wanted to help her do. We usually practiced at 7 PM, so I offered a 30-minute window at 6:30. Again, I have known this family for years and anticipated a very cordial and productive conversation. I thought our interests were the same; we wanted his daughter to improve, work her way up to varsity, and contribute to the team in the way we both felt she was capable.

When he didn't show up at 6:30, I assumed he had a change of heart. As practice was wrapping up at nine and I was turning out the lights to the gym, the father walked through the front door. Though tired from a long day at work and a solid two-hour practice, I opened the coach's office and invited him in for a talk. The conversation remained cordial but quickly became frustrating as he was not open to my suggestions for individual improvement and coaching suggestions. He seemed rather focused on why other freshmen, not hesitating to call out specific names, were playing Varsity ahead of his daughter. I reminded him of my rule about naming other players and the desire to stay focused on his daughter's skills. Ignoring my request, he decided to continue after the other girls. At that point, I respectfully ended the meeting. I encouraged him to have his daughter come early or stay later at future practices so I could work extra with her. Unfortunately, the offer was never taken advantage of, and the parents continued to verbalize their frustration.

Parental grumbling seemed to be contagious, and I began to hear little bits of frustration from the mother of one of my sophomores. In her freshman year, she played JV and was a swinger at the varsity level. She had some good basic skills, some height, a good outside shot, and took well to coaching. We enjoyed a good relationship during her freshman year as she sought out and embraced additional coaching to improve. She worked hard and made some meaningful contributions to the Varsity team as a freshman. The following summer, she factored into my planning as a key player in the next season.

As her sophomore season began, she had good practices, but she struggled with the speed of the game, and her jump shot wasn't falling consistently. I was encouraging her to get more aggressive in the paint on both sides of the ball and work on adding to her game that way . . . working inside, out. She showed flashes of brilliance but would let one missed shot or a travel call rattle her confidence and impact her effectiveness. I would substitute for her, talk to her about the situation, and then get her back into the game to work on what we discussed. As this pattern continued, the player approached me after one game and asked me what she needed to do to improve. I was very proud of her for asking that simple question and letting her know it. We then had a 15-minute conversation about what I saw as areas for development and how we could improve. This was a very positive development in the player-coach relationship until Mom got involved.

Without even having the courtesy to address me personally, the mother sent a pointed e-mail to the school's Athletic Director complaining about my efforts as the coach this year. Her e-mail complained of "daddy ball" when I didn't even have a child on the team. The mother referred to her daughter's participation in AAU as if that entitled her to a certain level in high school. Success only comes before work, in the dictionary. I was involved in AAU for about 10 seasons prior to this year and quickly realized that there are a variety of levels and some programs that are more competitive than others. While AAU experience can be helpful if the right effort is put into development, it is not a free pass to success in high school.

Instead of encouraging her daughter to continue working hard, she felt entitled because of AAU experience. The mother then included a sentence in the e-mail that still stings. "Coach Ault, I am sure, does not realize this, but he is mentally abusing the girls."

I spent 11 years at Mater Dei building a successful program and returning the school to consistent appearances in the Shore Conference Tournament and state playoffs. I was certainly not a "win at all costs" coach, and I took great pride in building strong, meaningful relationships with my players in any program I coached. I didn't view my position as a dictatorship; instead, I worked to develop a collaborative program where integrity and hard work would create a cycle of returning players, alumni, and pride in the community. I spent countless hours of personal time working the girls through summer leagues and team camps, all in an effort to help them get better at a game we shared a common love for and to help them prepare for the next level if they wanted to pursue a college career. The idea that a parent who didn't even have the courtesy to talk directly to me would accuse me of "mental abuse" was disheartening and very deflating. She accused me of politics and reduced the 15-minute post-game conversation I had with her daughter to "he said she needs to 'box out' more." The last dagger was a suggestion that maybe her daughter wasn't starting because the parents didn't complain enough. When I read the e-mail, I was livid and frustrated beyond words. I offered the following reply to my AD:

> This is quite surprising coming from the (family name). I don't have time to call you now as I am at work. I don't play politics. Don't care if somebody went to St. Mary's (the grammar school connected to the high school), Catholic school or public school. My own daughters came into this program and had to work their way through the ranks. Players much better than most of what I

currently have started out at JV and worked their way up or down accordingly. (The Player) had a bad game yesterday. Prior to that, she was starting to come back around. She is slow of foot and slow to get her shot off, things we have been working on throughout the season. Right now, (The Player) is not as consistent as she was last year on either side of the floor. She has moments of brilliance, then long lapses. I would expect that from a younger player, AAU or not. By the way, just because you play AAU doesn't make you a star. I used to coach a lot of AAU and have seen various levels of teams and individuals. I have been working with (The Player) and will continue to do so because she is one of my players with great promise. Again, I don't care where she went to school, what color, what religion or who she is related to. Seriously, "mentally abusing" the girls. That is a ridiculous comment and couldn't be further from the truth. Nobody has been the subject of more abuse than I have, and it is from parents with unreal expectations for their daughters and a saddening sense of entitlement.

I was able to connect via the phone with the AD, and we had a lengthy discussion about the situation. I agreed to meet with the mother but insisted that the player attend the meeting as well. I wanted the parent and player to hear the same message directly from me instead of my comments potentially being lost in translation. I had to swallow some frustration over a few of the comments that were made, especially since I wanted this to be a productive meeting, with the result being agreement from all parties on how we could work together, player and coach, to recognize the potential. The meeting lasted about 30 minutes and was very successful, which prompted a follow-up e-mail from the player's mother.

Coach - thank you for meeting with (The Player) and me last night. All three of us had different impressions of what is going on. (The

Player) now understands that you were not intentionally ignoring her and that she only heard certain things and misunderstood others. I appreciate the patience you had and how you spoke to her and explained things in a way that she now understands. I look forward to the rest of the season and seeing (The Player) being able to play as well or even better than she did last year now that this is all cleared up.

The player and I resumed our player-coach relationship. She began to work harder and focused more on skill development. Through persistence, she began to become much more consistent in her non-scoring efforts, such as defense and rebounding. I would often praise her for boxing out and using proper rebounding techniques. One of her best efforts helped spark a come-from-behind win in a first-round state playoff game at home. She ripped down 15 rebounds, 10 on the defensive glass. At one point, I caught a glimpse of her proud father striking the pose of a bodybuilder flexing his muscles. Her eyes and smile said it all.

The player-coach relationship was very important to me. My personal philosophy with my players was to encourage an open dialogue so they knew what I expected from them, but also so they had a channel to view what areas of their individual game needed improvement and how their game fit into the team. I also encouraged the same open dialogue with parents. As a team, parent and coach, I felt we had the best opportunity to guide and support the young athlete. One father, also a coach, with whom I have had the pleasure of working quite a bit over the years, always encouraged his daughter by telling her, "Don't get frustrated, get determined." I thought that was perfect encouragement as a coach and a parent. Too many times, when things aren't going well in our pursuits, we tend to shift the blame to somebody or something other than ourselves. This statement imbued a sense of accountability and focused effort that I looked for in my players. I borrowed the phrase and have used it with my players and with my own children.

Working with his daughter, it didn't take long to see her determination. This young lady had a tremendous work ethic. Undersized even as a point guard, she was never outworked by anybody and keyed in on mastering every aspect of her game. I had the great pleasure of working with her and her father in a township league and in some summer development camps. As a student at St. Mary's, the grammar school that shared the campus with Mater Dei High School, I would often see her at the Varsity games. As a friend of the family and somebody interested in her individual development as a player, I would often go watch her play. I began to imagine her as the point guard for my team, which was starting to develop nicely and would have a tremendous freshmen class coming in when this young lady was a sophomore. I spent hours off-season thinking of the quality of players and the types of plays we would be able to run. I guess you could say I was wearing rose-colored glasses at that time.

One of the difficult things for Mater Dei is the draw of two larger Catholic high schools in the immediate area, both of which have perennial powerhouse girls' basketball teams. Red Bank Catholic had a top-notch coach and a program on a tremendous run over recent years, including sectional and state championships. St. John Vianney was not only known throughout the state of New Jersey but often received national attention for the strength and success of its program. They were a fixture in the Shore Conference Championship and state Tournament of Champions. These were two significant hurdles in trying to build a program at Mater Dei. I was used to seeing girls graduate from St. Mary's with aspirations of playing at one of those two schools. It was frustrating. As I started to develop more relationships in the local community with parents and players, I was starting to draw more attention to Mater Dei. As an eighth grader, the diminutive point guard with a great work ethic had her eyes set on Red Bank Catholic. Don't get frustrated; get determined. By this time, we had a very special player-coach bond. I knew she was heading off to another school, but I didn't let that affect the relationship we had developed. In her eighth grade graduation card, I wrote a very simple expression, "You will always have a home wherever I am coaching."

I'll never forget the call the following summer. The voice on the other side was an excitedly nervous young lady who asked a very simple question, "Coach, do I still have a home with you at Mater Dei?" This was a player-coach relationship that developed without parental interference. We went on to have three great years together. As a sophomore, she took over a young team with tremendous promise. The freshmen class that year was, as expected, a special group of players who had worked with me on the AAU circuit for four years prior, loaded with gifted athletes and hardworking ballers. We also had a gifted two-guard sophomore with tremendous skill sets in every facet of the game. In addition to the young talent, I had a senior transfer from the local public school. In one of the most unselfish acts I have witnessed as a coach, the senior transferred to Mater Dei, knowing that she would have to sit out 30 days of the season. Her motivation was simple. She wanted to play basketball with her sister, one of the very talented freshmen, who had decided to come play for me. This was no small sacrifice as the senior was a solid post player at 6' tall and a formidable presence in the paint. The future was bright. As a program, we were heading in a positive direction. At the helm of it all was a 5' 2" dynamo who had recently returned home from the perceived greener pastures of Red Bank Catholic High School.

SEVEN
FRACTURED FRIENDSHIP

COACHING BASKETBALL HAS ALLOWED me to meet many different people and make wonderful friendships along the way. There have also been a few circumstances of strained relationships because of differences in opinion over the talent level of my friends' daughters and their growth within the game.

When my oldest daughter became a freshman in high school, I could no longer coach her AAU team, the Middletown Hotshots. Although most of the Hotshots were going to other schools and two were still eighth graders, five of the girls on the team were coming to play for me in high school, so coaching them in AAU would directly violate the NJSIAA rules. In my opinion, this was an inexplicable rule that was unique to New Jersey. I passed the clipboard and whistle on to a good friend of mine who was my assistant coach and whose daughter was coming to play for me in high school. We had a great team run together and enjoyed the experiences at practice and in tournament play. I knew I would miss the AAU season and the interaction with the girls and their parents.

A couple of years earlier, I had asked my youngest daughter if she wanted to play AAU. Unlike her big sister, who was committed to the game and passionate about playing, my little one wasn't yet that focused on basketball. She enjoyed playing it but also liked softball and running track for grammar school. In her initial response, she said, "Daddy, I play basketball during basketball season." I completely understood and didn't push the issue with her. She was a good young player and had a great mind for the game, but she also had other interests that she enjoyed. When I could no longer coach my oldest daughter, I revisited the idea with my youngest. The Hotshots already had two levels of teams and were coached by a great group of people who were truly dedicated to the girls and teaching the fundamentals of the game. Winning was important, but it took a backseat to work on the proper execution of the X's and O's, individual development, and most importantly, excellent teamwork. I thought starting up a third level would be a great idea.

My youngest daughter was playing for the school team at Holy Family. Some spirited girls on the team worked hard for their young coach, but they didn't have the time or drive to work on improving their skills. Instead of creating a team of superstars in AAU, I asked my daughter and a few of her teammates who were more serious about the game if they would like to start a team and spend some additional work developing their skills and getting more game experience. Including my daughter, there were four girls interested. I then networked through some friends and coaches I knew, explaining what we were trying to do. Before too long, we had a team of little Hotshots . . . round-faced, bright-eyed, and eager to learn.

With my high school coaching schedule and commitment to summer leagues and camps, I knew I would need assistance running the team. In addition, as happened with my oldest daughter's team, there would come a time when I would have to step away because of high school rules. Finally, I hoped to build the program and pass the torch so that the Hotshots could continue growing as an organization. With all of that in mind, I enlisted the assistance of a couple of fathers whose daughters were on the team. To a man, they didn't want the head coaching job, but they were willing to be assistant coaches and fill in as head coach when needed. I was friends with the guys, so I figured this would be a natural fit and transition. It was seamless for the two years we ran the program together, and we had fun working with the girls. After two years, I had to pass the torch again as three of the girls were coming to play for me in high school. The team played a third year together, but many of the girls who had gone to other high schools stopped playing basketball, so their interest in AAU dissolved. My friendship continued with the assistant coaches for the program as their daughters came to play for me in high school.

One of my friends had two girls playing in my program. His oldest daughter was a small guard with a quiet disposition, but she was a strong competitor. Her basketball skills weren't completely developed yet, and they didn't often get the necessary attention during the off-season. Softball was her primary sport, and the extra time and effort was put into those skill sets, and rightfully so. She was a tremendous All-Shore centerfielder with a great bat. With solid athletic skills and good speed, she did find her way to the Varsity basketball team as a freshman. Some of my trusted advisors questioned my decision to have her swing to varsity. Some people thought I favored her because she went to Holy Family, my parish at the time, where I had coached prior to Mater Dei. Others thought that she sat varsity because I was friendly with her father. The simple truth is that she worked very hard in practice, was very coachable, and I knew the competitor that was inside the player. My decision was vindicated early in her freshman year.

During a Varsity game against one of our division rivals, Pt. Beach, we were in a heated battle with frequent lead changes. Playing in their gym was an experience as it always seemed to be about 20 degrees hotter than any other gym, and the stands were always packed with a sea of red and white, supporting the home team. Over the years, we had competed fiercely for second place in the division. We were often chosen as one of the teams to eventually knock off the perennial division winner, St. Rose. On this night, my team was playing well, but we were not particularly sharp. For three quarters, we struggled to find a rhythm, saddled with foul trouble, but somehow managed to stay in the game. At a critical point early in the fourth quarter, one of my junior guards was already on the bench with four fouls, and my junior point guard had just been whistled for her fourth foul. As the ref reported the foul to the table, I studied the length of my bench for substitution options. At the far end, I spotted my freshman guard focused on the game and cheering for her teammates. As I shouted out her name, she popped up with enthusiasm and surprise. Behind the bench sat a good friend and confidant, and I could hear him quietly say, "What are you doing, Bro?"

With the benefit of hindsight, I would say I knew exactly what I was doing. The truth is I went with my gut. I didn't think twice about my decision, patting her on the back and encouraging her as she reported to the table. It was early in the season and a good time to see what my bench was made of. I knew the competitor inside but didn't know exactly how she would react in this kind of situation. On our next possession, down a point and the clock winding down, the little freshman guard curled off an elbow screen, took one dribble into the lane, and dropped in a floater without the slightest hesitation. Our fans went crazy as we took the lead. Our bench surged with excitement and growing confidence. The freshman sprinted back to play defense with the poise of a senior, not pausing for a second to celebrate her go-ahead basket. I smiled at my friend behind the bench and said laughingly, "Just like we drew it up."

We went on to win the game, but one of the best moments of that win came while reviewing the game tape later in the week. With the camera staged on the bleachers behind our bench, we had a tremendous view of the big shot from the freshman as the play developed in front of us and a great angle on the fans across the gym in the main bleachers. I took the time in the film review to highlight the accomplishment of the team and the cool-handed approach of the freshman as we watched her knock down the shot again. It was especially fun to see her dad jump to his feet in the stands across the way with both fists in the air. It was a precious moment for all of us to celebrate.

For the rest of that year and her sophomore year, she spent a good portion of the time playing JV but swinging up to varsity. Her minutes were limited, but I could see a steady progression. In her sophomore campaign, with two senior guards graduating, she had a great opportunity to step up into a significant role as the point guard for the team. There was work she needed to do, but with her competitive spirit and seeing the writing on the wall, I was certain she could step up to the challenge. I hoped the opportunity would encourage her to work extra on her skills to be prepared for the next season. I had arranged for her to work with our graduating point guard and her father, a coach, to help develop the necessary skills. Unfortunately, the summer softball schedule was hectic, and the time was never put into working on individual basketball skills.

Prior to heading off to the Naval Academy for team camp that summer, I received news that I would be getting a transfer in from a high school up north. As it turns out, she was a junior point guard. The first time I got to see her in action was at team camp. It was very evident that she had good ball-handling skills and a good shot from

3-point range. She lacked the speed and agility of my current junior point guard, but she was a more mature floor general. At camp, they split time at point and sometimes played together with the other as the two-guard. As I did every summer, I was trying to get an idea of what combinations might work well on the floor and what the general strengths and weaknesses of the team were going into the season. I looked at the addition of the transferring guard as a positive. Both players possessed complimentary attributes. I hoped they would feed off and push each other to be better. If not, I was sure I could utilize both in various ways that would improve our team.

After returning home from camp, we played out the rest of our summer in the outdoor league at Belmar. For me, this was a more lighthearted affair as it was difficult to field any consistent team because so many of the kids had conflicts with other team sports and vacations. As players came and went, I tried a variety of combinations on the court. Everybody got a good share of time and even got to experience some different positions. The summer went well, and I excitedly began to plan for the first few practices in November. Then I got the phone call.

My friend, whose daughter was the freshman who hit the big shot a couple of years earlier and was now going into her junior year, called to express concern that I "handed" the point guard job to the new girl. That wasn't the case at all. We talked for a while about what I saw in both girls, how I thought they complimented each other well, and, more importantly, what they meant to the team. I also told him that this was summer, and nothing had been decided about the season in July. There was plenty of time to prepare for the season with individual work. As he pressed and began to get more heated in his approach, questioning my integrity, I told him he was out of line and taking advantage of our friendship. I ended the call with him encouraging his daughter to work hard and get prepared for the season.

During the early part of that basketball season, his daughter approached me about what she needed to do to improve. I appreciated the initiative and walked her through different aspects of her game. She seemed to embrace the idea and went to work on improving her skills. Her father seemed to drift further away from engaging me and became a little more public in denouncing me because of how I "gave his daughter's spot away." A mutual friend of ours, one who liked to stir the pot jokingly, turned to him and asked what he was going to do when his younger daughter was on varsity, implying that she was better than the older daughter. We were never the best of friends, but we were certainly friendly. While his oldest daughter was on the team for the next two years, he was much more distant and less friendly. In his mind, his daughter was entitled to the starting point guard role, and I had taken that opportunity away.

As I have shared before, a very satisfying experience as a coach comes in the "light bulb moments" experienced by players. During her senior campaign, this player continued to grow and made many key contributions to the team. As we pushed deep into another successful season, we were playing a game against Toms River North to prepare for the state playoffs. North had a great coach who was building a strong program of her own. I felt this would be a good test for us before the postseason. As the game progressed, the player previously discussed was finding more comfort in her game and playing with tremendous confidence. She went on to post a career-high of 16 points in the game. That switch had been turned on, and she fully embraced her role on the team, which showed in the quality of play.

One of the more frustrating coach experiences is the overzealous parent who tries so hard to help their child during the game that they end up hurting them. I think everybody who has attended a youth sports game has encountered the "sideline coach," often gesturing or actually yelling out instructions to their child during live play or trying desperately to gain their child's attention while the team is huddling during a timeout to offer their two cents about what corrections need to be made. What those parents fail to recognize or don't care to respect is that they are often doing more harm than good. Don't get me wrong, the parent-child relationship is important in the overall progression and maturation of a young athlete. However, there is a right time and place for parental guidance, which should not be taking place during competition or immediately following a game, win or lose.

As a coach who was also a father of three wonderful young athletes, I carefully separated the moments and my role in their development. During their games for teams where I wasn't their coach, I limited my comments to words of encouragement for them and support for their team. I would never tell them what to do in the game, how to run their plays, and never yell the dreaded word "shoot!" Instead, I would encourage through phrases like "box out," "work to get open," "be shot ready," or "keep working hard." I would reserve specific coaching, if required or requested, for a later time, hopefully well after the game's emotion has subsided. I would later adopt this philosophy as the "24-Hour Rule" throughout my coaching career. I believe this is a great rule for all relationships in athletics, especially coach-player. There is a lot of emotion in competition. Sometimes, feelings can run a little high.

Although not always successful, I tried to reserve my more pointed criticism about my team's play until everybody could be removed from the situation and had adequate time to reflect on individual and team performance. This is particularly effective after a game when the team didn't play well. Win or lose, everybody knows when the team hasn't performed at its best—no sense in brow-beating the players. There have been a few occasions where I have entered the locker room after the game too angry or disappointed to have a productive post-game discussion. Instead of trying to find the right words in that emotional moment, I would write on the board the time of our next practice. I would use the quiet bus ride home from away games to "detox" from the stew of frustration, gather my thoughts, and reflect on that night's contest and what we could do to improve. What I would often remind myself is that the players were also stewing. They knew when we played well as a team and when their individual contribution was meaningful to the team output. They were often just as frustrated. By the end of the bus ride, I was generally collected enough to say a few words and offer some encouragement about our next opportunity for growth and improvement, which was the next day's practice. If our negative experience happened at a home game, I would use the time at home that night to put things in proper perspective, usually with some sage words of advice from my wife, a great game fan and an assistant coach by proxy. My next practice would start with a brief recap of areas for improvement, recognition of things we did well, and encouragement to pull everything together, starting with the practice at hand. The important thing was to allow enough time for the immediate emotion to subside and focus on building in a positive manner.

In all honesty, I believe most parents are trying to encourage their child-athletes to work hard and have fun while learning how to function in a team environment. However, some get too caught up in the game's emotion and the desire to see their child succeed, sometimes apparently at the cost of everything else. You can hear and see the difference between good parent fans and those who lose sight of the team aspect of most sports, only caring about the advancement of their son or daughter. The screams are not cheers and encouragement but often vocal disappointment in their child's effort, indiscreet comments about the "lack" of skill or performance in other players, or disparaging public remarks questioning plays or directed at the coach. From the bench, often across the gym from the fans, I didn't hear or pay attention to the antics of the fanatics. Sometimes, in huddles, I would see a player looking into the crowd, trying to acknowledge the "coaching" they were getting from Mom or Dad. If I felt that the player was becoming distracted by what they were seeing or hearing from the fan side of the game, I would sub for them and take a moment to help them focus on the game and their contribution to the team.

In one case, while I was the coach of the seventh and eighth grade boys at Holy Family, one of my best players was my power forward, a humble workhorse who often outwilled bigger, taller players. During his seventh grade season, I often talked to his parents, touting his work ethic and contribution to the team. Like their son, the parents were generally quiet and reserved. Something changed during the eighth grade season. This was my third or fourth year at the school. We had a good team, and because of increasing successes the previous season, we were expected to compete for our division title and have a fighter's chance at the league championship. If those prospects were going to be fulfilled, the team would need every bit of strength and resolve in our power forward.

He started the season off strong. Paired up with our center, who was a tremendously gifted athlete with uncanny leaping ability, we had a dynamic front court that was eclipsing our opponent's rebounding efforts at a three to one clip. I had seen a stat somewhere revealing that the team who wins the rebound war wins the game 85% of the time. This was undoubtedly bearing out. However, as the season went on and our successes grew, I noticed an increased tension in my power forward. I also began to recognize the sounds of a more vocal and animated father. Not only was he yelling out instructions to his son, but he would sometimes slip into admonishing him for what he considered bad play. The result was a conflicted, confused, and increasingly demoralized player. He was hard enough on himself in judging his game actions. He certainly didn't need negative reinforcement from his father. At first, the boy would shoot a glare at his dad or mouth a plea to stop. As heavy and public as the criticism was, the boy never disrespected his father. With each admonishment, the wind would slowly leave his sails. My power forward was not beaten by our opponent, but rather by a depleted self-confidence. His inner strength was gone, and I noticed a physical change in his outer strength. He would literally "shrink" in stature as if trying to find a place to hide on the court. It got so bad in one game that I had no choice but to take him out and sit him on the bench where I hoped he could gather himself. After putting him back in the game, the cycle didn't take long to repeat. Following my halftime discussion with the team, I pulled the young boy aside privately, giving him some words of support and encouragement to help him learn to focus on the game and not anything else going on in the gym. I was proud of his efforts as he worked not only to block out opponents and control the glass but also to block out the continued negativity.

We went on to win that game, but I felt very unsettled about the incident. This was early in my coaching career, so I hadn't yet adopted the 24-hour rule. After the game, I politely asked the boy's father if I could have a few minutes of his time. We moved to a hallway adjacent to the gym but still in the public eye. I wasn't worried about any physical altercation. My concern was for privacy because of the topic's sensitivity, and I didn't want to risk any sense of embarrassment for the father. When in the hallway, I thanked him for coming to the games and supporting his son and the team. I told him it was always good to see family, friends and students filling the gym. There is nothing like playing in a full gym; the buzz of the crowd, the back-and-forth banter between fans clinging to every play as if it were the last, and the occasional sounds of the local school band playing during timeouts, making communication in the huddle a challenge. I also told the father that I was proud of his son for the way he works and for how he shoulders both a physical role and a leadership role for the team. He quickly expressed gratitude and echoed my sentiments. After we agreed, I rolled the dice and asked him to please refrain from the negative comments shouted out to his son during the game. I explained how the words destroyed the boy's confidence, hurting his game and team. I followed by saying if he was somehow unable to do that, I would prefer that he not attend the games. This is where the situation could have gone bad, but it had quite the opposite effect. The father acknowledged that he gets wound up during the games. The last thing he ever wanted to do was hurt his son's feelings, and he was unaware of how bad it sounded. We shook hands after the conversation and parted on great terms. From then on, the father was positive in his words of encouragement, and the results were noticeable. Instead of hanging his head in shame or frustration, I often caught a glimpse of a prideful smile breaking out on my player's face. He went on to have a fantastic season. While we won our division, we fell short of winning the league championship. No matter what, the greatest accomplishment was the turnaround in a father-son relationship through the game of basketball.

Unfortunately, many of these situations don't end so well. During the game, crowd noise is generally that . . . noise. I can hear the ebb and flow of the game through the gasps and cheers of the crowd, but I rarely hear specific things fans are saying. Occasionally, I would scout another team in preparation for a future contest. During those games, I sat on the side of the fans and heard the game from an entirely different angle. Some of the things I heard in the crowds at those games would make even the saltiest sailor blush. Nobody seemed free of ridicule and criticism . . . team players, opponents, coaches, and certainly the refs. After a few scout games, I grew a much greater appreciation for sitting on the other side and not being able to discern the negative rants from the crowd's cheers. However, there were a few forgettable moments where crowd noise dissipated right as a parent chose to get loud.

One such moment was during a summer league game at Red Bank Regional. This summer league is held over four days, where the girls play two games a night in a hot, humid gym. The idea is to give players and coaches some additional exposure before the end of summer when winter sports coaches can no longer engage their players in keeping with NJSIAA rules. The league provides a great venue, along with team camp and team workouts, for the girls to get to know one another and for the coach to begin formulating some ideas of talent coming into the season. This is supposed to be a low-key event that promotes unity. Some people get hopelessly lost in the competition regardless of the circumstances.

During one particularly hazy, hot, and humid evening in early August, we were finishing up our second evening game. The girls were playing well but obviously on the tail end of their energy level. This was a summer when some of my older players were learning new leadership roles because we had graduated some key seniors the year before. There were times in the summer games when we obviously needed more chemistry and looked a little disjointed on defense, missing assignments and slow in rotation. Our lapses didn't come from a lack of effort but more from a lack of cohesion. Again, this is all part of the summer league, identifying weaknesses and areas of focus. At one point late in this hotly contested summer league game, I called a time-out to calm the girls and emphasize the teaching moment in a game that bore no significance on our season, at least not from a playing standpoint. At the relatively quiet moment after the time-out call by the ref, one of the fathers screams out, "Play some goddamn defense!"

This is the first time I heard this guy blurt something out, but, as I found out later, it was not the first time he had chosen to voice his opinions. It was deafening and heard by those on our court and the crowds from the two adjacent courts. I kept it light on the outside by telling the girls in the huddle that even the crowd noticed we could be better on the defensive end. Inside, I was disappointed that any parent, in the middle of a meaningless summer league game, would be so brash as to take the Lord's name in vain while disparaging his daughter and her teammates. In many ways, this was a growing pain and a foreshadowing of things to come.

EIGHT
A THOUSAND WAYS TO 1,000 POINTS

AS A HIGH SCHOOL BASKETBALL PLAYER, reaching 1,000 career points at the varsity level is a significant milestone. It highlights a player's scoring ability and unique skill sets, allowing them to spend most of their high school career on varsity. The individual achievement is tremendous and often celebrated with the game stoppage, acknowledgment of the individual, and most likely some flowers from Mom and Dad, as well as something from the school to memorialize the event. As the head coach for a girls' varsity program for 16 years and an assistant for 6 years, I have had the occasion to witness many of these celebrations. In a vacuum, these are wonderful moments. Behind the scenes, they can reveal so much more about the players and their supporters.

Whenever we got inside of 20 points to the mark for an individual player, I pulled them aside and had a personal conversation. This was a practice I would repeat for all my players on this threshold. I take great pride in my relationship with my players. I am the drill sergeant, trying to help them understand the potential that lies within them and challenging them to bring their best to every practice and every game. I am the guru trying to help them think the game, a mantra I often repeat to my players, encouraging an embrace of the intricacies that make good teams fluid in effort and make the sport fun to be a part of. I am the philosopher, speaking of love for the game and wanting each player, starter or role player, to practice like they play and to play with passion. Probably most importantly to me, I am their coach, an additional positive role model in their lives, protective of each player as if they were my own child, wanting them to develop and mature not only in the game of basketball but also take the lessons of the game into a productive and fulfilling adult life. The success of a coach is often measured in wins and losses. I would be lying if I said winning wasn't important. However, it was equally important for me to succeed in building strong, trusting relationships with all my players, each unique to the players themselves.

We > Me

My first opportunity to participate in the 1,000-point milestone came in the 2009-2010 season at Mater Dei. As a coach, I was blessed with a very talented group of players that featured gritty, hardworking girls who embraced their individual roles with fervor but also understood their importance to the overall team. The balance on the team was incredible, and we were fortunate to have not one but two players on the verge of the 1,000-point mark. I quietly kept track of the official stats over their four years on varsity and never mentioned the pending milestone. In my eyes, I didn't want to add any undue pressure to the girls. My greater concern was ensuring that the focus on teamwork and unified effort wasn't overshadowed by somebody trying to "get theirs." The two players went about the team's business and competed without a problem. As we got into the heat of the season, trying to win a division championship and qualify for the Shore Conference and state tournaments, the individual milestone became more in focus for both players and their teammates who wanted to celebrate shared success, as well as their part in making it all possible. The players were unique in their scoring methods. One was a graceful shooter with impeccable form and a soft touch, capable of scoring anywhere on the court. The other was the proverbial bull in a China shop, bullying her way into the paint and out willing opponents to loose balls and offensive rebounds, both of which led to second-chance points. As unique as their skill sets were, so were the experiences around accomplishing 1,000 career points.

The first player to approach the scoring milestone was my center, the graceful shooter and quiet force on the team. She never mentioned the 1,000-point plateau to me personally, but I wanted to have the talk with her. It was a simple conversation where I expressed my pride in her individual accomplishments on the court and, in this case, the maturity and elegance with which she handled the situation. She went about her business of contributing to the team in any way she could. I also wanted to relieve potential stress, letting her know that nothing would stop her from getting to 1,000 points. We had at least a dozen games left in the season, and she was inside of 20 points. Her scoring average alone would have her there in two games, if not sooner. I also encouraged her not to keep the score in her head and push for the number. Let the scoring come naturally as it had all throughout her career, through the combination of her skill sets, our offenses, and through the hard work of her teammates. We had a great discussion, parted with a hug, and returned to preparing for our next opponent.

On January 1, 2010, I called the player's parents. Wishing them a Happy New Year, I went on to share with them that their daughter would most likely eclipse 1,000 points in our next game, which was the following day at Keyport. I let them know that the game is customarily stopped for a brief moment to acknowledge the player, so if they wanted to give flowers and take pictures, there would be time to do so. Since we were on the road, I also let them know that I had planned to acknowledge the event at our next home game more formally. The parents were grateful for the call and the efforts toward recognition. Like their daughter, they were humble, quietly doing their business. During the game at Keyport, things went off without a hitch. With an elbow jump shot, her sweet spot on the court, she scored the points that pushed her over the mark. Keyport was very gracious in allowing a few minutes of recognition and joined in the celebration. We cruised to victory and had a very enjoyable bus ride home, topped off with a raucous rendition of our school fight song as we pulled into our parking lot, a tradition when returning from games. As a coach, I was beaming with pride, very pleased with the way everything unfolded, and even more excited about the opportunity for the other player on the team, who wasn't far behind in the hunt for 1,000 points. Unfortunately, like the players themselves, the next run at the mark would prove to be completely different.

The Raging Bull

The power forward on our team was the one I dubbed the female Charles Barkley for her uncanny aggression, strength, tenacity, and ability to play bigger than her 5' 5" frame. As I said earlier, she was the bull. A soccer player by trade and a very good one, she used the combination of speed, athleticism, and raw determination to make her good at everything she did. Another player that I was lucky to have a great relationship with. Like many of her teammates, I had the opportunity to coach her for several years before high school in township leagues and AAU. We worked well together, mainly on the same page, but sometimes butting heads. Her will was as stubborn as her efforts to put the ball in the basket, sometimes missing a layup in traffic but getting multiple attempts just by beating opponents up on the offensive glass. With equal enthusiasm, she would sometimes challenge my direction because she didn't agree or didn't understand the purpose. Gentle nudging with a firm but fair hand, as well as a few hundred suicides (a sprinting drill used for conditioning), got us through to a level of mutual respect and admiration. This player knew she was getting close to 1,000 points and was pushing to get there. Although she would often ask me, I never revealed the exact total.

My efforts for discretion and focus on the team instead of the individual were made more difficult by doting relatives, a pseudo aunt and uncle, who kept score on the sidelines for every game. I understood that they often paid her for points scored or offered her other rewards for her efforts. I thought their intentions were simple and innocent, but they didn't realize the situation they were creating. Or, maybe they did and just didn't care. Thrown into the mix, the player's parents often touted the individual accomplishments of their daughter. The mother was fiercely competitive and often showed it with vocal outbursts at the team, the opponent, the officials, and the coaches. The father, also very competitive and very proud of his oldest child, was much more reserved but equally intense. The combination of personalities and situations led to one of the most disheartening experiences in my coaching career.

At the appropriate time, I pulled my player aside. Again, I talked with her, congratulating her, encouraging her to relax and let things come naturally, and embracing that this isn't just her achievement but something the whole team contributed to and wants to celebrate. As before, we shared an embrace and got back to work. Going into the week, she was less than 30 points away, and we had three games coming up. At the start of our second contest that week, a road game at Keansburg, she was 17 points away, a very achievable game total. I promised myself I would coach as normal, working the team through our offenses and defenses to win this game and prepare for a bigger challenge at Rumson-Fair Haven on Saturday. I didn't want to shift any focus during the game and add any pressure on my players by trying to force the 1,000 points. The game was a blowout early, and we were on our way with Keansburg. I subbed liberally throughout the first three quarters to keep some integrity in the game and honor the spirit of sportsmanship. Beyond good game etiquette, I was also trying to preserve our players for a much more physical and challenging contest on Saturday and take the opportunity to get minutes for my bench players to develop their game skills and team depth. At the end of the third quarter, up by 30 points, I glanced at the scorebook and saw that my player was 6 points away from eclipsing the personal mark. I decided to go for it and let the starters, who had played together with her for several years, get after it a little to see if they could hit the mark. As a courtesy, I told the opposing coach why my starters were going in. He was very gracious about the whole thing, offering me a handshake and the challenge that they were not going to "let her have the points." Challenge understood and accepted. I can't begin to tell you how frustrating the fourth quarter was for all involved. Her teammates, in a collectively unselfish manner, did everything they could to help tally those 6 points. True to the words of the other coach, the points were not coming easy, a testament to his players and their desire to compete in spite of being down by 30 points. In fact, with less than two minutes left, she was still four points away. I decided to pull the other four players and cycle in my bench, which included two spunky freshmen. They worked hard all season long and deserved the opportunity to get game minutes. When the subs reported to the scorer's table and were buzzed into the game, an unfortunate mess began to unravel.

In a shrill voice that carried across the gym, with very little discretion or concern for the players and their respective families,

Auntie blurted out, "Why is he putting THEM in!" Not fazed by the expression of doubt and disdain, my freshman point guard proceeded to pick the pocket of the opposing team's guard and pass the ball to my freshman forward, who instinctively advanced the ball to her senior teammate . . . bucket! We were now two points away from hitting the mark. Against my previous decision, I called a timeout and drew up a play to allow the key bucket to be scored. The less experienced group on the floor executed the play flawlessly, leading to a layup opportunity. Missed! The next possession led to a series of screens and passes, getting the ball into the right player's hands again. The opposing player was whistled for a reaching foul. Two points away from the career plateau, my player was headed to the foul line for one and one. This was it, or so we thought. With the tension inside undoubtedly mounting and her competitive spirit raging, she made the front end of the free-throws, pulling her within one point, but missed the second. Time was now the real opponent in the game. There was no doubt she would make 1,000 points, but it looked more and more like it would be the next game. With only seconds on the clock, I tried one more time, drawing up a side out of bounds play that was made for her style of play. A play we had run successfully many times over the years, which resulted in her scoring. Her eyes lit up, and the team was anxious to finish the job. As the play unfolded, she received a pass leading her down the lane for a layup. Missed again! A foul was called, resulting in a two-shot opportunity from the charity stripe. Needing one point to finish the task, and with the entire gym knowing what was developing, she approached the line.

We all watched in disbelief as both free throws rattled out. The waning seconds ended without another scoring opportunity. While we were all happy and celebrating the team win, a definitive cloud hung over the gym. Little did I know that a storm was brewing.

As was the ritual following the final buzzer, after shaking hands with the other team, our team filtered into the locker room for post-game review. I held the locker room door open as the girls filed in, except for one. I noticed that my power forward was still down by our bench, visibly upset. I told the girls to get dressed and then gathered up our remaining teammate. She was crying and very distraught over the fact that she couldn't get the one point needed to seal the deal. I gave her a consoling hug and encouraged her with the fact that we would be playing again on Saturday in a much more exciting environment and more meaningful game. What better arena for such a grand occasion? I also reminded her that her team was in the locker room waiting for her to join in the celebration of our victory. This is where her stubbornness kicked in, and she railed about how she didn't care and that she was mad that she didn't get the extra point. A little miffed at her attitude and actions, I quietly told her that she was acting selfishly and needed to focus on being part of the team. I walked to the locker room where the team waited and held the door for her to enter, eventually.

As we exited the locker room to board the bus, we were greeted by parents, friends, and supporters congratulating us on the win. On my way out to check on the location of the bus, I passed the player's mother in the school hallway. With flames coming out of her eyes, which rested above cheeks emblazoned red from boiling blood, she abruptly greeted me with, "Don't even fucking talk to me!"

Stunned by the brazen outburst from somebody I considered a friend, I did my best to ignore it, not wanting to get caught up in the emotion of the moment, potentially making a bad situation worse. Before I could gather the team on the bus, I noticed a verbal altercation between some family members of the team and the aunt of the player. I was filled in later that the spark was the aunt blaming the "asshole coach" for not allowing her niece to accomplish the personal scoring plateau. A couple of the other parents who had heard the verbal transgression commented on her lack of discretion in calling me names and doing so in front of my players. I moved quickly to get the girls on the bus to insulate the team from further mayhem.

While on the bus, the nonsense continued as the player sat in the back, still crying and acting out verbally. At first, her teammates tried to console and encourage her, empathizing with the frustration she must have felt. As the relatively short ride continued, the rest of the team, particularly the senior co-captains, became increasingly frustrated and started to hit me up with texts admonishing her behavior. I told them to hold tight, and we will get past this tension. When we arrived at school, with a much more subdued school fight song in spite of the convincing victory, the girls got off the bus and headed home. The senior co-captains let me know what transpired in the back of the bus and voiced their frustration and concern over the selfish attitude and outburst. I told them that we all needed to take 24 hours on this to allow for things to settle. I would address any remaining issues the next day at practice.

At home, I had a lot of time to stew over the events of the game. In addition, my wife shared her perspective with me, both as a fan in the stands for the game and as a concerned parent. My oldest daughter, one of the four senior captains, was also visibly upset about things said and done on the bus ride home. In addition, she was concerned about the negative impact this might have on the team as a whole. After a lot of reflection, I decided to talk to the player. When the girls arrived for practice the next day, I pulled my power forward aside. Along with her senior teammates and co-captains, we discussed the horrible displays at the gym and on the bus. She apologized for her actions and for those of her family, noting that she could not control their behavior. I had it in my head that I was going to suspend her for the next game, but her act of contrition to the team seemed to satisfy all parties. We went on to prepare for the big game against Rumson and the pending big moment. What promised to make the 1,000-point mark even more special was the fact that three of the girls from the Rumson team played AAU on the team I coached, with six girls from our team.

In addition to the big game environment, playing in front of a packed gym, the moment was made even more special as one of the fathers from the opposing team, a family from our AAU team, had planned to have a sports photographer on hand to capture the moment. It didn't take long as our press created a steal, resulting in a driving layup for the basket. The bull was not going to be denied this one. With barely any time off the clock, the game was stopped, and a brief celebration took place. I was the first person out on the court to give her a congratulatory embrace. The rest of the team quickly followed. Her mother and father came out on the court to give the flowers and take a few pictures. The agony was over. The sad part about the entire thing was that the actions at Keansburg had dampened the overall enthusiasm for this moment. In hindsight, we couldn't have planned a better venue for the moment to occur. It was truly a storybook moment, playing a powerhouse team in a great basketball environment, getting the key points with senior teammates assisting and members of the other team being involved due to shared experiences in AAU, as well as having a photographer there to memorialize the entire day. The icing on the cake was a team photo at half court following the game, not of the high school team, but of the AAU team made up of members from both teams that competed that day, as well as players from other schools who had come to watch, and the AAU coaching staff. The cherry would have been a victory for my high school team. Unfortunately, we fell short of that, but we did end the day and the quest for 1,000 on a very high note. I was glad it was behind us and that nobody else would be close for a while.

Keeping the Faith

While there wasn't going to be a 1,000-point scorer on my team for a few years, we did have the occasion to celebrate the mark in our gym the following year. During my tenure at Mater Dei, I became friendly with a family from Keansburg High School. In my third year at Mater Dei, I noticed the blue-collar effort of the center at Keansburg. I grew to admire her strength, determination, and leadership. She was the caliber of player not generally seen on the "lower" teams in our division, my team included, but quietly went about her business as Mother Hen and put in strong effort night after night. After games, I would talk to her and acknowledge her strength of play and character. I eventually met her father and two younger sisters. Her father's pride was evident for all his girls, but especially for his eldest daughter, who had been forced into a maternal role when her mother passed away a few years earlier. The more I learned about the family situation, the more I admired the individual courage demonstrated by this young lady. I began to follow her efforts in the paper. When our games against Keansburg approached, I was excited to not only plan on how to stop her but also to have the opportunity to talk to her and check in on the family. Through our conversations, we developed a friendship that would extend for many years.

When the youngest sister became interested in basketball, her father approached me about AAU. By this time, I had stopped coaching AAU for a couple of years, but I still knew a lot of the local coaches. I introduced the father to the coach of the Jersey Shore Wildcats, and a match was made. Her innate skill sets were tremendous, and she was a true scorer with incredible athletic ability. As she got closer to high school age, her father wanted her to play for me. One significant obstacle was the fact that I was at a Catholic school with a tuition burden. Although the school itself would have been a great place for her to mature, and she would have been a perfect fit on our team, the financial hurdle proved to be too much for a single parent raising three daughters. Instead of having the opportunity to coach her, I had the honor and dubious challenge of coaching against her. Through it all, we maintained a friendship.

Sadly, during her junior year, her father passed away suddenly. Now, the three girls were left to face the world without their parents. Family and friends did what they could to help, but the task was not easy. All three girls were forced to grow up a bit quicker than they should as they faced life's new challenge. However, through it all, they were able to use their love for the game of basketball as a comforting familiarity and the communion with coaches and teammates as their new family. The two younger sisters went on to lead their team to a very respectable season. The youngest worked her way into the scorebook in grand fashion, eclipsing the 1,000-point mark. I felt a swell of pride when I read about it in the newspaper, happy for her, but also knowing that her parents were smiling down from heaven. Looking at our schedule, I saw that we were due to play Keansburg at home in a couple of weeks. I talked to my assistant coach, and we agreed that we should take a moment on our home court to recognize our opponent for her accomplishment, something that isn't usually done.

My assistant found a beautiful crystal basketball perched on a stand. She had it engraved with the player's name and the date of her 1,000 points. Before our game, without forewarning Keansburg, I announced the situation to the attending crowd and presented our gift. Typical of her personality, the youngest sister was bashful in coming forward to receive the award, but the gratitude was evident in her eyes, now swelling with tears. It was a beautiful moment; sports and competition were done right, and I am glad I could share them. She was a terrific young lady and a great player. Bolstered by her sisters' love, her love of the game, and the support from the basketball community around her, she went on to complete one of the best high school careers and played all four years in college.

The D-Train Never Made the Station

I was in the best seat of the house for one of the most remarkable seasons in Shore Conference girls' basketball. In some ways, it is unfortunate that it happened on our team and not one of the more media darling-type teams. I say that only because not enough people knew of the strength, courage, passion for the game, and maturing leadership one of my girls demonstrated. Going into her senior campaign, a player I nicknamed D-Train needed 551 points to reach 1,000. I didn't give the mark much thought because that is a lot of ground to cover; we ran a system to get multiple players involved, and this player was unselfish. Those weren't exactly variables in an equation that required an average of over 22 points per game. However, during our fall SPARQ training, D-Train declared that she would be the next 1,000-point scorer for Mater Dei.

As a freshman, she played most of the season on JV, hampered by an early season knee strain and a lack of confidence. Her older sister was a senior on the varsity team and a very gifted basketball player. In some ways, I thought D-Train was afraid to play up, even though she had the raw skills to do so, because of her sister's skills and the team's strength around her. I wasn't going to put pressure on the situation, so I figured we'd bring the younger sister along when the time was right. I'll admit, it was frustrating. I wanted D-Train to see and understand her talent like I did. Eventually, she began to heal, and through repetition and experience at the JV level, she began to build confidence. On January 29, she made her varsity debut, coming into a game late against Asbury Park. D-Train scored her first two varsity points in that game and unwittingly marked the first step in an incredible journey of personal growth, team leadership, and an unbridled enthusiasm for the game of basketball.

In comparison to her predecessors, who had accomplished the 1,000-point mark, her 11 varsity points as a freshman paled up against 214 and 231 points, respectively. Her sophomore campaign was marked with the typical inconsistency of a young player trying to learn how to play the game and contribute at a high level. She struggled with timing and decision-making, causing her confidence to waiver. I wasn't about to give up on the promise I saw and knew it was just a matter of time before her potential was revealed. During our second regular season game versus our division rival and my personal nemesis, we traveled down to Belmar to play St. Rose. They were the perennial winners of our division and a powerhouse in the Shore Conference. Early on in my tenure at Mater Dei, we were on the wrong end of several beatings at the hands of the Purple Roses. Over the few years leading up to this season, as the Mater Dei program improved, we had come very close to beating them on several occasions, including a one point loss in overtime the previous year. Our two teams and coaches knew each other well. We needed something new and different to have a chance at breaking the stronghold that St. Rose had on the B-Central division. At this point in the season, we were both undefeated in the division and tied for first. If we were going to win our division, we needed to make a stand and break through. We needed a secret weapon.

On a team blessed with a strong senior class, with one 1,000-point scorer and another on the way just three games later, the opponents' focus was on making somebody else beat them that night. As shots opened, other team members did their part in contributing, but we weren't quite closing the gap. As the battle raged, a couple of my players got into foul trouble, and I was forced to go to my bench. Looking to uncork that potential, I called on D-Train. With seven varsity games under her belt, she had started to demonstrate an ability to get her shot off. Although only amassing 27 points in those seven games, 10 of them came in the last contest. It was time to step up and put it all together. It wasn't long after entering the game that the ball reversed to her at the right wing, where she promptly buried a 3-pointer. The bench erupted, and a spark had definitely been lit. On the next possession, D-Train dropped in another 3-pointer. Hope was rising, and the team began to really dig in for the fight. The coach of St. Rose couldn't make an aggressive defensive adjustment to shift focus to the sophomore because doing so would uncover the lid his players were putting on the two 1,000-point seniors. It was a "pick your poison" moment, and he chose to let her go. It would be nice to say we claimed victory that night, but we once again fell short, leaving Belmar with teary eyes and broken hearts. While the loss stung, the rising tide of potential realized was an amazing sensation. The sophomore talent dropped 21 points that night, including five 3-pointers. A long way from 1,000 points, or even thinking of it, there was a definite understanding she could contribute, and her confidence began to grow.

Unfortunately, the knee injury that plagued her freshman year started to flare up again, and the pattern of inconsistency returned. D-Train only scored 61 points in the next 12 games. Worst yet, she was forced to sit out the remainder of the season due to the injury. Unfortunately for the team, we were in the heart of the Shore Conference and State tournament season. Although inconsistent, her contributions would be sorely missed, and we would ultimately fall short of some of our season goals.

Her junior campaign was nothing special. We were in a rebuilding mode as a team, having graduated a strong senior class . . . the best collection of individual talent I had ever coached. We lacked senior leadership and had a pretty good junior class led by an emerging talent junior, a strong but inexperienced group of sophomores, and a promising young freshman. We finished up the year 14-11 and lost in the first round of both post-season tournaments. There was a palpable hangover at the end of the season, with all of those returning feeling like we just missed on many occasions. The talk quickly turned to summer camps and workouts, and there seemed to be an unusual excitement spreading around the team. The talented junior and two of the sophomore players drove the enthusiasm, which became infectious. When we got to fall workouts, the three of them approached me with the declaration of a special season that would get us a championship and see D-Train, the now-senior leader, reach her 1,000 points.

We started out the 2009-10 season with a convincing win over Keansburg. We were expected to win, but the girls played exceptionally well. It was obvious during the first two weeks of practice, building up to opening night, that this team had very good chemistry. The question was, at least on paper, could we be consistent in our efforts and overcome some glaring weaknesses? My point guard was a towering 5'1" bundle of energy and effort. She commanded our offensive sets and was an absolute pest on defense. My center, who was also my youngest daughter, was 5'8" and had the arduous task of going up against taller, stronger girls every night. It seemed like every other team had at least one 6' tall girl, and more than a few had girls 6'2" and taller. Even my senior captain was only 5'5" but packed a lot of basketball in every inch. We were always the shortest team on the court but never short on effort or desire, and always played with a strong team focus. They may not have been my most talented team in terms of individual skill sets, but they were the best TEAM I had the pleasure of coaching.

The funny thing is that after our convincing win against Keansburg, we came out the next game and laid an absolute dud at Asbury Park. I did a horrible job of motivating the girls prior to the game. Honestly, Asbury wasn't very good, and we all expected to roll to a win and roll out of town. Asbury Park came ready to play and seemed to hit every shot they took. Shooting an impressive 72% from the floor, Asbury stormed out to a 23-11 first quarter lead. Needless to say, I was annoyed at our overall effort. I knew I didn't do a good job in the pre-game, but the girls were doing an even worse job of executing our sets. Asbury Park was clearly the inferior team, but we were putting forth an inferior effort. I challenged the girls between quarters to play with more intensity, stating that great teams play great regardless of their opponent. They answered the bell as a group, with D-Train leading the effort. She went on to put up 45 points in the game, shooting 18 of 23 from the floor (she didn't shoot one 3-pointer) and went 9 of 11 from the free-throw line. She also pulled in 10 rebounds in the game. We outscored Asbury 64-21 over the remaining three quarters. The team effort was a lot better, but the individual effort displayed that night was incredible. D-Train put the team on her back and demonstrated just how special they could be.

That game against Asbury served as the ignition to a great run. It was also the first time I began believing that 1,000 points wasn't out of the question. It also became very obvious that this wasn't an individual goal but truly something the entire team was working toward. The team went on to win 13 of the next 14 games, with our only loss, of course, coming at the hands of St. Rose. We played in the Brick Memorial Holiday Tournament in that run of wins. We were a small parochial team going up against much larger Group 3 and Group 4 schools. As I preached all season, "We may be undersized, but we will never be undermanned." The girls really took that to heart. Led by the senior sensation, they went on to win the Brick tournament, collecting the championship they promised. Dropping in 62 points in three games, D-Train led the team to the statement wins and collected the tournament MVP award. At this point in the season, through 5 games, she was averaging 25.6 points per game. That pace would get her to the 1,000-point mark, but there was a lot of season left to play. She and her teammates kept telling me they would get there.

The season went on, and the scoring pace slowed a bit, but D-Train was still chugging closer and closer. Coming into the last week of the regular season, Mother Nature hit New Jersey with a couple of whopper snowstorms. We ended up having three games canceled due to snow. Normally, we would have rescheduled the games without a problem, but we were running up against the Shore Conference Tournament schedule, followed by the State Tournament. Once states begin, no other games can be played. We were unable to get the games in before the states began due to additional snow. As states began, with three games taken away from the season, she was still 74 points away from 1,000. I even went so far as to call the offices of NJSIAA to see if we could somehow get special dispensation to schedule the canceled games because of the unusual amount of snow that winter. No such luck. Our only option was to keep winning and go as deep into the tournament as we could.

As it ended up, we lost a heartbreaker at home in a 4 vs 5 matchup that had us playing St. Joseph of Hammonton. We were flat all game and just couldn't find the basket in a poor 9 for 32 shooting night from the floor and coughed the ball up 21 times against a tightly packed two-three zone. Plain and simple, we didn't play well. What was a well-oiled machine all season long just ran out of gas. We lost, and a valiant march to 1,000 ended just 46 points shy. Being 46 points shy doesn't sound all that close, but remember that three games were snowed out, and D-Train started the season needing 551 to even hit the mark. She ended up with 505 points in one of the most remarkable individual seasons I have witnessed. The best part about it was that this was truly a team effort. All of the girls wanted to get there, and that common goal built an iron-clad bond within the team. We had our post-game talk in the locker room, then came out to talk with friends and family. For the next hour, the girls hugged and cried at center court, taking picture after picture and defying the idea that this very special season was over. In the end, the season was extremely successful at 18-8, but the true success was in how the girls came together as a team and how an individual goal manifested itself in team accomplishment.

NINE
A GROWING PAIN

AS MY COACHING CAREER PROGRESSED, I noticed a trend of parent attitudes becoming increasingly hostile and more daring in words and actions. There were multiple news reports across the country about parents rushing fields or courts to engage a coach or a game official violently. I have always worked hard to build relationships with the parents in my program. I tried to create a sense of community or extended family. Even with that effort, one father seemed to become more agitated with every passing day.

His daughter came to our program as a very talented freshman. She made it to the varsity team in her first year and started for the team. The more success she and the team had, the more irritated this man became. At one point, he asked me to meet with him to discuss basketball. I had known him and his family since I started coaching in the community. His brother was a good friend and somebody with whom I had previously coached. He was among the nicest, most giving people ever met. He was always doing something for the kids and the church in the community. My player's father didn't have the same reputation, but I thought it would be good for us to talk and level set expectations. We shared a few beers at a local pub and enjoyed a nice conversation. I thought we were in good shape.

During her early years with the team, the father often stormed out of games if he felt she wasn't playing well. That sense was mostly driven by whether she was scoring a lot, as opposed to how she was growing in the game and what the team was accomplishing. The player had already developed a reputation as being a good scorer, often drawing extra attention from the opponent's defense. She was the type of player other coaches had to game plan for, creating some difficult scoring situations. She was still young in the game, developing her skills and confidence. In addition, our team was relatively young and still learning how to play as a unit for each other. Everybody in the area enjoyed watching her play and, even more, appreciated her growth in the game. Except, it seemed, for her father.

The storming out of games deteriorated into more vocal outbursts. Some were directed at his daughter, others toward other players, and many toward me. I never understood what the angst was all about. His daughter always came to play, worked well with her teammates, and spearheaded a great run for the program during her four years; she was a starter since her freshman year and exceeded the 1,000-point mark in her high school career. She was a joy to coach, which made the sideline antics even harder to tolerate.

During a game at Middletown North one Saturday morning, the girls were not playing an inspired game of basketball. We were sluggish on offense, slow to set screens, and even slower with cuts to the basket. Our shots were short, and our legs heavy. As we were struggling early, I heard a bellow from the opposite corner of the gym to "set some screens." I recognized the voice and honestly didn't fault the suggestion at the time. There were screens in every offense we ran, especially Motion, where the focal point was to screen away and bring a teammate to the ball. The offense then develops from the screening action. However, the girls were lethargic in not setting up to receive a screen and even less effective in setting screens. Defensively, we were nowhere near our normal intensity with no pressure on the ball, no rotation to help, and giving up a lot of easy baskets. As the game went on, the frustrations within the team were palpable, and the frustration from the father boiled over. He chose a quiet moment during the stoppage of play to scream out some negative and colorful words aimed at the girls on the court. Again, the frustration was understood, but the delivery was wrong, especially when representing a Catholic school. Hearing a father yelling at them from the stands in such an embarrassing manner was deflating and only added to the pain they were already feeling. We ended up losing the game, and I was left bewildered by the lackluster effort and frustrated by the growing irritant in the stands. As it turns out, many of the girls on the team decided to take advantage of a Friday night, staying out late and partying through the wee hours of the morning. It is no wonder that the 10:30 AM game proved to be too much for them to handle. Unfortunately, those few girls' selfishness and lack of discipline hurt the team. The following practice involved a lot of running and "conditioning."

At one point, the father called me, threatening to take his daughter out of Mater Dei and send her to Red Bank Catholic. Having put up with his antics long enough, I told him to go ahead and make that happen. As much as I would have hated to lose his daughter, the truth is that no one person is bigger than the team. Fortunately, she finished out her four years with us and had a great career. Unfortunately, I had to continue to deal with increasingly brash and vulgar interactions.

Her junior and senior years were fun to watch as her talent grew. Despite the very talented roster around her, the father continued to feel like everything should run through her and all plays should be made for her. To the player's credit, she worked with her team to realize success. Our team struggled some during her junior campaign, finishing 15-12 on the season, but the talented junior continued to mature in the game. She was our most productive offensive player, with 394 points that season, but she still needed to round out her overall game. While she was the frame around which we ran, our engine was a fiery 5' 1" senior point guard and one of the team captains. She was a dual athlete with tremendous speed, defensive quickness, and a good decision-maker with the ball, and she also had a fantastic year. At the end of the season, I was left with a tough decision around who would be awarded the "Player of the Year." Anybody who watched our team regularly could make a successful argument for either player. After reviewing the season, the efforts of both players, the leadership roles they both had, albeit in different ways, and scrutinizing the stats for whatever story they told, the award was given to the senior point guard.

Well, that was like lighting the fuse to a keg of dynamite. I did not, nor should any coach, ever consider the parent's reaction to an award issued to a teammate. A string of angry e-mails was written first to me, then the AD, then the principal, then anybody who would listen. With every step up the school's chain of command, his e-mails back to me became more belligerent. His main points were:

If she wasn't considered the best player, by far, on your team, then why did you:

- *Make her team captain*
- *Play her the most minutes than any player on the team*
- *Ask her to shoot any technical free throws*

- *Put the ball in her hands with the game on the line*
- *Ask her to defend the best player on the other team*
- *Have her throw the ball in, help take it up the court, and design specific plays for her, which, according to you, have never done before*

In addition, she has never missed a game, practice, workout, or camp in her 3 years at Mater Dei.

All valid questions and points to consider. This falls back to my "rose-colored glasses." The same thing could be said for at least two other players on the team, both seniors. The junior did lead the team with scoring, but the senior point guard was second, with a better overall shooting percentage. The senior point guard led the team in assists by far, often being the catalyst to the junior's made baskets. She also led the team in steals by a three to one ratio, which created many easy scoring opportunities. Perhaps her most eye-opening statistic was the fact that she was second in team rebounding at 5' 1" tall. My very talented junior was fourth in rebounds. It wasn't an easy decision, but the selection of the senior point guard was the right decision for that year.

As a side note to the rebounding prowess of my mighty point guard, she didn't attempt rebounding that much prior to the beginning of her junior season. One can imagine that looking in at much taller and stronger players jockeying for position and wrestling for rebounds might have served as a deterrent for a 5' 1" point guard. During the first game of our holiday tournament, early in her junior season, we were battling a very big front court for the host team, including a 6' 2" tall, strong, aggressive center. We were struggling in the rebound battle. At half-time of the game, I asked my point guard if anybody was boxing her out when shots went up. She jokingly referenced that the opponents probably don't feel the need to. I told her that should make her mad. They were discounting her presence in the rebounding game. My challenge to her was that while everybody else was fighting for position and she was being ignored, she should see the lane, sprint the lane, and find the ball. "Yes, Coach!" I wound her up. Now, it was time to let her go.

In the second half of that game, she darted in and out of traffic, often emerging with the ball. Those rebounds occasionally provided second and third opportunities for our offense. She amassed 10 rebounds, and we went on to win the game. A slight adjustment to her game, her willingness to be coached, and her desire to contribute to the team in any way she could, added another layer to her game and helped us win the tournament. Later that year, at one point in a game against Rumson, another strong, Division 1 talent-laden team, I turned her loose on a 6' 1" Princeton recruit that was running point for the other team and shredding our defense. Her impact was immediate, smothering on ball defense, creating turnovers, and frustrating a very talented player. The opposing coach had to pull his marquee player out of the game to regroup and figure out a different way to run his offense. Unfortunately, I came to that realization too late in the game. We were fighting an uphill battle coming into the contest, but that kind of adjustment could have leveled the playing field.

Getting back to my very talented player with the disgruntled father, she continued to amass points, creeping closer to the 1,000-point mark, and the sidelines grew more intense. One of my most hard-working players struggled with the defensive pressure by the sidelines in one game. Frequent double teams made things difficult and forced her to rush her decisions. After a few turnovers on the same side of the court where the father was standing, he publicly derided the struggling player and shouted, "Take her out. She is killing us." The player was so distraught over the comments I had to remove her from the game to console her. During our conversation, she expressed her concern because that father was "tearing the team apart." The stands were buzzing with people in disbelief that a parent could say something like that about a player on the court, let alone one from the team he was "rooting" for. As the game played on, I could see my oldest daughter, now a player at Drew University, talking to the father on the sideline. I watched for a minute out of concern, but she seemed poised and unthreatened. We ended up losing the game to the division standard bearer, St. Rose of Belmar. The girls played hard as usual, but the moment was just too big for them at that point in the season.

Once I got home, I asked my daughter what that conversation was all about. She told me that people in the stands were getting irritated with the father's constant remarks. As an alumnus of the program and somebody now playing in college, she was trying to explain to him some of the plays and the roles and responsibilities of the various players, emphasizing the value of team along the way. She also offered assurances that the plays we were running were very similar to what is expected in college. He, of course, wasn't hearing any of it. I appreciated my daughter's effort, but I was concerned about the father's more vocal and aggressive antics. I decided to invite him to meet with me at a local diner for a discussion to clear the air and create a more constructive and enjoyable environment.

We met at a local diner. Things were cordial but tense at first. I really didn't expect anything else. We had been friendly over the years, enjoying some conversations around basketball even before his daughter started playing for me. I thought we would have an open discussion, clear some air, and be in a more favorable position to move forward. I guess that is the optimist in me. After some small talk around our families and the season, he started in on the idea that our offense needed more screens. I shared with him that every one of our offenses is designed with continuous screening action to create openings for players on the floor. The idea is to develop multiple threats and make things more difficult for the defense. Everybody on our team was encouraged to be a scoring threat and challenged to be hard to guard. My initial efforts were met with skepticism, so I began the practice of drawing out one of our set plays, including a sequence of an up screen from the post for the point guard after they initiated a pass to the wing. This movement allowed for a give-and-go opportunity right away. If not there, the point continues to work through a block-to-block movement. While the up screen was beginning, the opposite side post and wing were setting up for a staggered screen that would allow the point guard to continue through to the opposite side, setting up for a three-point attempt. An on-ball screen was set for the person receiving the initial pass, allowing them to reverse the ball and setting up pick-and-roll action on the ball side. If the ball got reversed, the opposite wing lifted to receive the pass. Depending on the action from the staggered screen, the wing may have entry passes into either post or could continue reversing to the point guard for the shot attempt. If nothing was available, the team was drilled to flash up toward the ball, allowing for continuity in the UCLA offense. The girls ran the play very well, often getting looks out of the initial set. The team was also very well-versed at running UCLA, so if nothing developed, we could get great looks out of the continued movements of the offense. As I showed this to the father, I also explained that his daughter was the one receiving the up and staggered screens to shed her of the defender who often played her tight because of her scoring prowess. One set play, four screens, three of which were set for his daughter. I thought he would appreciate the visual and hoped that it would ease his mind around the intentions of our offensive sets.

The "chalk talk" drawn out on a diner napkin didn't have the desired impact. In fact, it almost seemed to frustrate him as he began to call out other players and verbalize their perceived lack of talent. At that point, I had asked him to refrain from talking about other players. I expressed that I was happy to talk to him about what his daughter contributes to the team and how we can improve her game, but other players were off-limits. He continued down a destructive path, ignoring my request. Again, I encouraged him to leave other people out of this conversation and went a step further to ask him not to be disruptive at games with the negative outbursts and jeers toward his daughter's teammates. He challenged me with how I would know what he was saying or how he was acting on the sidelines. I replied that several people have expressed their concerns to me, especially around the impact on the overall morale and welfare of the team. His response was, "Yeah, who? Your disrespectful fucking daughter?"

The words hit me in the heart and confused me. I was stunned that a grown and educated man with two daughters of his own would feel at liberty to speak in such a manner about another man's daughter. It took everything in my power to gather myself and not react to the anger and emotion that was in my head. The demons in me wanted to lash out in anger and respond with violence. I'm guessing that is exactly what the father wanted. Some sort of fuel to get me in trouble with the administration. Thank God for my better angels. I rose slowly from the table and let him know the conversation was over. I turned and headed for the exit. As I worked my way through the diner to the parking lot, the father shouted out in a room full of people, "You fucking coward!"

Later, I shared this incident with one of my family members just to outlet my frustrations. "You are a better man than I am," he replied, "I would have been in jail." I also let the Athletic Director know of the situation right away, so there wouldn't be any opportunity for false reports to be filed. He asked if I wanted him to suspend the man from future games, but my first thought was about his daughter.

I know the frequent outbursts were embarrassing to her, and that dynamic had to be difficult to manage on the court and at home. I didn't want additional fallout for her and also didn't want to create any fuel for the already red-hot hatred the father exhibited toward me.

I was never sure why he acted the way he did. His daughter had made varsity for me as a freshman and started every game for four years. She was a great player in our program, loved by her teammates, easy to coach, and grew to be a leader among her peers, named co-captain of the team, both as a junior and a senior. Now, she had 1,000 points in her sights as she started her final season. During the summer before her senior year, I sent 20 letters and supporting game films to college coaches to help her find a school to continue her basketball career. None of it mattered. The player's senior year brought out the ugly in the father. He just seemed angry at the world. Despite that, the team marched on and worked together to put up another strong effort in the Shore Conference. By this time, the daughter had matured very well in the game of basketball and was one of the best players in the Shore. We finished second in our division just about every year, always behind St. Rose.

Every season we played St. Rose twice a year for division play. In my first year at Mater Dei, the Purple Roses put a beating on my team, winning by 40. The following year, the St. Rose win gave their coach his 200th career win. "Don't worry, kid, you'll get there one day." Not what I wanted to hear after a loss, but words that did resonate with me as a goal for my high school coaching career. As our program developed, we began closing the gap against St. Rose, with several near misses, including a one point overtime loss in their gym during my oldest daughter's senior year. Always close, but no cigar.

Beating St. Rose would prove to be a little more challenging for my team that season. They had a 6' 3" center that was magnificent at creating space in and around the paint. Had wonderful footwork and great hands. If opposing teams sent two at her when around the paint, she would step out to the 3-point arc and stick one in their eye. We didn't have the size to match up, but we always had the heart. As it was, the girls played a hard-fought game, losing by 14 points. While we always coached and played to win, it was important to recognize a tough loss and the lessons that come with it.

After the game, I was talking to my assistant coaches outside our makeshift locker room and the father, still in the gym, took that moment to shout, "Why don't you do us all a favor and resign." It was shot after shot with this guy, and nothing ever seemed to please him. The player went on to have a great senior year, capping off a brilliant career by surpassing the 1,000-point mark. She made the All-Division team and was named to the annual All-Star game for the Shore Conference. At our annual awards banquet, I had the opportunity to share with the entire group of athletes and their parents just how special of a player and person she was. I was also privileged to award her the Player of the Year for our program.

The award was well-deserved, but the moment was bittersweet. The school had determined earlier in the year that all varsity level games for winter sports were moving to a 5 PM start instead of 6:30 or 7 PM, which was custom for the 11 years I was coaching the program. I worked in the private sector, so my schedule was a little different than that of an employee of the school. Making 5 PM starts, which would require me to be at the gym by 4 PM for game prep and warmups, would be a challenge to my work schedule and responsibilities. As it was, I had been taking ½ vacation days to be on the bus for away games and present to fulfill my obligations as a coach. I expressed my limitations to the Athletic Director at the time and stressed that I wasn't the only person impacted but that many parents would be unable to attend our home games due to the earlier start. Those concerns fell on deaf ears, and ultimately, I was unable to commit to continuing as the coach for Mater Dei. So, as I presented the Player of the Year award that season, I knew it would be my last at Mater Dei. We had a good, young team, and I was going to miss out on their future development.

Once my presentation of the team and their accomplishments was over, clearing me of responsibilities for the evening, I worked my way over to have a beer in a quiet celebration of my time at Mater Dei. As my cold Miller Lite appeared, a couple of fathers of past and current players came over to say hello. We were talking briefly when I noticed the disgruntled father walking over to where we were all standing at the bar. I thought there might be some sort of conciliatory gesture now that the season was over, recognizing the quality high school career his daughter achieved and appreciating that she would be moving on to college. There was a brief exchange of "pleasantries," followed by a declaration from him that, "I'm the one who got you fucking fired." The other fathers immediately stepped in to address the situation, one of them meeting a push in the chest. I guess my hope for conciliation was misguided, but certainly no more than his assessment of the situation. It may have made him feel better about the bitterness and spiteful antics, but he had nothing to do with the end of my time at Mater Dei.

His antics created a distance between my future coaching endeavors and relationships with parents. The inexplicable anger and the willingness to deride and disrespect others was something I hadn't seen in my 23 years of coaching to that point. While some select parents had acted out, there wasn't anything that despicable. I noticed, however, that more stories were popping up in the youth sports world that were eerily similar and even far beyond what I had experienced to date. Something strange was happening in the sports world, causing ugly incidents to occur more frequently. Most of those centered around parents who were trying to live vicariously through their child's athletic experiences and holding on to unreal expectations for their child's future in sports. Some parents came into situations with a sense of entitlement and passed that along to their child-athletes. Fading away were the days of accountability for self and commitment to the team, all built around a trust in the coaches.

TEN

MOVING FROM THE METS TO THE YANKEES

ONCE WE COULDN'T WORK out a compromise around start times for home games, the Athletic Director at Mater Dei asked me for my letter of resignation. After prayerful consideration, I responded with the following:

You asked me for my formal letter of resignation the other day at our end of year meeting. After considerable thought on the situation surrounding my position as coach at Mater Dei, I cannot write that letter. The truth is I am not resigning, but rather I was put in a situation by the school administration where I can no longer coach. Might be semantics, but you have made the choice to relieve me of my position as coach at Mater Dei, not for cause, but for 90 minutes, a 5 PM varsity game time versus a 6:30 PM game time.

One of the goals behind the strategic planning was to make Mater Dei Prep a "destination campus." Offer better programs, build up the academic and athletic reputations, increase extracurricular activities, enhance the Catholic enrichment in the school and the engagement in the community -- all key elements in trying to attract quality student-athletes to our campus. The move of game times from 6:30 to 5:00, costing you the employment of a very successful coach, makes no sense at all. I have discussed/argued this point with you to the point of nausea already, but I can't get over the ridiculous nature of this action.

Girls' basketball is one of the most consistently successful and most attractive programs at our school over the last 11 years. I am not tooting my own horn here, merely stating the facts. We have competed with some of the state's best programs year in and year out. A couple of goals for every sports program in the area are to qualify for the Shore Conference and New Jersey State Tournaments. These are benchmarks for success that the girls' basketball team has achieved . . . 9 years in a row for Shore Conference and 10 years in a row for States. The program's success has drawn girls to the school specifically for the opportunity within basketball. There aren't too many sports at Mater Dei that can say that, girls or boys.

There is no one person that is bigger than the school. Although there are many people who don't feel that way by what they see taking place on campus, I get that idea and support that sentiment. However, what I don't get is the driving force behind a decision of this magnitude. It's not like I have been a problem staff member. It's not like I have been a polarizing figure. I have never done anything to harm the girls in any way, or the reputation of the school. Quite the opposite, in fact, even in the spotlight of a very public, constant barrage sent my way by one father. Something that the school administration let carry on for far too long. My tenure at Mater Dei has been a model of consistency, success, and positive outreach. I have devoted my time, talent and treasure to enhancing the school programs and enriching the experiences of the female student-athletes, their families and the community. To cast that all aside, without cause, at the whim of a handful of public schools in our division who struggle to maintain a team, let alone a program, makes absolutely no sense on any level for Mater Dei.

Yes, I have "had a nice run" at Mater Dei, but it was never about me. I have never coached for personal gain or glory. I certainly didn't coach for the money. Maybe I was naive, but I always gave to Mater Dei trying to make it a better place for others, because it was a place, an ideal that I believed in. You have made a choice. I hope in the end it was made for the right reasons and in the best interest of the girls and the school. At the end of the day, that is what I want for Mater Dei. I just don't see how this decision leads to improvement of what Mater Dei Prep has to offer. Perhaps I can get an explanation of the goals and vision that led to this decision, if not from you, then maybe (the principal).

To prevent the normal scuttlebutt that runs through small communities, I sent the following e-mail to current players, alum, and their respective families:

Before the rumor mill starts grinding away in its typical embarrassing and erroneous fashion, I wanted to get the word out to you personally. As of this morning, I will no longer be the coach at Mater Dei.

There has been a change brewing at our school, one that really started last year. I was told coming into this season that varsity game times were going to be moved up to 5 PM, instead of the 6:30/7 PM slot they have filled for years. Through some lengthy discussions, I was able to convince the administration to keep our game times at 6:30 this year, which allowed me to keep coaching. I was told at the start of the season that the game times were changing next year, something I didn't accept then and didn't want to believe. Unfortunately, that was confirmed by the school administration this morning. While I don't understand or agree with this decision, I must respect the choice the school made.

Over the last 11 years, I have used my vacation days to take bus rides to away games. Home games used to be at 7 PM, then were moved up to 6:30 PM. I don't work in the school system, so the later games along with the later practices, allowed me ample time to complete the obligations to my profession while affording me the time to be committed to my passion. Moving home games to 5 PM will make it impossible for me to fulfill both commitments as I have in the past. Enough on that . . . things change. This is the school's decision.

What hasn't changed and will never change is my passion for coaching the game of basketball. I have been blessed since moving to this area in 1994 with the opportunity and pleasure of coaching basketball at Holy Family for 12 years, at Mater Dei for 11 years, and at various levels in AAU, Mid Monmouth and Rec. While coaching required a lot of personal time and commitment, I always viewed my experiences with my coaches and my players as an extension of my life and my family. I also saw coaching as an opportunity to have a positive influence in young lives and to be a good Christian witness. While we were working very hard at being successful, usually measured in wins, we were also very focused on building an enduring quality program, especially at Mater Dei. When I inherited the program at Mater Dei back in 2000, I had one simple goal and that was to build a successful, competitive program that represented the school and our community with pride and dignity. I wanted Mater Dei to be a place where grammar schoolgirls would want to come, maybe first drawn by basketball, but later to realize that it was a good school as well. Along the way to that goal, I met a lot of great people, made some good friends, fought off one or two enemies, and enjoyed great success in helping a group of young individuals come together as a team, a program.

Obviously, parents are included in this e-mail. First, I want to thank you for entrusting me with the care and teaching of your daughter, some of you more than one. That was a privilege I never took for granted. While you may not have always understood or agreed with my approach, the one thing you could always be certain of is that I always had your daughter's best interest in mind and the greater need of the team at heart. Some have struggled with letting your child grow up. They will face adversity as they move through life, especially as they move up to different levels. Being successful at one level doesn't guarantee success at another. Let them struggle . . . let them fail . . . but be there to guide them and encourage them. You can't play for them. Success only comes before work in the dictionary. The key is to keep working, keep learning, and keep finding ways to improve. If your daughter is struggling, don't take the easy way out and blame the coach. Don't measure her against what a peer is doing. Simple truth is that the peer may just be working harder, have a better attitude, or has matured better in the game. Work with the coach. Understand what your daughter needs to do to get better. Then it comes down to one thing . . . her desire to work.

I have included alumni in this e-mail because I wanted to thank them for everything they have done over the years, not just as players, but in coming back to support the program as fans, as guests at practice working to help the younger teammates get better, and as trainers and coaches, giving back to Mater Dei Girls' Basketball. You will always have a place in my heart. Thanks for the many great memories and for the lessons. Don't be strangers.

Finally, to my girls this year . . . I am very proud of the effort you put into this season. Unwanted and unnecessary distractions aside, you worked hard throughout the season and finally started to grasp what you can achieve as a team. We were very young this year. That was a point I tried not to focus on, but it was a stark reality reflected in the inconsistency of our play, especially against the better teams.

However, you kept grinding away and improving. Our best games were our last, which isn't always the case. Sometimes teams get burnt out or distracted by the end of a season and trip up where they shouldn't. This year we rallied together at the right time, coming from behind to beat Marist in our gym. Then, going down to take on the defending state champs and current number five in the state at Trenton Catholic. One of my favorite memories is how quiet that gym was at half time, as we went to our locker room tied at 24. You ladies gave your best and played some good basketball in the process. Yes, we fell short in the end, but I firmly believe you have a tremendous foundation to build from. (My two senior players), it has been a tremendous pleasure coaching you over the last 4 years. I wish you both the very best of luck in college and in what you do in life. (My two junior players), you both bring a wonderful work ethic and a strong competitive spirit to the team. I'm sorry I won't be there for your senior year. You are the leaders now. Set the tempo and help drive the future success of the program. Give my replacement the same drive and determination you gave me. For the four sophomores and 6 freshmen on varsity, and those that made up the JV team this year, you are the future of the program. I was truly excited at the end of this year and looking forward to building for next year. The raw talent is there. Now you need to match that talent with grit and determination. As I said before, don't wait until November to play basketball. Don't just play, but work hard to improve as an individual, but importantly as a teammate. Don't just play, but play with passion. Love the game.

God bless,

Coach Ault

Once the dust settled on the move away from Mater Dei, I enjoyed the respite from coaching that followed. For the first time in a very long time, I had no plans for the spring or summer. There were no clinics to run, no camps to take my team to, no summer league, no AAU, and no summer training sessions with the team. It was nice to have all that time back, enjoying time with my family and new experiences. All three of my children were off to college at this point, so my wife and I tried to figure out what empty-nester life was supposed to look like. I enjoyed the early days away from coaching, but a hole was starting to develop in my heart.

In early October, I began to have more intense reflections on the possibility of life without basketball, especially with the upcoming season right around the corner. No roster reviews, no preparation for tryouts, no practice plans, and no opportunities to develop young players and build relationships. I reflected on the many words and e-mails sent to me from former players and parents of children in my program:

"Coach, you taught us things that we couldn't have possibly learned from anyone else. Both on the court and off the court. Thank you for everything you have done for all of us! I have seen that things in the coaching world can be very frustrating. You love the game, you love the girls, but somehow stupid bullshit gets in the way of playing the sport and doing what you love. Don't stay out of the gym for too long!!"

"I know that both of my girls are better people for being a part of your program, (my wife), and I thank you for all of your time and effort over the years, I am confident that both (my oldest daughter) and (my youngest daughter) will use the lessons they learned while playing for you throughout their lives. For what it is worth, I always thought your teams were well prepared and often

'overachieved.' I see the reaction you get from the players that come back to visit you after High School and those reactions speak volumes for you as a person and coach. You certainly left it 'all on the court.' Thanks again for everything!"

"I am very sad to hear the news that you will no longer be coaching the basketball team. You are the best coach that has ever been there. You have played a huge role in my life, and I wanted to thank you for all of your time and effort in helping to make me who I am today. Our team has and always will be my family to me. I am truly blessed to have you in my life. You were always there when someone needed you not just as a coach, but as a mentor and someone that we could look to and know that everything would be okay. You are a wonderful coach and person. I look forward to seeing you soon! You really are a wonderful person and have been an amazing inspiration in my life! 'Coming together is a beginning, keeping together is progress, working together is success.' Espirit De Corps!!!"

I began to really miss basketball and struggled with the thought of not being involved in a program for the upcoming season. I prayed for strength and guidance through the mental challenges I was working through. God does answer prayer, and sometimes that answer is no. This time, I received a resounding yes.

My cell phone rang one afternoon, and the caller ID showed me the name of one of the best basketball coaches in the state of New Jersey, Dawn Karpell. We had faced off a few times in the past as she was working her way up the coaching ranks and back to her alma mater, St. John Vianney. At this point in her career, she was home at the helm of the most historic basketball program in New Jersey and winners of multiple Tournament of Champions. Dawn had played for one of those TOC teams and was looking to elevate the program back to the days of dominance. We spent a few minutes catching up on our families and the season's prospects. Her words were music to my ears and an unexpected but welcomed surprise, "Do you want to be my assistant coach? I need somebody to work with the bigs and help us with some offenses." My answer was an immediate yes, followed by, "That would be like moving from the Mets to the Yankees."

No disrespect to Mets fans, some in my family, or to the previous high school team I had coached for 11 years, but St. John Vianney was the cream of the crop, the measuring stick for all other programs. In addition, Dawn was a fantastic young coach who, over time, had become one of the best high school coaches in all of basketball and somebody I felt I could learn a lot from. Of course, I wanted to join the program. Ironically, the following week, I got a call from the head girls' coach at Red Bank Catholic, who was also the Athletic Director and another historic coach in the Shore Conference. He asked me to join the staff at RBC as the assistant coach on the boys' program. I was honored by the offer and thought about it for a while, as my nephew would soon be attending that high school, but I had already made a commitment to SJV. I was going to become a Lancer, made not born.

ELEVEN
HOW CAN I ASSIST?

ECSTATIC TO BE BACK in the coaching fold, I was confident but admittedly nervous about joining the staff at St. John Vianney. However, even with the successes of former programs, I had never coached a program of this caliber at this level. SJV was always at the top of the Shore Conference and the New Jersey state rankings, even times when the team was ranked nationally. The expectations for coaches and players alike were always high, drawing top players from around the state to play for this coach at this parochial school. Where most teams in the Shore Conference were blessed with a few good athletes and had to work at rounding out a starting lineup and a quality bench, the great majority of players at SJV could start anywhere else. The roster was full of Division 1 basketball players. The last time I coached Division 1 prospects was with young men at the Naval Academy Preparatory School, and 20 years prior to this experience, well before any of these girls were born. I wasn't sure the girls at SJV would be able to relate to that experience nor appreciate the challenges and successes of building the program at Mater Dei.

I had experience as an assistant coach before, and I knew how to support the head coach's vision, work with the players, and build relationships with the people behind the jerseys. At the end of the day, that is what leadership in any organization is truly about . . . the people. Jocko Willink's words came to mind, "Leaders must always operate with the understanding that they are part of something greater than themselves and their own personal interests." With that in mind, I asked Dawn, "How can I assist you?"

The first practice was interesting. I didn't know any of the girls, but was certainly aware of the capabilities of the returning juniors and seniors. I was completely unaware of the sophomore and freshmen players, but had been told that there was a lot of talent, especially in the freshman group. That was a safe assumption, sight unseen, for any season at SJV. After introductions of the coaching staff to the players, we broke into a full-court shooting drill to get the blood pumping and the legs working. I moved up and down the court, observing the different players and offering some simple words of encouragement to all. After the drill was over and the team was gathered at one baseline, one of the seniors approached me to introduce herself. She was very pleasant and engaged me with a bright smile as she told me her name and welcomed me to the team. She followed those pleasantries with a warning, "We will break you." I knew she was having fun but also challenging my grit and fit to this program. I quickly responded with a firm, "Challenge accepted." Our relationship and mine with the rest of the team was forged right then and there. From that point, the team went to work on preparing for the season, with the lofty goals of a long run into the postseason and hopefully a Tournament of Champions appearance.

Coach Karpell worked me into the fold a little bit at a time, weaving my coaching style and game knowledge into the fibers of what she had already built.

A Lady Lancer basketball player can come in any size, shape, or color. There is no common denominator except a love for the game and a desire to get the most out of her abilities. She is first of all concerned with the good of her team and knows that individual recognition will come through team excellence.

I watched Dawn's interactions with the girls and marveled at how she was able to push all the right buttons and get the most out of her players. I enjoyed watching the girls push each other. Every practice was high-quality competition. The girls expected a lot from themselves and demanded even more from their teammates. Instead of a 5' 8" player trying to play the role of a center, we had several legitimate players over 6 feet tall who could play inside and out. They needed coaching in post-play and footwork, but they also had tremendous shooting and ball-handling abilities. The talent on the team was a dream roster for any coach. Once we broke the ice of the gruff exterior, the reputation and honor of the program being upheld by every one of them, they were all just young players looking to fulfill the dream of playing basketball at a high level and seeking to understand what it meant to be part of something bigger than themselves. They all wanted to be coached and challenged to be better. I had found a new home. In addition, I was an assistant to a great coach, shaping up a tremendous program, and I didn't have to deal with any of the negative parent stuff. At least, that is what I thought.

This is a good time to reiterate that 99% of my interactions with parents were pleasant. In fact, to this day, when I see the parents of players I coached in my career, there are warm hugs and great memories shared. As an assistant coach, I got to know the parents in a different way because I wasn't the one making decisions around individual matters like positions, starters, and playing time. In a lot of ways, this made players and parents alike much more comfortable in approaching me. Those engagements could be funny, curious, or sometimes put me flat on my heels as a study of human behavior.

The season kicked off, and the team looked good early. We lost our best senior player to a bad knee injury about five games in. Her injury forced my challenger from early in the season — also a senior, a great player, and somebody I admired as a person – to elevate her presence both on the court and in the locker room. She was a vocal leader, demanding a lot of herself and trying to push a younger team that would require a talented underclass group to step up and punch above their class at the time. She poured her heart and soul into the team, every practice, and every game. Jocko Willink once wrote, "In order to convince and inspire others to follow and accomplish a mission, a leader must be a true believer." This player was a believer and driven to be the tip of the spear for the rest of the team, the steel example for the younger players. I believe her example significantly impacted our freshman group, specifically our point guard, who would now be relied on even more heavily than expected.

As the season progressed, the road was bumpy for SJV standards. Games were more competitive, play was uncharacteristically flawed as people were learning new positions, or there were early struggles as younger players were forced into big varsity action earlier than expected. As coaches, we were studying and learning, working to find the right chemistry and rotation. The team struggled to find that groove early, suffering through five losses in a seven game stretch. One of those losses was by 2 points to our parochial school rival, Red Bank Catholic. A painful loss, to say the least, but those games were always close. The true signs of our struggles were found within our division, losing two games to less talented teams, adding credence to the expression, "Hard work beats talent when talent doesn't work hard." Saint John Vianney having six losses in a complete season is a very uncommon sight. Suffering six losses in the first 15 games was not only an indication of just how impactful the loss of our senior leader was, but it was also a reminder of how much work we still had in front of us to play as a team.

Heading into the biggest game of the year against Ossining, a tremendous program out of New York with a UConn recruit and several other fantastic players, we found out that our star center would miss the game due to a softball recruiting trip to Notre Dame. She was a tall, powerful lefty with a lightning-fast step. As good as she was at basketball, she was even better as a starting pitcher and, as a junior, was being heavily recruited for softball. Already struggling with a significant loss due to injury and trouble finding our rhythm, we now found ourselves down another key player going into a college showcase against a formidable opponent. This is the beauty in the depth of a program like SJV . . . one great player goes down, and another great player emerges. We went into the game with two freshmen in the starting lineup, one for the first time all year. The addition to the starting lineup that night was a 6'0" forward, slight in frame and very quiet but loaded with untapped talent. She and I had started forming a special bond through some of the post-play work in practice as our season progressed. I would encourage her to take advantage of every game moment and unleash that potential inside of her. We often talked about her ability to contribute 10 points and 10 rebounds every night. She struggled to find her comfort zone through the first 15 games, like our team in general. Now, she was forced into the starting lineup on a big stage.

Our team could have made excuses, but that isn't the Lancer way. When the final buzzer sounded, SJV found itself on the losing end of a 106-100 triple-overtime game. The packed gym was amazed at the play on both sides. The players were exhausted. The coaching staff was both bummed by the loss and proud of the incredible effort. Our team found something in that game, and a spark ignited. Our senior leader lit up the gym with a career-best 37-point effort. Our newest starter contributed a solid 10 points and made key plays on both ends of the court. Our freshman point guard dropped 18 on the opponent and played with incredible grit, demonstrating a will to win that would serve us well for years to come. Four freshmen played significant minutes in that game and accounted for 48 out of the 100 points. A bond was formed on the court, and the team played with balance. Working through our early season struggles and putting forth a valiant performance against Ossining made me think of a part in the Lady Lancer Prayer read by a player before every game, "A Lady Lancer basketball player never realizes when the odds are stacked against her. She can only be defeated by a clock that happens to run out of time."

These girls were evidence of that, for sure. We lost in one of the best basketball games I have ever seen or been fortunate enough to coach. However, in that loss, a metal was forged that would prove to be invaluable for the younger players on that team. On the heels of that game, I realized how special the SJV program was and, even more so, how lucky I was to be a part of it.

TWELVE
YOUTH MOVEMENT

AS MY SECOND year at SJV began, expectations rose as we looked around the gym. During the summer, we added five freshmen to an already talented roster: a powerful 6'3" center from Jackson, a strong 6' freshman swing, and three good guards, each with separate skill sets. In addition, we had a transfer come in — a wily, very energetic sophomore forward from Secaucus. Our special bond was immediately forged when we were broken out into guard and post drills early in the season. I worked with the post players and introduced a library of post footwork to help them succeed in and around the paint. We got to the point of an up-and-under move, which she worked flawlessly until she lifted her pivot foot to finish. I told her that she might want to introduce a dribble to that move because she would be called for a travel. In a style unique to her charm and personality, she began to argue with me, adamant about the fact that the move she made was not a travel. She told me that her father, who was a well-known, respected coach, talked to officials about it and was told that it wasn't a walk. She left our drill frustrated and confused. After that practice, I went home and read through the rule book to review the rule and check my knowledge. She was right!

At the next practice, I pulled her aside to inform her of my discovery, which proved her correct. After a few minutes of celebration on her part, literally dancing and turning in circles of joy, we got back to business drilling post moves and getting ready for game action. Our little experience around the up-and-under move helped us form an indelible bond as player and coach. Credit to her parents, who let us work through our disagreements together, independent of any parental involvement. We figured it out and worked well together for years. With the new additions, the team roster now boasted nine sophomores and five freshmen. This group would become the core of great things to come, but there was road to be paved. We marched through the season posting a 23-5 record, losing the five games by a total of 10 points to tough competitors like St. Rose, Christ the King, St. Mary's of NY, Manasquan in the Shore Conference Tournament semi-final, and Immaculate Heart in the state tournament final round for Non-Public A. Every practice was intense, and every game was a learning opportunity. The talented underclass was soaking it all in, building game awareness and a court presence. The Shore Conference and the basketball community were beginning to understand the potential of this team. With that understanding came rising expectations.

My third year at SJV started off with three victories against very good opponents in Roland Park Day from Maryland, one of our division rivals Rumson-Fair Haven, and Montclair in their holiday tournament. Our first loss came against Franklin in the final game of the holiday tournament. Franklin was also a team on the rise with a lot of talent, who would go on to be a frequent player in late-season playoffs and the Tournament of Champions. Our team didn't play well and, for the first time, showed a lack of chemistry. The mix of young talent and the extremely competitive nature of our daily practices had everybody jockeying for starting positions and playing time. As we exited the locker room after the post-game talk, parents were gathered by the corner of the bleachers on the way to the exit. Most of them were conciliatory about the loss and encouraging about the opportunities in front of us. After all, this was only our fourth game in a 30-game season. Walking through the group of parents, I noticed a mother of one starter looking in my direction, so I walked over to say hello. My greeting was met with a very stern rebuke of, "This team isn't as good as you think they are." I tried to reassure her that we would be working hard to improve the areas of weakness that showed in the game and that we would be ready for things to come. My words had zero effect on her as she walked away in anger. When you play for one of the best teams in the state, expectations always run high, and you can count on getting the best out of every opponent. To me, we lost the game, took a lot of lessons out of it, and we would work on improving all aspects of our team. To that mother, there was something deeper burning that I didn't understand; her daughter was a starter and leader on the team.

For the first time as the assistant in a couple of years, I began to see a bubbling up of parent frustrations and subsequent involvement. Coach Karpell had asked me to join her on a few early-season parent meetings to help navigate discussions around what players could do to get better and earn more playing time. This was a little different for me as an assistant coach, but it was very eye-opening to the growing sense of entitlement that began to leech into high school sports. AAU basketball had become much more prevalent, distinctions of premier teams or sponsored teams were on the rise, showcase events were being played across the country through the spring and summer months, and parents were dumping more and more of their money into personal skill trainers for their children. With these "investments" came an expectation of return, advancement in high school, and opportunities to play in college.

Like a broker watching the stock market rise and fall with every day, some parents were just overwhelmed by the emotion and stress that come with the expectations of performance. All of this was mounting after just one loss.

Coach Karpell did an amazing job of blocking out the noise and focusing on the growth and development of the team. We worked every day at being competitive while improving chemistry. As the season progressed, the discipline and internal strength started to show more and more. The team rattled off 11 consecutive wins, including a victory over Manasquan in the third game of that streak. Every SJV game versus Manasquan carried extra weight. The two tremendous head coaches, both with amazing accomplishments as players and leaders of teams, had a very healthy respect for each other. The players on both sides were hard-nosed and ferociously competitive. One of the players for Manasquan, their best player at the time and younger sister to a player who spent one year at SJV before playing for Manasquan, took exception to the loss that day. During the game, she teetered on the line between aggressive and dirty and often had emotional outbursts with very colorful language. After the loss, while both teams were meandering through the crowd of players and spectators, she took that opportunity to throw a few choice words toward Coach Karpell. Not only did the player decide to act out disrespectfully, but her mother joined the party with a barrage of insults directed at the coach. I had to work my way back to Coach Karpell to help her navigate through the crowd to the locker room. Instead of taking the moment to teach her daughter some courtesy and respect, the mother throws in and only adds to the chaos.

This was a high school girls' basketball game. Yes, it was intense and competitive, but it was one game that Saint John Vianney won, and there were many more games to play. There was no acceptable rationale for the player's behavior and no excuse for the mother acting as she did. As competitive as the world has become, especially in sports, there is virtue in losing with grace.

During the 11-game winning streak, besides beating Manasquan, we also defeated several quality teams, including St. Anthony's (NY), Christ the King (NY), and Morris Catholic. Our team was playing extremely well, and our early season loss seemed to be a thing of the past. Then came our second game of the season versus Manasquan. At that point in the season, we were 14-1, and Manasquan was 15-1, with their only loss suffered in our gym several weeks before. There was no need to build up the anticipation and excitement around this game. Unfortunately, we ran into a buzz saw that night and showed that we still had things to work on. Manasquan came out hungry and determined to make a statement. The fourth quarter was the exclamation point as they outscored us 26-7, finishing off an impressive 25-point win. We left the gym beaten but by no means defeated. There were a lot of games left on our schedule, and we needed to get back to work. The collective feeling was that we would see Manasquan again in more meaningful games.

We finished off the regular season with five more wins and added two early-round wins in the Shore Conference Tournament. To this point, in an already illustrious career, Coach Karpell had never won the Shore Conference Tournament as a coach, which is one of the marquis accomplishments in New Jersey. Our early wins set us up for a semi-final game against Manasquan—round three of the heavyweight matchup. With the teams splitting during the regular season, all eyes in the Shore Conference were on this matchup. Both teams were focused and determined in their preparation to win the rubber match.

Early in the game, Manasquan had picked up right where they left off from the earlier 25-point win. At the end of the first quarter, Manasquan had a 19-6 lead and seemingly owned all the momentum. I think the practice of having a player read the Lancer Prayer resonated the most in moments like this. *She can only be defeated by a clock that happens to run out of time.* We played poorly for the first eight minutes, and Manasquan played very well. The only thing that mattered on the scoreboard was the clock, and there were 24 minutes left to play. We broke the huddle to start the second quarter with our common expression of "together" and a raw determination to play our way.

The second quarter saw the pendulum swing in the other direction to favor St. John Vianney. Our nerves calmed, the effort intensified, and we were back to playing Lancer basketball. As halftime drew near, we had outscored Manasquan 14-5 in the 2nd quarter and went into the locker room down 24-20. The fight was on, and the two best players in the gym, the dominant forward for Manasquan and the floor general for SJV, were doing everything they could to elevate their respective teams. This was a toe-to-toe fight between two heavyweights in the center of the ring.

Halftime locker room discussions can often take on a similar cadence for coaches. Common phrases and game references will often be repeated throughout the season. One constant theme from Coach Karpell was the importance of the first three minutes of the second half. This was the time to go out and set the pace and attitude for the remainder of the game. The revered three-minute window could often be the wedge between good and great teams. For this game, those words served as a reminder of the importance of coming out with the same intensity and same focus showcased in the last eight minutes. I am sure similar words echoed through the opponent's locker room as well. Two great coaches, leading two great teams, but only one could win and advance to the finals of the Shore Conference Tournament.

The third quarter picked up as if there was no break. Both teams went after each other in every phase of the game; every shot was contested, every rebound battled for, and every loose ball fought for like it was the last opportunity to win. As was to be expected, the rest of the game went on at a thrilling pace. When the game ended, Manasquan secured a five-point win and a seat in the tournament finals. As important as the first three minutes are to open the second half, they are equally key to the beginning of the game. Unfortunately, on this day, SJV had dug too great a hole to overcome. To their credit, the Lady Lancers never lost faith and battled back. At game's end, the power forward for Manasquan had 22 points and 10 rebounds in the winning effort, and our point guard posted 25 points, four rebounds, and four assists. Not only was this a battle of two marquis programs in the state, but a battle of will between two of the best players the state has ever seen.

From that loss, SJV went on another win streak, notching six straight victories in late-season play. After the loss to Manasquan, this team had an attitude that was taking shape and starting to mature. For some programs, losing games is a possible and sometimes acceptable outcome. For this team, winning was expected, and any loss, while loaded with lessons, left a very nasty aftertaste. Practices were even more focused. Players started not to worry about starting positions and amount of playing time but were more committed to what they could do to help the team. Devotion to each other began to show as we worked our way through the state tournament. Our first three victories in states came with an average 26-point margin, including a 61-36 thumping of our rival Red Bank Catholic.

We were only up four at halftime in the game against RBC. As the teams headed into the locker rooms for the half, Coach Karpell gathered the staff outside before heading in to speak with the team. We reviewed our play through the first two quarters, discussed what wasn't working, and suggested adjustments for review during the break. Calmly, Coach Karpell soaked it all in and quietly reflected on what she needed to say to the team. Then, she grabbed the door handle and threw open the door like the gym was on fire and she needed to get the girls out. An innocent garbage can was in the path and swiftly thrown to an empty section of the room. Coach was the one on fire and the players were a very captive audience. The importance of the third quarter's first three minutes paled compared to the power of the next three minutes in that locker room. The words were pointed and sometimes colorful. The sting of poor play emanated throughout the room, and no excuses were to be tolerated. This was win or go home against a hated rival in our gym, and the lack of teamwork demonstrated in the first 16 minutes was not acceptable. No adjustments were made to the scout or the execution of our game plan. Adjustments were expected to be made in the collective mentality and within each player, but that was something they owned as a team. With that, Coach Karpell exited with the same fever pitch with which she entered. The staff followed quietly behind her while the players were left to their own devices. I only offered to "Make sure you pick up the garbage." I guess that could have also served as a metaphor for the moment.

As the four coaches entered the gym, the crowd hushed and probably wondered about the state of the SJV players. The RBC team had already taken the floor to warm up for the second half, obviously content with their effort thus far. Several minutes later, with little time left before the start of the second half, the SJV locker room doors flung open, and the team sprinted over to the bench led by our junior point guard. There were no smiles, no conversations, no last-minute words with coaches before resuming the game. The girls dropped their water bottles at the bench and took a couple of shots to loosen up; then the horn sounded to get the teams back to the bench. The team huddles broke, and that was the end of the game. . . for RBC. We outscored the Caseys 38-17 over the final two quarters, taking care of business as we advanced to the finals for Parochial A-South. The girls had answered the bell and returned to the form that carried them most of the season. The coaches breathed a collective sigh of relief because of the way the players responded, but there was still a feeling that something was missing. We were a great team but marred by inconsistent play in critical moments.

In the Parochial A-South finals, we quickly dispatched Gloucester Catholic 53-25 and earned a rematch with Immaculate Heart for the state championship in Parochial A. Like Manasquan earlier in the season, Immaculate Heart jumped all over us early, taking a 14-point lead to halftime. Immaculate Heart had beaten us in the same spot the previous year and seemed destined to do it all over again. They played with incredible confidence and knocked down big shots early. Our team looked sluggish and disconnected, much the way we appeared early in our game versus Red Bank Catholic. As we headed toward the coaches meeting outside the locker room at half, I was curious as to what the approach would be this time. Was another garbage can going to be the target of frustration? We gathered and reviewed the statistics and shared thoughts about what needed to change.

There were no outbursts, and no frustrations were expressed about the poor play. How many times can that be done before losing its effect? The conversation was pointed but focused on the adjustments that needed to be made for our success in this game and the right to advance to the Tournament of Champions. The team was laser-focused on the coach and the whiteboard review. When she finished, Coach Karpell, as she often did, asked the staff if there was anything else. Without pause, I told the girls that our next 16 minutes had to be the best 16 minutes of our season. We left the locker room as a team and headed out to warm up before the second half ensued.

From the entry of the ball to the start of the third quarter, we were back in business. The intense, in-your-face defense we were known for was in full swing. A team that hit six 3-pointers in the first half was struggling to find room to breathe in the second half. Our offense started to flow better, and we began to see impact with our 6' 3" sophomore center, "Cuz," as I called her because her last name was the same as my mother's maiden name. Chipping away at their lead, we ended the third quarter down six. We were playing better, but our best was required to pull this one out. Momentum carried into the fourth quarter, and we found ourselves in a hotly contested game in the late minutes but still behind by two.

Our next offensive possession started with the break from a defensive rebound. The primary break was stalled by great transition defense. Secondary break movement found the ball swinging from right to left, where one of our best shooters, a smaller guard with a huge personality but also extremely hard on herself, was waiting in a shot-ready position. She had struggled offensively all game, only scoring a single two-point basket to that point. I used to call her Chicken Little because of the way her head went down and her shoulders dropped on every missed shot. She would often come to the bench for conversation with me about not allowing the game's mental aspect to impact her performance. I would remind her that great shooters shoot their way out of slumps. I encouraged her to keep working through the flow of our offense and be ready for the next opportunity. The pass swinging in her direction was that next opportunity, and she nailed a three to give us the lead.

That bucket was huge, but what happened next was even more impressive. The diminutive guard, who had every right to celebrate the go-ahead basket, wasted no time in sprinting back on defense ahead of a quickly transitioning team. As one of her teammates picked up ball to push the threat to the outside, our guard headed to the next threat, getting between the offensive player on the right and her driving line to the basket. The pass was made to the player on the right wing, who attacked the basket and promptly ran over our waiting defender. Charge! Chicken Little jumped to her feet and pumped her fist into the air. Our bench went crazy after witnessing the sequence of the go-ahead 3-pointer and the flawlessly executed transition defense by the same player leading to the charge call. Her game awareness, court presence, and desire to compete helped capture the momentum that would ultimately lead to victory. Saint John Vianney had overcome that 14-point halftime deficit to exact revenge from a year ago and capture the New Jersey State Championship for Parochial A, punching our ticket to the Tournament of Champions, something that eluded us the year before.

The state was divided into public school groups one through four, based on enrollment size, with Group 4 being the larger schools. The parochial schools were divided into Parochial A and B. The state tournament would play out in each group and parochial level first until six champions were standing. Those six champions would then be seeded in the TOC, playing until only one remained. This was a grand tradition that played out every year for basketball for boys and girls since 1989. In its infinite wisdom, all sarcasm intended, the New Jersey State Interscholastic Athletic Association decided to end that experience after the 2022-23 season. Luckily, that was a few years off from this point.

We were now in the Tournament of Champions (TOC), and our first game was against the Group 2 champion, New Providence. While a smaller school, New Providence had a great coach who created a consistent winning program. They had good talent and a bright future led by a sophomore and freshman sister combination that would prove lethal to many opponents in years to come. Our swarming defense and more battle-hardened roster proved to be too much, as we went on to post a 63-39 victory, advancing to the semi-final round against a very good St. Rose team.

Ugh, St. Rose again! This was a team that haunted me as a head coach at Mater Dei, having never beaten them (record of 0-26) and a personal demon I had not been able to exercise to this point. The haunting continued as St. Rose pulled out the semi-final victory, beating SJV 47-43. The teams were tied at half and played to a 14-14 draw in the fourth quarter, but there was a moment in the third quarter where St. Rose eked out a four-point difference. Maybe it was the first three minutes of the second half. Either way, the lesson taken from this was the importance of putting together 32 minutes of quality effort for every game.

We went home as Parochial-A State Champions but came up short in the TOC. St. Rose went on to lose in the TOC finals to Manasquan, a team we so eagerly wanted to play for that title. This left us with a feeling of unfinished business.

THIRTEEN
#UNFINISHED BUSINESS

I THINK every coach looks for something to drive their team to the next level; something inspirational and encouraging, but also a statement of commitment and devotion, a mission. As soon as we started discussing summer plans before the upcoming season, the concept of unfinished business started floating around. It wasn't long before that became our official mantra.

Our summer was packed with great workouts focused on conditioning and sharpening our collective skills. The team played in the Best of Maryland showcase to get some early challenges against teams from all over the map. We bulled our way through fall leagues, building a stronger court presence and team chemistry. Added to the mix this year was a fundraiser to help the team on a trip to Florida to play in a showcase event to kick off the season. In every situation, with every effort, on every Twitter post, and in almost every conversation, the reminder was said and acknowledged: #unfinished business. What was especially enjoyable was the complete buy-in from parents. If there were any grumblings, they were faint whispers spoken in quiet spaces away from the gym.

Everybody seemed to enjoy being a part of this basketball family and supported the ambition of the girls and the coaching staff. The player-to-coach relationship could develop and mature without intrusion. It was a fantastic feeling.

The season couldn't start early enough. The SJV girls were primed and ready to go, but we were facing an early challenge. Our senior point guard and team captain had suffered a foot injury that was going to sideline her for a few weeks. Every coach dreads injury to players, especially to somebody so key to the operation of the team. However, most coaches will also see the opportunity for growth and development of other players on the roster. We had some very good young talent, but both of our reserve point guards were relatively untested at the helm of the varsity team. Our junior point guard was a spirited player with an unparalleled enthusiasm for the game. She had spent the last two years primarily on JV, crafting her skills and getting comfortable with our offenses. As coaches, we never had to worry about her effort or desire. She was extremely coachable and wanted nothing more than to step up and lead. She assumed the starting role as floor general until our team leader returned. Her backup was a freshman who, although unproven in meaningful gameplay, showed remarkable tenacity and fit right into the program's culture. She also carried the yolk of being the head coach's daughter, which can bring a lot of self-induced and outside pressure. Now, she would be pressed into action on the big stage, allowing her to earn her stripes and showcase her talents.

Our first game of the season was against a lesser opponent, but it was a good game for us to have come out of the gates. The strength of our team allowed our two point guards to pick up some game experience, allowing them to work on their ability to grasp and run our offensive sets. Both girls were tenacious defenders and already blended right into the team effort to smother our opponents. The repetition of offense and building rhythm on that side of the court was key to our early games. We easily won our first game, then picked up a good win against Rumson in our second game. This was the first test of our new backcourt players, but they prevailed in this effort, combining for 19 points, four assists, and four steals. Now, we were off to Florida for a big showcase event and a couple of big matchups.

We won our first game in Florida against McKinney North out of Texas. It is always interesting to see the competition measure from outside New Jersey. There is a lot of pride in the quality of girls' basketball in our state, especially in the Shore Conference. So, when New Jersey teams play out-of-state teams, it is a study in contrasting styles and a chance to prove your metal. At SJV, we played a quality out-of-state schedule, mainly with New York teams. McKinney was a good team, but Cuz, our junior center, was too much for them to handle, with 21 points on the day. It was a good win and additional experience for our girls as they continued to develop as a team without our starting point guard.

Our next game was against Villa Maria Academy from Malvern, Pennsylvania. This program won eleven District One championships and came off another deep run in the previous year's state tournament. We played well, and our confidence in the current team grew daily. The game against VMA would be a great barometer of how well our point guards were maturing in this early season. The game was in our favor early, up 27-23 at half, but this was a quality opponent with excellent guard play and great depth. Both defenses stepped up the pressure in the second half, and the game remained very close, with Villa Maria outscoring SJV 19-15 to finish regulation tied. By the time we had finished the third overtime, players on both sides were spent from putting every ounce of energy into a quality basketball game. It was one of those games where neither team should lose, but we did. The game ended at 67-64, with SJV falling short despite the valiant effort. Everybody contributed in some fashion; our point guard tandem combined for 17 points and six assists, our wily power forward from Secaucus added 14 points, including ten free throws, and my 10 and 10 forward ended up with 9 points and 19 rebounds. There were so many positive lessons from the loss that would propel us forward into the remainder of our season.

After the Florida trip, with our senior floor general back in action, the Lady Lancers rattled off 18 victories in a row, with quality wins against Ossining (NY), Christ the King (NY), Manasquan, Morris Catholic, Red Bank Catholic, Lenape, Gil St. Bernards, and Blair Academy. One of the most satisfying wins for me came against my personal nemesis, St. Rose of Belmar. We were deep in the Shore Conference Tournament at this point of the season, meeting up with the Purple Roses in the semi-final round.

These games were never easy; they were two very well-coached teams with incredible players and programs rich with a winning culture. By the end of the third quarter, SJV was down 43-36, struggling with some foul trouble. In the fourth, SJV had overcome the seven point deficit and inched ahead in the score. Both teams continued to battle through the fourth quarter, with St. Rose closing the gap, but SJV never relinquished the lead. The remaining seconds were exciting as neither team wanted to be at the short end of this game. Those seconds were a gut-wrenching eternity for me as I watched the events unfold and time tick away. We pulled out a 59-54 win against St. Rose, a first in my coaching career. Our reward was a game versus Manasquan in the SCT finals.

We had beaten Manasquan twice in the regular season, once by four points in overtime and the second game by six points in regulation. Still, the Warriors were last season's defending Shore Conference Tournament and Tournament of Champions winner. Every game was a battle from start to finish. As mentioned before, these were two of the premier teams in the tri-state area, two historic programs led by excellent coaches, with multiple Division 1 prospects on both rosters. There was a lot of respect between the two teams, but no love was lost. Now, round three was about to begin on the big stage of the Shore Conference Finals.

The Lancers got the best of the finals contest that day, handing Coach Karpell her first SCT championship as a coach. We took a 22-17 lead into halftime, then put together a strong third quarter that helped propel us to an 11-point victory. As was the case throughout the year, there were many contributors to our success. Our senior point guard strung together a 16-point, five rebound, and seven assist effort to lead the way. The sharpshooting two-guard, Chicken Little, added 14 points, including four 3-pointers. It is difficult to beat a team three times in the same season, particularly your biggest rival, but we pulled that off on the way to the Shore Conference Championship. That title was a key component of our unfinished business. We were not done yet.

The team had to quickly refocus our energies on the state tournament and the six games that needed to be won to fulfill our mission. Our first five games were wonderfully executed against familiar foes like Red Bank Catholic and Immaculate Heart. As good an offensive team as we were, our defense proved to be the differentiator as we held our opponents to less than 32 points per game over that stretch. With our win over Immaculate Heart, we won another Parochial A state title and secured our spot in the Tournament of Champions.

After earning the first-round bye for the TOC, our first opponent was Lenape, who we quickly eliminated after a sluggish first quarter. Our prize was a fourth matchup against Manasquan, who had secured another Group 2 state title and were fresh off a great win against Rutgers Prep, another powerhouse New Jersey team. There were no secrets between our two teams at this point in the season. Everybody in the area wanted to see this matchup in the finals, a fourth game between Manasquan and St. John Vianney with a winner-take-all reward. It didn't matter that we had won the three previous games. They were all close, hotly contested scrums, including one overtime game. Manasquan was the only thing standing between us and finishing our business.

SJV had the better of the first half, heading into the locker room with a 32-24 lead. The third quarter was an absolute slugfest, with both defenses coming up with big plays and both offenses being put into an uncomfortable pace, resulting in a 5-3 quarter won by Manasquan. The fourth quarter was the opposite, as both offenses started flexing their muscles in a race to the finish line. The respective stars for each team were on full display. Our senior point guard, a DePaul recruit, led the effort with 23 points, 11 rebounds, and six assists. The star player for Manasquan was a power forward bound for the University of Maryland, who was on a tear that day with 27 points and nine rebounds. The question for both teams was not about the will to win, or whether their star players would show up, but rather where the key contributions would come from the supporting cast of each team.

As the fourth quarter wound down, the game was still up in the air, but momentum favored Manasquan, who had put together a furious comeback, and the lead seesawed in the waning seconds. In a season where SJV had only suffered one loss and where we had won 27 games in a row, all seemed to be in question. Our successes in the season came from an incredible team effort with contributions from everyone. This game had already seen our best defensive player put forth another stellar performance by being an absolute pest all day, and she added an unexpected 10 points to the effort. Her inspirational play gave us a great lift of energy. In a fashion very appropriate to the rivalry, regulation ended in a tie at 49-49. The first overtime was a 4-4 struggle, indicative of some mental pressing on both sides as everybody fought to finish on top. Heading into the second overtime, each team was waiting for somebody to take charge and pull their team to the championship. Nobody seemed to be able to get enough separation to win the game. *She can only be defeated by a clock that happens to run out of time.*

Late in the second overtime, we seemed stuck in this loop with the game still tied. The team never seemed to panic, but we needed a basket in the most significant moment of the season. As we worked through a set on our side of the court, the ball ended up in the hands of our forward, who was a key contributor all season long, but to that point in the game was scoreless. Her offensive struggles in the game weren't even a thought as she pulled up with a 12-foot jumper to give us the lead. It was a huge basket taken with confidence that players with less mental fortitude may have shied away from. The Lancer defense intensified to slow down the Manasquan offense in the fleeting moments. Our floor general stepped up to help us complete the mission. She commanded the ball every time we had possession, and Manasquan was forced to foul to stop the clock and extend the game. Ultimately, she made 9 of 10 free throws in that overtime period, and our team defense proved too much for our opponent. SJV went on to win 65-58, earning the 2015-16 TOC crown, completing a 31-1 record. Looking around the gym and seeing the players' smiles and tears of joy, I reflected on the last line of the Lancer Prayer:

> *She is what a small girl wants to become and what an elderly woman can remember with great pride that she once was.*

The season, that championship game, created lifelong memories for all of us and an overwhelming satisfaction of finished business.

FOURTEEN
A FIRE INSIDE

AFTER THE EUPHORIA of our win and the subsequent celebrations died down, I began to feel the desire to be a head coach again. My experiences at SJV were all stepping stones in an incredible learning journey. I loved every moment and the relationships shared with the coaching staff, all the players, and their parents, who were enjoyable and fully committed to the team. I felt like I could take the lessons learned, add them to my 11 years as a head coach for girls, and find another program to develop. I wasn't in a rush, but I did start to look around for what I thought was the right opportunity.

During the offseason, I looked for and applied to a couple of coaching jobs in college. I had always wanted to try coaching at college. I felt very comfortable that my experiences at the Naval Academy Prep School, playing college competition, and my time at Mater Dei and St. John Vianney preparing young women for college made me a viable candidate. I wasn't shooting for the stars. I applied to a couple of Division III schools and a small Division 1 school in New Jersey. My challenge wasn't a lack of experience or knowledge of the game, but I had this little thing called a career outside of basketball, my primary source of income.

My time at Holy Family was all volunteer work. Once I started coaching high school, I received a modest stipend, but I always had my career to manage and my family to support. I intentionally focused on lower divisions and smaller schools because I knew the coaching demands weren't as stringent as mainstream Division 1 schools and marquis programs. I was also in sales, so I had some inherent flexibility in my work schedule without any travel out of the state. I knew I could manage both and wanted the opportunity to grow as a coach. The schools I applied to didn't feel the same way. Even with strong letters of recommendation from current college coaches, I couldn't get an interview.

I took some shots and missed. As I often coached my players when they missed shots or made mistakes in the game, I focused on the next sequence. For me, I had the luxury of still being the assistant at SJV, and we had a season to prepare for. As usual, we always had high expectations, both internally and externally. We had just come off the high of winning the TOC the year before, and we were returning a lot of key players who benefited from that experience. We did lose a lot to graduation, but we had five seniors and three juniors returning, along with some talented sophomore players.

We had another great season, with big wins over Christ the King (NY), Long Island Lutheran (NY), and Rumson-Fair Haven on our way to a 23-5 record. However, we did fall short of goals, losing to St. Rose in the Shore Conference Tournament finals and ultimately to Red Bank Catholic in the semi-final round of Non-Public A South. Thus, the season was cut short by our standards.

The next year, my last at SJV, we started the season 19-0 and seemed unbeatable. We had a younger team than normal, with only two talented seniors. We did have four strong juniors and a good underclass, but we were missing the big game savvy and leadership that we enjoyed in previous years. That said, the team was shaping up very well, and we were hot out of the gates. Both seniors were committed to Division 1 schools, one at American University and the other at West Point. As a Naval Academy graduate, I had a lot of fun with that one and enjoyed a strong relationship with the player and her family.

Our first loss was to Christ the King (NY). This was always a fiercely competitive game and a longstanding tradition. They got the better of us that day. Rebounding in grand fashion, the SJV team got back to winning ways, including a big win over St. Rose in the Shore Conference Tournament semi-final game. These games were never easy; they were two very well-coached teams with incredible players and programs rich with a winning culture. By the end of the third quarter, SJV was down 28-27 in an incredible battle between two defensive-oriented teams. Late in the fourth quarter, under a minute to go in the game, we found ourselves down one point after two St. Rose free throws. The ensuing inbound entry pass went to one of our quickest players who could push tempo, albeit sometimes out of control. As she came up the right sideline with seconds ticking, I suggested a timeout over half court to Coach Karpell so we could set up a sideline play. Coach went with her gut and felt it best to let the girls play on instinct. She was right.

While our quick guard pushed tempo up the right sideline, the fastest player on our team, a junior forward with lightning speed, was running the left side of the floor. Going with the flow of the play, she continued through the paint left to right, popping out in the baseline corner on ball side, beyond the 3-point arc. This was not typically one of our three-point shooters, but she had hit one earlier and was having a great game. She was an amazing athlete with a God-given combination of size and speed. In the blink of an eye, our streaking guard advanced the ball to her speedy teammate, who pulled the trigger without hesitation. Swish! SJV was now up two as the buzzer sounded. My arms went straight up in the air in a celebration of victory. A local photographer captured that image and quickly found social media, where my brother-in-law dubbed it as "A fat guy finding free doughnuts." With that win complete, we were now set up to play Manasquan in the Shore Conference Tournament Finals again.

This championship game was different and something Manasquan had been planning on for a while. They jumped on us early with an 18-12 first quarter and never looked back. Any chemistry we had built going into the game seemed to evaporate throughout the game. The team didn't react well to the loss, and we struggled in an abbreviated state playoff run by losing to St. Rose in the semi-finals for Non-Public A South (renamed from Parochial).

Another successful year was completed, but the team was left with a void of not winning the big games that year. I also struggled with the void in my heart, the yearning to lead my own program again. Making the decision to leave wasn't easy, but I knew it was something I needed to do.

Building programs was something I thoroughly enjoyed. There were two openings that I explored, Trinity Hall and Holmdel High School. After speaking with the respective athletic directors, Holmdel seemed like the right place to go. This was a team that had some good talent but never seemed to get over the hump in creating a consistent winning culture. There were some rumblings about parents forcing the coach out, but I didn't pay much attention to those rumors. What I knew for a fact was that there was an opening at a school close by, and I was interested. I wanted to bring some of the SJV culture to a small public school about three miles down the road. So, I traded my black and gold in for the Hornet blue and white. I was beyond excited to get started.

FIFTEEN
WELCOME TO THE HORNETS' NEST

DURING MY TIME AT SJV, Holmdel High School was in the same division of the Shore Conference. We played them twice every year, so I had a front row seat to how the team played and some of the returning talent. At the end of the previous season, the divisions were realigned, and SJV was moved out. While I was bummed about not being able to play against my old team, I was relieved not to have to face them twice in the season. The caliber of talent and the depth of the programs were vastly different. My relief was short lived, however, when I learned that the division would now have Manasquan and St. Rose added, to go along with Red Bank Catholic and Rumson-Fair Haven. We needed to get to work fast on the foundation of our program and getting the players committed to a new way of thinking. Considering the challenge of facing each of those teams twice in one season, we were looking at 0-8 before reviewing the rest of the schedule. I knew I needed some help.

Having been an assistant coach for the last six seasons and previously in AAU, I knew how important that role was to the overall success of a program. Working with Coach Karpell and watching how she delegated responsibilities throughout her staff and relied on them to manage and enhance relationships with players provided me with a great blueprint to follow. I gained a deeper appreciation for that key presence on the bench, especially during games, where the title sometimes moved from assistant coach to team psychologist.

One of the areas of difference I learned early in making the transition from coaching boys to coaching girls was the tremendous self-doubt and lack of confidence that most of the female athletes had. It wasn't that they were less intelligent, possessed fewer skills, or weren't competitive in nature. They simply didn't believe in themselves or trust those aspects of the game. The boys were confident, even brash, and maybe to a fault. If they missed a shot, they would take the next one or try to make some other spectacular play to compensate for the miss. If a girl missed a shot, her body language told the story, shoulders slumped and head down, overthinking the miss and becoming paralyzed in game play, often compounding the miss with mental errors. Having somebody on the bench to recognize those moments of mental anguish and the presence of mind to work through the player's stress and doubt was an invaluable asset. I needed to find a trusted partner to create a new culture at Holmdel and help to round out the staff and our approach to this new group of players. Interviews for the assistant coaching job began right away. The AD had told me there were a few candidates.

The first was a young lady who played at Red Bank Regional, a Shore Conference team, played at Richard Stockton College, and worked on the staff of NJIT as the Director of Basketball Operations. I had never met her before, but I knew her aunt well, the current coach of St. Rose of Belmar. Her aunt was a coach I had worked with in the AAU ranks for the Jersey Shore Elite program. We had competed against each other in many of those heated games between St. Rose and SJV, and we were friends. I was curious to learn more about her niece, now a candidate for the role as my assistant, and wanted to evaluate her based on her merits and nothing else.

Our meeting was at Holmdel High School in the Athletic Director's conference room. The connection was immediate. For the next hour, we talked about basketball and her experiences as a player and coach in the AAU ranks. We had common enthusiasm around a defense-first mentality, the need to have competitive, intense practices, and the importance of the team in creating a winning culture. I shared my thoughts about the Motion offense, Flex, and UCLA sets that I had run for years. She walked me through Wisconsin's Swing offense, which I was unfamiliar with. It didn't take long to recognize that we meshed well and that she would provide a great balance to the program. I hired her on the spot as the JV head coach and assistant to Varsity. Interviews were over.

We went to work scheduling summer workouts and joined the summer league at Hoop Group in Neptune. We needed to learn the players, their individual capabilities, and the team dynamic. We inherited three seniors, two juniors, and five sophomores from the previous season. Participation in girls' basketball at Holmdel had declined over the last couple of years. When we started the summer league, we had 16 girls eager to participate in the basketball program —sixteen girls to support both JV and Varsity teams. The positive side of only 16 girls in the program supporting two teams is that there wouldn't be any cuts. In fact, I put some effort into trying to find additional players and managed to talk one of my sophomores into getting her freshman sister to join us. Her first response was a chuckle as she didn't think her sister was very good at basketball and probably wouldn't be interested. Ultimately, the younger sister joined the program and was part of the JV team. As allowed by state rules, we used the summer and fall periods to start laying the foundation for the season ahead.

Knowing that the previous coach had some issues with a group of parents in the program, I decided to employ a practice I had used every year previously as a head coach. I scheduled a meeting with the parents and the players following one of our early practices. It was important to put faces with names, introduce the coaches, and lay out our expectations for the players and our need for support from the parents. In addition, I wanted the parents to know what they could expect from the coaches. The parents were welcoming, conversations were fruitful, and I felt great about the season ahead.

In New Jersey at the time, basketball could not start until deep in November. Teams were allowed to conduct tryouts Monday through Wednesday of the week leading up to Thanksgiving. Official practices were not allowed to begin until the Monday following Thanksgiving. Teams had to have five practices completed before they could scrimmage, a minimum of three scrimmages before the first game, which couldn't be scheduled until the third Friday in December. Looking ahead at our schedule, we opened at St. Rose and had a game at Manasquan before the Christmas break. In other words, we had a lot of work to do in a very short time to get a foundation laid and begin building player-coach relationships. Everything was new, and there was no telling what baggage the returning players carried with them from their previous experiences.

We laid the groundwork for the season ahead without worrying about "tryouts" with only 16 girls in the program. I had a plan for the first five practices as to what the foundational components were going to be, starting with conditioning of body and spirit. We were small in stature, with my tallest player being a slender 6' 1" freshman. To compete with the larger programs and the pool of talented players, we would need to be in great shape and ready to punch above our weight class. In addition, the defensive mindset I would require demanded quickness, endurance, and teamwork. We needed to be able to work five bodies functioning as one, which requires a lot of work, sacrifice, and selfless play. Players had to maintain pressure on the ball while not giving up a driving lane, while those off the ball had to be in the right position to disrupt passing lines and not allow for any penetration toward our basket. Great defense and effective rebounding led to easy offense through transition opportunities. All those things meant we had to be in great shape, which was not the condition the girls came into the gym.

As I looked at our scrimmage schedule, I noticed a lot of fluff and not much substance. We had three scrimmages planned against mediocre teams. If we were going to get ready for the tough season ahead of us, we needed to add some meat to our scrimmages. We didn't have a lot of options of when we could add a scrimmage because of the way our current schedule butted up to the beginning of the season. So, I had to squeeze something in early. I also didn't want to scrimmage anybody in the Shore Conference because I wanted something unfamiliar and challenging for the girls. One of the assistant coaches from SJV had left to coach a little closer to home. She joined the staff at Saddle River Day, a private school in northern New Jersey, a topnotch program that lost to Manasquan in the TOC semi-finals the year before. This was the kind of matchup I was looking for, so I sent a text message to gauge interest.

Saddle River Day had an early scrimmage with Old Tappan, which they were willing to make a tri-scrimmage. The date was very early, but it allowed us to have the minimum practices required by the state and gave us opportunities to work against two different teams. The tri-scrimmage format was Saddle River vs Holmdel for two quarters. Old Tappan vs Saddle River for two quarters. We then finished with Old Tappan for two quarters. Saddle River Day was a machine, much like the higher-caliber teams in the Shore

Conference, but that didn't faze me. To build the right kind of culture at Holmdel, the girls needed to see what great basketball looked like and they needed to be willing to compete no matter what. We were playing two teams of this caliber in just a couple of short weeks. Old Tappan was more of a mystery to me, but they offered us a reprieve from Saddle River Day and a very different look to work against. Five practices weren't a lot for a new program, but we were ready with what we knew at that point.

Saddle River Day blistered us in the two quarters we played against them, our first two as a team. They were a swarming defense with a suffocating press and very efficient offensively. The chemistry of the team was amazing and fun to watch, something I knew as a coach happens over time and a lot of repetition together. My team struggled on offense and didn't quite know how to play team defense. We tried a few things with moderate success, but we were outclassed. I watched my girls to gauge their reaction to a very adverse situation. Thankfully, the two quarters went by quickly, with plenty of learning opportunities. As Saddle River Day and Old Tappan warmed up, I pulled my team to the side for a "half time" conversation.

There were a lot of downcast glares in our group and an air of failure. You don't often have pivotal moments so early in a season, but I knew my approach and reaction at this moment were important to setting the tone, etching out our new culture. We needed to find the bright side of this experience. Similar to concepts presented in Jon Gordon's book *The Power of Positive Leadership,* "Optimism, positivity, and belief are the fuel that positive leaders need to keep moving forward and drive results . . . The fact is, if you don't have optimism and belief, you can't share it. If you don't have it, you can't transform your team and organization with it. It starts first and foremost with you."

I commended the girls for fighting hard against one of the powerhouse teams in New Jersey, acknowledging that we only had a couple of weeks together at this point. I didn't speak negatively about the quality of our play. Instead, I chose to highlight the qualities of our opponent and held them up as a standard for the direction of our program. I assured them that, given time, good effort, and teamwork, we would be able to compete with the best teams in the Shore Conference. That was a glimpse into the future. At this moment, we need to work on the things that we can improve today. I asked for patience running through our offensive sets, working to get teammates open. I encouraged hard nosed, aggressive team defense and better effort on the glass. Yes, we got punched in the nose by Saddle River Day, but that didn't matter. We had to think of the next sequence and that meant our scrimmage against Old Tappan.

The girls responded positively. Our efforts in the second part of the tri-scrimmage were significantly improved. The downward stares and lost looks turned into eyes up and looking for teammates. Our offense began to take form, our press created some easy baskets, and the lift in spirit was palpable. We had marked improvement and left the gym with many positives, one of which was a show of resolve by the players and a glimmer of understanding that our program goals were achievable. On the way to the bus for our trip home, I stopped to talk to a few parents. Saddled by some of the same self-doubt and uncertainties that their daughters felt after the Saddle River Day scrimmage, they questioned me as to why we would play them at all, let alone the first scrimmage of the year. Changing the culture involved changing the expectations of the parents and the conversations held at home. Rather than focus on the negative perceptions offered by the parents, I shared some of my positive feelings about the day's experience in both scrimmages and my excitement for the season ahead.

The parents knew we had a very tough schedule and were quick to point out how "unfair" it was for a small school like Holmdel to play such powerful programs, not to mention eight games of our schedule. The general feeling among parents is that we had no chance against such programs and that they shouldn't be on our schedule. My response was that we needed to be ready to play whoever was on our schedule and that we would play to win. A group of parents from the school clamored about this all the time and even petitioned the mayor's office to force some change. I saw it as noise and didn't want that mentality to impact the team. Being prepared to compete with the powerhouse teams in our conference required us to test our metal.

The strongest metal is forged in the hottest fires. Our opening night game at St. Rose was blazing hot. If Saddle River Day was a learning experience, this was baptism by fire. For the first quarter, we looked like we were going to be in a slugfest with one of the best teams in the Shore. Down 10-8, our team was excited and feeling good about our preparation. We had showed up ready to play. However, as any coach will tell you, games are not generally won in the first quarter. I always preached about "32 minutes" in an effort to provide focus and balance to our game presence. We had some successes in the first quarter, but what we really did well in those eight minutes was make St. Rose mad. As a team, they were bigger and faster than we were. For the next 24 minutes, the Purple Roses flexed their basketball muscles and went on a 59-17 rampage. The "I told you so" looks were out, and parents continued the song about how we shouldn't be playing these teams.

The bus ride home was solemn, more than expected for an early season loss. I spent time reflecting on the game and felt that several of the girls had shied away from adjustments and coaching throughout the game, maybe taking things too personally. It was only the first game of the season, but I sensed that something was off. As we pulled up to the school for drop off, I stood at the front of the bus, offered some additional words of encouragement, and told them we would get back to work at practice the next day. Before leaving, I asked my senior captain for a few minutes of her time. I shared my concerns with her and asked why some of the players were so down after just one game. Listening to her input, it became evident that there was still a dark cloud hanging over the team due to how the previous coach communicated, especially during challenging times, often leaving the girls feeling isolated and unsure of themselves. Their confidence was shredded. We had to focus on our next opponent, a winnable game at home against Raritan. Still, I had to embrace the challenge of winning the internal battle and building certain players up after what appeared to be a deflating experience. We were going to have to build one brick at a time.

The Rockets were a Group 2 school like Holmdel. They had three very good seniors returning to their roster, so I expected this to be a close game. I wasn't worried about the opponent as much as I was about the effect of the old Holmdel coach being on the bench for the opponent, now an assistant for Raritan. Several girls were rattled by the idea of seeing him again for reasons unknown to me. Once those jitters passed and the game got underway, we were in a very competitive game. Like the St. Rose game, we played very well in the first quarter, but this time, we came to the bench after eight minutes up six. The energy was different because the belief was different. The girls knew this was a team that we could beat.

The second quarter was close, but we maintained our lead going into the locker room with a score of 22-18. The battle continued through the third quarter, but Raritan's trio started to hit some key baskets, giving them a one-point lead as the teams headed to the sidelines for the break. I was happy with how my girls improved throughout the game, especially on the heels of the St. Rose debacle. Instead of quitting, the girls dug in for a couple of good practices and responded well with quality play throughout this game. The lead changed several times in a very exciting fourth quarter. One of my players, a sophomore forward, began to have an impact on the game. She was a hard worker in practice and very receptive to coaching. If she lacked anything in basketball skills at that time, she more than made up for it with hustle and desire. She was a blue-collar player with a love for competition and began showing that in the game's most critical part. We weren't having any luck on the perimeter in this game, so she took it upon herself to get downhill and challenge the paint.

Time after time, she would drive and draw the foul, sometimes shooting two free throws and others in a conventional three-point play attempt. During the fourth quarter, through grit and determination, she went to the foul line nine times. I watched with great pride in what I was seeing unfold, a player having a lightbulb moment in realizing that she can play and that hard work pays off. I offered empathy and suffered for her as she missed seven of the nine free throws. I kept encouraging her to return to the line and reward herself for a job well-done. She bravely stepped up every time but couldn't get the shots to fall. We lost by two points. The pain and anguish on her face were evident. Nothing I said offered any consolation. She didn't lose the game for us, but there was no telling her otherwise. The fact of the matter was that we wouldn't have had the chance to win had she not experienced the epiphany of her capabilities. I hugged her and told her we would work on everything we needed as a team at practice the next day. As a coach, I knew I had discovered a very special player, and I was excited about the fact that she was only a sophomore.

Walking into the gym for practice the next day, I saw a single player working at the far end of the main basket. There she was, my blue-collar kid, putting in overtime by herself. She was shooting free throws, then running to get her own rebound. Over and over again. I sauntered over to say hello and check in with her. She had a smile on her face and a special look in her eye. She cared. Feeling like she let the team down, she committed her time to resolving what she perceived as the problem. We talked briefly. She asked for some input on her shooting form. I made some subtle adjustments, then let her return to work, rebounding for her until a teammate arrived. Another sophomore replaced me, best friend to the shooter, also a blue-collar player who was a good athlete, both physically and mentally, and very coachable.

There is a great section in *The Power of Positive Leadership* that touches on talking to yourself instead of listening to yourself. "If I listen to myself, I hear all the reasons why I should give up. I hear that I'm too tired, too old, too weak to make it. But if I talk to myself, I can give myself the encouragement and words I need to hear to keep running and finish the race . . . Too often we listen to ourselves and hear all the unhappiness, failure, and unfulfilled goals." I was watching this unfold before me through one of my players. After missing seven free throws in a game her team lost by two points, it would be very hard not to listen to the voices of self-doubt and discouragement. This player recognized the opportunity to improve and talked to herself about what she could do as an individual contributor in support of her teammates. She was a sophomore in high school, showing a keen sense of accountability and a willingness to lead herself and others by example. Coaches are not supposed to have favorites, but she became one of mine at that moment through the demonstration of commitment and the desire to turn a perceived failure into a positive experience.

Walking away from that conversation, I turned to find another sophomore and two freshmen in the gym early. Each was at an individual basket, working on skills they wanted to improve. The sophomore was a very skilled offensive player with a program of shots that she would work through before and after practice. The freshmen players were both tall, lanky athletes but with unique skill sets. One had nervous energy about her and sneaky speed. While still developing, her game and talent were probably the most complete. She could score from multiple spots and use her athleticism and length to be an effective defender against different positions. The other freshman, a slender 6' 1" center by default, had a very quiet, humble demeanor but had a good shot, defended well, and had a knack for rebounding and blocking shots. I found myself in the gym early, looking at foundational pieces for the program to go along with the senior and junior talent on the team.

Watching this unfold before practice made me feel better about the team's direction. My challenge now was helping the girls build on that feeling and the team's commitment to improving. We had an upcoming game against Manasquan, the defending TOC champs and one of the best programs in the Shore Conference, with only one day to prepare. I was concerned that a drubbing at the hands of a powerhouse team could be deflating for the girls, but we went about our business, reviewing the scout and putting up game shots, getting ready for our next opponent.

SIXTEEN
LAST SECOND ADJUSTMENT

ON THE BUS TO MANASQUAN, the girls were loose and singing songs together. Although it wasn't American Idol, the show was fun to watch and music to my ears. We had a quality practice the night before. We knew the task at hand, albeit monumental. I told the girls we would prepare to win every game we played, regardless of the opponent. We had prepared to beat Manasquan. Whether or not the girls believed they could win was still unknown. We needed a little miracle.

As previously noted, Manasquan won the TOC in the previous season. They were returning two key players that were both seniors, one a Harvard recruit and the other Maryland bound, and both were excellent scorers. Although somewhat unproven early in the season, their bench was loaded with talent, including four very good freshmen. As I watched the teams warm up, I gave thought to our scout and my pregame review. In a moment of vividness, I decided to scrap our original game plan. With about five minutes left in the warmup, I pulled the team back into the locker room, which was a classroom at the high school.

"I know we haven't practiced this, but we are changing up our defense. Along with being better, we need to be different than what they expect us to be tonight." I began to draw up the Triangle-and-2 defense, with the intention of playing denial defense on their Division 1 recruits. I didn't know if we could stop them, but we were going to make life more difficult for them and force the younger players to be productive. We reviewed the man-to-man component of the defense and defined the matchups, including rotational players. I drew up the "triangle" zone component of the defense, reviewing the movement and responsibilities. All of this in about four minutes. It was a proverbial crapshoot, a roll of the dice, betting on my team's ability to overcome uncertainties from the previous games and pull together against a formidable foe.

We charged back to the gym, put up a few more shots, and then came to the bench for the pregame announcements. I reminded the girls of our plan, encouraging the girls in the triangle to have eye discipline in seeing player and zone, the girls in the man portion to deny driving lines and access to the ball, and stressed the need for great communication and movement as a team . . . five moving as one. We broke huddle, and the starting five took the floor.

Early in the first quarter, our defense was sharp, flustering the senior stars and confusing the Manasquan offense. After a couple of minutes of us getting the better of game action, our defense frustrating their players, and our offense having early success, the opposing coach burned a timeout. I took great pride when my team's performance forced the other coach to call a timeout for adjustments. This timeout was especially satisfying because of the quality of the opponent and the coaching staff. The head coach was incredibly successful and had built a tremendous program. One assistant coach was the former head coach of St. Rose, a friend but a nemesis. The other assistant was a friend and the father of a former player from one of my AAU teams. As they crafted their response to the Triangle-and-2 defense, I had a few adjustments of my own.

As the ball was inbounded by Manasquan, we were still set up with the same defensive look. Once the ball broke half-court, the triangle part of the defense broke out and engaged in man-to-man. The confusion led to a turnover, and the ensuing possession led to a three-pointer by my senior captain, who was smaller in stature but strong in spirit. My team put together a great effort for the first quarter. Eight minutes done, and we were down 16-11 to the defending TOC champs. Holmdel players were fired up, stoked by a stellar performance. I reminded them that games aren't won or lost in the first eight minutes. We would need to put together our best 32 minutes to pull this off while keeping them off balance.

Starting the second quarter, feeling some oats of my own, we opened with our 2-2-1 full-court press. The talent on Manasquan was just too good, and we gave up a couple of easy baskets. I quickly shifted us back to Triangle-and-2, with the girls picking up where they had left off. They executed with great precision despite having yet to practice this defense. The second quarter continued with a similar theme defensively, and our offense started to find more of a rhythm than we experienced in our previous game. My senior shooter also found more success from behind the arc, draining a couple more 3-pointers. We were holding our own and went into halftime down nine. Honestly, if you had asked anybody in the Shore Conference, they would have expected the deficit to be at least 20 points.

The second half carried on a similar theme and my team did not let up. This team that had struggled in a loss to Raritan just two nights before, leaving the gym with a lot of self-doubt, was now standing toe-to-toe with a monster program, a perennial powerhouse. We were a smaller, less talented team, but we were playing with great heart and hustle. When the final buzzer sounded, we had lost by 12 points. During the post-game handshake line, the opposing coaches were very complimentary of the way we had played. On our way back to the classroom, the team was happy and in a celebratory mood, recognizing that they had played well and were starting to come together as a team. The two freshmen on my team bounced up to me and said, "Coach, that felt like a win!"

I would revisit those words several times over the next few years as the moment when our foundation was established and a team spirit cemented. The players showed great resolve and focus, adjusting our game plan in a four-minute chalk talk. Everybody contributed in so many ways. We challenged a better team and forced them to adjust their style of play. Along the way, we discovered a pretty good outside shooter, as my senior captain dropped 20 points on the strong defense of Manasquan, including six 3-pointers. It wasn't a win, but it all felt great.

Two days later, we lost in the first round of the Score at the Shore holiday tournament to the host team, Southern High School. We didn't have the same focus and intensity that we displayed at Manasquan and were still learning how to string positive sequences together. For only the second time in my career, my team had lost four games in a row, and we went into Christmas 0-4. The season was still young, but that wasn't where I was hoping to be. We needed a spark to get some momentum going.

SEVENTEEN
HOLIDAY SPIRIT

THE DAY AFTER CHRISTMAS, we resumed our season right away with our second game in the holiday tournament. We played a good game against Millville, securing our first win of the season. Our junior power forward began to show signs of comfort in our program, flexing some muscle with a 17-point, eight-rebound and five-steal effort. She was a gifted basketball player. . . strong-bodied, graceful, and agile. She could power her way through the key, had an excellent shot with extended range, and she could break down defenders to get to the rack. On any given day, she could be the best player in the gym. There were no physical limitations to her game. When she struggled, it came with game awareness and confidence in her abilities. Her running mate was a junior point guard, adept with handling the ball and blessed with raw determination. Although not a captain at the time, she was our emotional leader, often burdening herself with helping her teammates get to the right competitive spirit. The two of them together formed a strong nucleus for our emerging team and helped secure our first win, setting up our next tournament game versus Mater Dei.

Playing Mater Dei was a little strange for me, having spent 11 years there as the head coach earlier in my career. The assistant coach was one of my former players, the point guard who had gone to Red Bank Catholic as a freshman, then transferred to Mater Dei. This was a moment of pride for me to see a former player now working in the high school coaching ranks. I wasn't the least bit surprised to see her on the sidelines. As a player, she always demonstrated great leadership and a strong work ethic. Her father was a township and AAU basketball coach, an excellent mentor to many people, including me, and a strong positive influence in her life. It was wonderful to see them both on the sidelines before the game. With big smiles and even bigger hugs, we spent a few minutes catching up with each other and news about our respective families. It was a heartfelt but brief reunion. We had a game to play. Holmdel got the better of Mater Dei in a hard-fought game. We were still lacking consistency in a unified effort, but each game brought new discoveries, and our second consecutive win inspired increased confidence in our team.

We carried the positive momentum into a game against a divisional rival, Shore Regional. Like us, they were trying to establish a winning program. Shore was a small Group 1 school caught up in the same top-heavy division of the Shore Conference at the time, with eight games against Manasquan, Red Bank Catholic, St. Rose, and Rumson-Fair Haven. Like us, they were trying to figure out how to balance the schedule against those assumed losses while maintaining the confidence and enthusiasm of a team filled with hard-working but less talented basketball players. The coach brought a fiery competitiveness to the program and a raw determination to push his program over the hump against tough odds. We first met while I was the assistant at St. John Vianney. He had a great mind for the game and was trying to institute some structure into the program. As documented earlier, SJV was too much for most teams, but the games against Shore were particularly lopsided in those days. That didn't matter to him. He wanted his girls to play at their best regardless of the opponent, which is how he prepared them. I always admired his grit and desire to create a positive atmosphere for young female athletes to grow. In many ways, I felt like we were kindred spirits. This commonality in effort and position in our division made these games very competitive. We were each counting on this game as a win since we were fighting against a presumed number of losses and needed a .500 record to qualify for the Shore Conference Tournament and State Playoffs. We were opposing coaches with a common mission.

We beat Shore for our third consecutive win, improving to 3-4 on the season and carrying a lot of confidence into our game with one of those formidable opponents, Rumson-Fair Haven. This was another well-coached team full of Division 1 recruits. The coach was another friend on the sideline, and we shared the bond of having served as officers in the U.S. Navy. I had a great deal of respect for him and certainly for the quality of play from his girls. My team was playing better, showing an improved understanding of the game, and building stronger chemistry. Parents were excited and encouraged by the quality of team play. There was a building belief that we might just be able to beat RFH.

It didn't look good early as Rumson jumped out to a 7-0 lead, hitting on their first three attempts, while we were struggling to find a flow. We ended the first quarter down 15-5, seemingly unable to compete. Another good sign of our growth was a developing down but not out mentality. We won the remaining three quarters 35-30. The team looked good, and my dynamic duo of juniors led the way, combining for 29 points. Unfortunately, we ended up on the wrong side of the final score at 45-40, serving as another reminder of the importance of playing focused basketball for 32 minutes. We didn't win, but we showed fight and a willingness to compete. More progress and reasons to be encouraged.

We took care of business against Monmouth Regional, which we should have. Our next opponent was Trinity Hall in our gym for a Saturday matinee. Trinity was a good team and an opportunity for us to pick up a win outside of our division. The feeling from their camp was similar, as their record was also 4-5, and they were looking to hit the .500 mark. The game was over shortly after tipoff. My girls put on an offensive display in the first eight minutes, hitting shots from every angle, including six 3-pointers. We were up 28-10 when the storm passed, and Trinity Hall had no idea what hit them. It didn't matter what they did defensively or how many timeouts they took to make adjustments. We were just much better that day. My team applied pressure through a strong press and suffocated the ball in the front court. Our offense was balanced and very fluid. We won in all phases, finishing with a 62-38 victory. After starting the season 0-4, we had won five out of the last six games, righting the ship at 5-5. The girls were playing well and celebrating with each other. The parents were ecstatic. There was a positive buzz around the Hornets' Nest.

EIGHTEEN
SOMETHING WICKED THIS WAY COMES

OUR NEXT STRETCH of games was a true gauntlet. We were staring down the challenge of six games in eleven days; RBC, St. Rose, Raritan, Manasquan, Matawan, and Rutgers Prep in that order. Four of those teams were ranked in the top 10 of the state at that point in the season. We prepared for each game individually, planning to not only compete but to win. Parents continued to approach me about the complexities of our schedule, which was out of my hands, but I offered words of encouragement. Several parents told me that we needed to focus on Raritan and Matawan, which were considered our "winnable" games. My only hope was that the parents weren't giving their daughters the same gloomy forecast at home.

We were not competitive against Red Bank Catholic. As always, they were too big, strong, fast, and deep for us. The roster was loaded with Division 1 talent, and that was evident. After a good first half against St. Rose in the next game, down only nine points, the wheels fell off the cart in the second half, and we got whooped, including a 26-5 fourth quarter. It was like we didn't expect to win, so why bother trying? I wasn't happy with our effort, but like everybody else, I looked to the Raritan game, where we could avenge our two-point loss from earlier in the season.

The game started off great with us taking a 15-12 first-quarter lead. It looked like we were off to the races. Something happened during the second quarter. We started to lose all sense of unity and cohesion as a team. The ball stopped moving through our offenses, with players taking uncharacteristic shots. At halftime, down two points, I went to work trying to pull the team back in and get everybody on the same page. We talked about the first three minutes and left the locker room.

As well as we had played in previous games like Manasquan and Rumson, we looked the exact opposite here. Raritan outscored us 48-24 in the second half on their way to a 26-point win. My team had fallen apart right before my eyes, but I wasn't sure why. Was it the string of tough games? Were we in a physical rut due to the grind of the season? Whatever it was, we would have to get it corrected quickly.

Later that night, I got a text from one of my sophomore players asking if I had time for a call. During our call, the player was complaining about some things other girls on the team had said about her. She was telling me about texts between other players shared with her by another teammate. There were feelings of exclusion and dislike. She told me parents were shouting things from the stands directed at her during the Raritan game, like, "Don't pass it to her; all she does is shoot the ball." I was listening to tales of mean girls being played out within our basketball family. In all my years of coaching to that point, I never had to arbitrate anything like this. Honestly, I didn't think it was my position to get involved in personal relationships between the girls. After listening for a while, I offered some comforting words and suggested that the best thing to do would be to talk to her teammates directly. Let them know that her feelings were hurt. I encouraged an open and honest dialogue. These were relationships that they needed to own and manage, along with being accountable to each other. I suggested that if she wasn't comfortable with the idea of doing it alone, ask our senior captain to sit in to help facilitate the conversation. The captain was mature, levelheaded, and well-liked by everyone. I further offered that if they were unable to come to an agreeable solution, I would step in to help work through the issues with everyone. The player agreed to make the effort.

I guess it was too much for me to expect teenagers to try to find a peaceful resolution. The heated text that I received the next day from the player's mother suggested that I ignored her daughter's plea for help and that I didn't care about the girls. Instead of addressing the "bullies" and supporting her daughter, I played it off as "girls being girls." The next thing I know, I am getting a call from the school's principal to attend a meeting with administrators, the player, and her parents. Twelve games into my first season with a new program, and the administration is catering to a parent over gossip and rumor instead of backing the coach's position.

After about 10 minutes of listening to the same recap I had in the initial call from the player, the tone shifted to every bad thing my predecessor had done the season before . . . the derogatory tones, public rebuke of the player, punishment for errors on the court by reducing playing time or benching, and even actions taken during AAU season. All of this had nothing to do with me, but I was the dumping ground for their frustrations. I let the parents know what my hopes were by having the girls talk to each other to work things out. I assured them I cared about their daughter and treated her with kindness and respect, as I did all my girls. I also reminded them that their younger daughter, a freshman who wasn't going to play for the high school, came out at my request and was a member of our JV team. The principal didn't have much to say in the matter, but the vice principal, a woman, was also in attendance. After listening to the conversation for a while, she stated in a matter-of-fact way that this sounded like "typical girl stuff" and that they should be able to work it out themselves. I was thankful that she expressed that sentiment to the mother and her daughter. Coming from her, it was received much differently than had it come from me, the principal, or any other male figure. Emotions settled and we left the table in a cordial manner. In fact, outside the meeting room, the mother gave me a hug and thanked me for coaching her daughters.

With that behind us, I began engaging the sophomore player like before with encouragement and support. At the next practice, I addressed the entire team in a general way about the importance of our bond with each other, on and off the court. I chalked Raritan up to a fluke and asked them all to come together for the remainder of our season. While this struggle was going on within the dynamic of our team and extended family, we had a game with Manasquan to prepare for. We were still in a broken state and Manasquan was eager to make the statement that, although we only lost by 12 points in our first matchup, we didn't belong in their stratosphere. For the second time in the season, we lost four games in a row, allowing our opponents an average of 71 points per game. As quickly as we rose to 5-5, we had sunk faster to 5-9 and seemed to lose our way in the process. The one bright spot in the Manasquan game was the sophomore who had lodged the complaint. She lit up for a 16-point performance, including four 3-pointers, one of which was a "logo three" before they became all the rage. Some would say that she was being a ball hog and doing things to spite her teammates. I felt like we found another weapon that added to a balanced attack, and we needed to figure out how to get everybody working together again.

We managed a 3-3 record over the next two weeks, still working through a tough schedule laden with Rutgers Prep, Rumson, and

RBC. By the Shore Conference Tournament cutoff, we were below the required .500 mark and missed the opportunity to participate. With that prospect gone, we had to pick up a couple of games and begin our focus on preparing for the state tournament. NJSIAA had changed the .500 requirement for participation in the state playoffs, so we were going to be in, but I wanted us to be in a position for a positive experience. As if we didn't have a tough enough schedule already, I picked up a game against Lincoln out of Jersey City. They were ranked 12th in the state at the time. If we wanted to advance in the state tournament, we needed to be ready for stiff competition.

Prior to our game with Lincoln, my son joined the coaching staff as a volunteer. He had just completed his first season as the head coach for the boys' seventh and eighth grade basketball team at St. Mary's Grammar School. Starting to catch the coaching bug, he wanted to work with older players to continue his growth and development as a coach. I already had one dynamic assistant, who I adored as a person and thoroughly enjoyed working with. Now, I had the pleasure of adding my son to the lineup. I had coached him in seventh and eighth grade, my last two seasons with boys before moving to high school girls. I knew how much passion and positive energy he had for the game. He was also a post player by nature, a very good defensive player, and always had a desire to improve his game. The three of us made a good team, sharing different viewpoints but providing great balance to the team. The timing was great, as we were headed to Lincoln, a team with two dynamic bigs.

Like our Jekyll and Hyde performances of previous games, Lincoln, who had only lost four games all season, jumped out to a 20-5 first-quarter lead. I had begun to question myself about my abilities to help this team recognize their potential. Lincoln had two big girls, both over 6 feet tall, and a speedy point guard. We were trying to match up early, but there was no effect. When we switched to our 2-3 zone, the point guard was penetrating at will, causing our defense to collapse and exposing the post. During the break at the completion of the first quarter, I decided to utilize a junk defense. We doubled the most effective post player. I put my best defender on the point guard with instructions to slow down the penetration, and to deny her the ball when she doesn't have it. I placed a helper playing zone between the top of the key and the free-throw line to stop penetration should the point guard get by our primary defender. Her other role was to help defend the wings on either side of the court, favoring one player and leaving the other more exposed. Then I had my next best defender on the other big, who was more of an outside-in player. She was also in denial, with instructions not to help other defenders. Basically, we committed four resources to their three best players. My other defender was a rover between the remaining two offensive players. Desperate times call for desperate measures. The fun of it all was watching it work. We won the last three quarters 59-50. However, like our first Rumson game, the first quarter deficit was too much to overcome.

I felt like this was another one of those games where the talk at home was about our chances of victory being slim and none. Once we got beyond the doubt of others and began believing in ourselves, this team could play with some of the best around. At one stretch late in the Lincoln game, we turned up the heat with a full court press. The added pressure was effective, and we turned great defense into easy offense. My sophomore long shooter, playing more focused basketball since the incident a few weeks prior, scored from deep on four consecutive possessions. She finished the game with 22 points, fueled by six 3-pointers. Everybody had caught the fever of believing in us as we had the host team on their heels. Even my two lanky freshmen showed great signs of maturity and elevated their gameplay. We lost 70-64, but we had taken significant steps in our preparation for the postseason. Shortly after the Lincoln game, we found out that our first-round opponent for the Central Jersey

Group 2 playoffs would be Raritan. The chaos of our last game against Raritan had taken a lot to overcome. The effort in our Lincoln game and subsequent wins against Jackson Liberty and Toms River South would suggest that we were in a much better place. Time would tell.

Seeding for the state playoffs is based on power points, which is a method by which teams are rewarded for playing tougher schedules. Wins against certain programs carried more weight. If you were a Group 1 school and managed to beat a Group 4 (larger school), you would pick up power points. With our schedule and some key wins, we ended up collecting more power points than Raritan. So, even though they had beaten us twice during the regular season, we were seeded higher and hosted the first round of the playoffs. The winner of our game earned the right to play Rumson, the presumed winner of their first-round game. We were 0-4 in our games against these two teams, but I was excited about the prospect of these matchups and went about laying the path forward for my team.

We had two good days of practice leading up to the game against Raritan. Normally, I would work in some film review, but I chose not to look backwards for this occasion. I shared my thoughts with the team before our first practice; I told the girls that this game was about us, our mental state, and our execution as a team. We had come a long way since the meltdown twelve games before. Our only option was to continue to build better habits together.

When play began, there was no doubt we were a different team. My two juniors led the statement of effort early, with the point guard getting downhill at will and the power forward putting a lot of pressure on the defense's interior. In addition, my senior guard hit a big three-pointer early to spot us a 17-13 first-quarter lead. The game was physical from the start, and we picked up some early fouls, but the bench provided the required support to keep our effort strong. With all the contributions and a concerted team effort, we built a 15-point halftime lead. It was a good feeling in the locker room at the half. The girls knew they had played well but also knew that our opponent wasn't going away. Without my input, they were reminding each other about the importance of the first three minutes and the need to put together 32 minutes of quality basketball. It was a proud moment listening to the players coach themselves.

The third quarter was rough, both in nature and in the quality of play between the two teams. The physicality increased on both sides, and fouls began to rack up. Early in the third quarter, my power forward was called for her third foul. Shortly after, my sharpshooting sophomore picked up her third foul as well. In addition to our foul woes, Raritan's two best players began to flex their offensive muscles. By the end of the third quarter, our 15-point lead evaporated to four points. Raritan took the momentum into the fourth quarter, taking the lead early. The rest of the game was nip and tuck, with a lot of emotion on both sides. Raritan believing they could win, and our team working to fight off the demons of the past.

Late in the fourth quarter, our defense was still struggling to slow down Raritan's two best players. I decided to make a change and inserted my two talented freshmen, who had been growing and gaining experience all season long. As I sent them to report at the scorer's table, I told them they weren't freshmen anymore. They were now responsible for the two best offensive players. They had the length to bother their outside shooting and the quickness to keep them away from the basket. It was time for them to step up. The fresh energy and enthusiasm they brought propelled our defensive effort and helped us close out the victory at home, 60-55.

We earned the right to play Rumson-Fair Haven in the Group 2 quarterfinals. In simple terms, RFH outclassed us in our final game of the season. We fought them to a tie after the first quarter, but their talent and depth proved to be too much for us again. We ended the season at 12-14. When we were at our best, the girls let go of self and relied on team. Unfortunately, those moments were inconsistent throughout the year. We were a team with potential, but too often got mired in the opposite spirit, putting self before team. Those struggles may have been signs of our relative immaturity and inexperience, or maybe weariness from the challenges of our highly ranked opponents. Earlier in the season, we had adopted the phrase, "No excuses, only adjustments." The program's direction was very positive. The talent returning was evident. We had to go to work on the commitment to develop physical and mental strength, to continue developing our skill sets, and to work from the frame of reference that the rising tide lifts all boats.

NINETEEN
BUILDING ON SOLID GROUND

PREPARATION for the high school basketball season begins during the summer months. By NJSIAA rules, once school has ended for the year, sometime in June, coaches from all sports, regardless of season, can work with their athletes directly. This allows for workouts and summer league basketball. Eager to build on the strength of our foundation unveiled throughout the previous season, we went to work planning workouts to enhance our collective skill sets, build our strength and conditioning, and scheduled games to help develop our chemistry and character as a team.

Our returning roster was solid, and we had a year of experience in our system. The fiery point guard and the very talented power forward from last year were now seniors and selected as captains for the team. The junior class was diverse in talent and provided great stability and depth to the roster. I had the two blue-collar players who continued to show great improvement through a commitment to excellence, a hardworking and talented offensive player who could score from anywhere and worked at refining her craft with extra practice every day, and the long-range shooter who had other weapons we needed to tap into. Of course, we had the two lanky freshmen from last year, now sophomores, both very gifted in the game and loaded with potential. We just needed to gain more experience and tap into the depth of skills they each possessed.

The incoming freshman class was small, both literally and figuratively. Last year's eighth grade team from the middle school affiliated with Holmdel High School was a talented bunch. Unfortunately, before the season even started, one of the best players on the team had made up her mind that she would pursue bigger and better basketball opportunities at St. John Vianney. She ultimately went on to have an amazing high school career and ended up playing at Holy Cross. However, she would have been an incredible addition to our growing Holmdel program. I did get to know another very talented player on that team and built a relationship with her family. This young lady had a knack for basketball. She had a strong, athletic frame and a hard-nosed attitude to go with it. Her offensive skills were well-developed, and she had great defensive instincts. We talked throughout the previous season and deep into the AAU season. She was coming to Holmdel, and I was very excited about that prospect for our program.

Unfortunately, she was pulled away by the temptation to go play for Manasquan—a huge blow for us and the Holmdel community. Anytime you lose one of your own to outside programs it hurts. This had become a pattern in New Jersey over the years, and in the game in general, where players and their parents sacrifice the local team for pursuits of aspirations at powerhouse programs. So many times, those moves become delusions of grandeur, leading to frustrations for the player, often demoralizing them and causing them to lose their passion for the game. The NJSIAA has rules in place to help minimize the impact of player movement to build stacked teams, especially when it involves two public schools, but the rules had more holes than Swiss cheese, and the governing body was limited in its reach and will to enforce them. Having been through this previously when I was at Mater Dei, I wished the player and her family the best of luck, and I let them know that she was always welcome back should things not work out. We did get one of the very talented players from that eighth grade team. She was a small guard with big fight in her, and she was the younger sister of my senior captain from last year, the one who nailed six 3-pointers in the game against Manasquan. I went to watch the eighth-grade team a few times throughout the year, always enjoying her level of effort and caliber of play. She could handle well enough but needed to work on her confidence going left and her court vision, both things that could be developed through practice. She had nice shooting form and wasn't afraid of big moments in the game, frequently knocking down key baskets from outside. In the eighth grade league championship game, she showed strong defensive effort throughout, but several times was caught in a mismatch against a much bigger, stronger player. She didn't back down an inch and was committed to the effort of helping her team in any way she could. Her parents were great people, always very pleasant and supportive. She was Holmdel-bound and eventually earned her way to being the only freshman on the varsity roster.

During the summer workouts, I encouraged the girls to take ownership and pride in our team. If we were going to build a more dynamic and durable program, they needed to build enthusiasm and interest among their peers. We needed players to fill rosters at JV and varsity levels to allow for competitive practices and strong benches that would promote natural growth and maturation within the game for players during their time in high school. Another issue with players and parents is an increasing mentality that the only path to college ball is to be on varsity as a freshman or to be a starter at that level. Not all players can compete at the varsity level right away. They may have physical attributes, but their mind for the game isn't developed yet. They may understand the game well but not have the strength and skills to match at that time. Both of those cases are not bad things. The beauty of being part of a team and working within a program is that every individual can contribute in their own way, at the level appropriate to their abilities, and have the opportunity to grow and mature in the game. There are limited spots on a varsity basketball roster, and only five players can start a game, but every team needs depth on the roster. We needed more players in our program to have sustainable growth. The girls encouraged a few of their classmates to come out, and we grew our program from 16 to 21. We worked through the summer and fall to prepare ourselves for the season to come.

I felt the early part of the 2019-2020 season would be a good litmus test for our team. We opened at St. Rose, a perennial powerhouse team that played a level of basketball we strived to attain. Then, we were off to the Lady Lion Holiday Tournament at Lincoln High School in Jersey City, a new experience for us beyond the comforts of the Shore Conference. I wanted to test our metal, the mental strength of this team, hoping to transform potential into reality. I thought we were ready for the next level of play, but I needed the players to believe in themselves like I believed in them.

Our game against the Purple Roses was a bust! We rolled into the bandbox gym in Belmar, New Jersey. I didn't want to just compete and firmly believed we were ready to win. My assessment was incorrect. We were defeated by the name on the front of our opponent's jersey, an old habit that still plagued the girls' psyche. The entire basketball community favored St. Rose, including our supporters. In their minds, Holmdel was still a collection of ragtag players, not ready for prime-time Shore Conference basketball. Our girls bought into those feelings lock, stock, and barrel and stumbled through a 28-point loss. I always preached to my girls that the game of basketball is just as much mental as it is physical. While we were ready physically, we needed to strengthen our mental resolve. I felt as though I had failed as a coach by not having them better prepared. I cared about my players and wanted to help them realize their potential, but we fell short in the first game of the year. Failure during the season is inevitable. In fact, I would encourage my girls to push themselves to fail. In that effort, a person will better understand their limits and will have the opportunity to identify the commitment and resolve required to turn failure into success. A lot of thoughts for our first game of the season, but these girls were special and capable of much more. Back to work.

As often encouraged, our next few practices were all about the next sequence. Improve, build, and prepare for the tournament. We opened the Lady Lions Tournament with a one-point overtime win against West Orange, an athletic, guard-oriented team. The next day, we had another close game against New Providence, losing by one point in overtime. We rebounded from our opening-day loss, playing two competitive overtime games against very good opponents. The girls were playing better, and our bench was starting to take shape, but we were still missing that boost of energy in our early rotation. One of our juniors, the same player who had missed seven free throws in the Raritan game last year, had earned a starting spot to start the season. During the tournament, she was struggling with the flu and was unavailable for the final game, so we needed to find someone to fill that starting role. In stepped the athletic, sneaky, quick sophomore. Her minutes had increased during the first two tournament games and the results were impactful. With that, I decided to insert her into the starting lineup for our third tournament game against the host team, Lincoln Lions. Her promotion to starter and the absence of the sick junior created a gap in rotation off the bench, so other players would have to step up into new roles and more minutes. We slugged our way through the first half, working through the wrinkle of a new starting five and a slightly different rotation. Although not as crisp in our early execution, we went into halftime with a 23-20 lead. After I detailed some game adjustments, I felt like we needed something to elevate our energy and intensity. I put my dry-erase pen down and asked the girls, "Why do you think Lincoln scheduled a game against us in their tournament? They could have played several other teams. Why us?" After some quizzical looks and shrugged shoulders, I said, "Because they think they can beat us. They don't feel like you all measure up, and they will take home an easy win in their tournament. We need to go out for the next 16 minutes and prove them wrong!"

The girls took the message to heart and went on to post a 30-11 halftime effort, securing a 22-point win against a top-20 team in the state. My senior power forward led the effort with 21 points, five rebounds, three steals, and two blocks. She flexed in a way she had been reluctant to do in previous games. Her play inspired others to step up, including our new sophomore starter, who chipped in eight points, 10 rebounds, and five steals. This was her third solid performance in a row, earning her a nomination to the all-tournament team. The quality of play was far better than opening night, and some of that potential was starting to show. I also had to make a decision around the starting lineup for future games. The chemistry of the group that started and played most of the minutes in the Lincoln game was dynamic. Suppose I moved the sophomore into the starting lineup, who would I have to move out? Two juniors would be the best choices, my blue-collar player who missed due to illness or the long ball shooter.

Thinking through the psychology of the players involved, I didn't believe the shooter would have taken the news well and that the change would have a negative impact on her game and, more importantly, the team's chemistry. On the other hand, the hardworking junior earned every minute she played, always contributed heart and soul, and didn't deserve to lose a starting role due to being sick. Admittedly, I didn't communicate that change well, and the news fell a little hard on my blue-collar junior. Her mother called me to discuss the situation and share some of her daughter's emotions around the news. Mom was very respectful, listened to my explanation, and understood my philosophy behind the change. While the frustration was obvious, the player managed the situation well. I wasn't surprised by her grace and maturity in handling the circumstances. You could tell she reflected great parents who trusted the coach-player relationship and taught their daughter how to navigate difficult situations. I listened to her feelings and shared my thoughts around the power and energy she could bring to the game as the first person off the bench. I also encouraged her not to be too focused on who starts the game but to pay attention to who finishes games and who is on the court during pivotal moments.

TWENTY
A TEAM IN NEED OF A LITTLE POP

OUR NEXT GAME was at Raritan. On paper, we were a much better team than Raritan, but they still had a tremendous player who could score in multiple ways. I knew the girls also felt like we were a much better team than Raritan, even though we were not far removed from the previous season, where we had lost twice to them. This was a trap game. We played very well and grew with every experience from our previous games. I was concerned about taking a step backward but focused on driving the girls forward.

As the team was going through pre-game preparations, I must have made 10 trips to the water cooler, trying to wash away the concerns of a potential stumble in our progression. I needed a boost, something that calmed my nerves and provided much needed focus. On my last trip to the cooler, as I poured out another drink, I could feel somebody standing next to me, watching my every move. I was so consumed by my worries around the game that I didn't even recognize the face of an old friend staring right at me, someone I hadn't seen in years. We embraced and spoke briefly since the game was getting ready to start. I asked him to hang around afterward because I wanted to talk. I also charged him with observing my team and sought his input on what we could improve.

Pop, as we call him, was the coach for St. Mary's seventh grade boys while I coached at Holy Family. We used to have some fierce competition in our head-to-head games. Still, we always shared a mutual respect and admiration for each other, and it showed in the way our teams played and in our friendly banter on the sidelines, often standing right next to each other, commenting on the play of our boys. We went on to commission the boy's league together for many years. I admired his coaching style, focusing on defense first, and his uncanny ability to get every ounce out of his players. He coached a seventh grade only team in a league of seventh and eighth grade combined programs. It may not seem like much, but the difference in maturity, physical and mental, and basketball ability between seventh and eighth grade can be very stark. St. Mary's had decided to split the two levels and sent their eighth grade program off to a different league, with an air that they were too good for our Northern Monmouth Parochial Basketball League.

The teams in our league took a little offense to that gesture and always seemed driven to take that out on the seventh graders, or at least try to. Pop didn't flinch at often being undersized or not as talent laden as some of the other teams. In fact, he relished the chance to have his boys compete against insurmountable odds. They often came out on top or just missed, leaving the other team marveling at the heart, hustle, and execution of a younger team. Pop excelled at developing the talent he had into a true team, working together and relying on each other to overcome obstacles thrown their way. He didn't do it by browbeating his players into submission but through a consistent, encouraging, and loving way, all part of the reason he was called Pop. Our philosophies around how the game should be taught were very similar, especially the style of teaching, how players should be coached and developed, not only as players but as people. Seeing Pop put a charge in me and helped me focus on the task at hand, beating Raritan.

The Rockets were fired up, fueled by the emotion of having lost to us in the state playoffs last season. My new starting lineup stumbled early, and our bench rotation, especially the junior recently relegated to that spot, struggled to find cohesion. We found ourselves down by two at the end of the first quarter. As we settled into the game and began to find a rhythm as a team, we worked our way into a five point lead at halftime. Our conversation during the intermission was around not looking past Raritan and understanding that they weren't going to fold for us. They believed they could win the game, and we needed to snatch that belief from them.

As expected, Raritan had another emotional surge coming out of the locker room. While we maintained the lead, they won the quarter and were very much in the game, down four. My team needed leadership, somebody to take over and drive a unified effort. I challenged our senior captains to grab the reins and lead the team in both effort and game awareness. Although not playing our best, we were the better team on the floor that night. I implored the girls to not only believe it but to show it. Our captains responded, as did the rest of the team, and we closed out the game with a strong fourth quarter effort and secured a 14-point win. With our post-game talk complete, I went back out to the gym to find Pop.

After catching up on family and general news, I asked Pop if he would come to our practices for the next couple of days. I wanted a fresh set of eyes and a different voice for the girls in some of our drills. We had a big game at home against Manasquan in three short days. I wanted him to take a hard look at our defense and help us push past any barriers in the way of working five as one in stopping opponents. He gladly agreed and we spent a few days together preparing for one of the best teams in the Shore.

Early in the day leading up to the game, I learned that my starting point guard, one of my senior captains, was sick and not in school. I wasn't worried about who to insert into the starting lineup because I had the junior who had previously been a starter. I knew she would be ready to go as always. What I was concerned about was who would play the point and what that would do to the continuity of our offense. Of course, we would work other players in at some point during practice to prepare for moments like this, but you can't replicate the level of intensity and competition that Manasquan brings to every game during practice. Ideally, with a team that is deep in talent and experience, a coach would be able to have fiercely competitive practices. We just weren't there yet, and one of my most competitive players was now saddled with the flu. I looked for one of my juniors to take over the helm. She had a calm, mature presence about her that would suit the role well. Looking ahead to next season, she was the leading candidate to take over the point guard role. Point guard wasn't her natural spot, but she had a poise in her game that I felt could lend itself well to that position. She was a hard worker, committed to improving her craft, always putting up shots and working on her game. I had two other options, one a diminutive sophomore who was a spark plug every time she was on the floor, but somewhat limited in ball skills, and the other was my lone freshman who just wasn't ready for that level of play yet. The decision was simple.

Since game day was already upon us, we didn't have the opportunity to practice with the new roles and responsibilities in the lineup. Like our first game against Manasquan the year before, we had to make game time adjustments and draw things up on instinct. With Pop's watchful eye, we had been working on defensive intensity in our last few practices. As noted before, there are no excuses, only adjustments.

I give a lot of credit to my girls. If we had lost such a key player the afternoon of a big game last season, the air would have been let out of the balloon for the team. The naysayers would have occupied all their head space, and we would have been rolled over. Instead, the rising confidence and belief in our team from the girls was palpable. The desire to contribute and sacrifice to propel the team forward was evident. We shot out of the gate in the first quarter with an incredible focus, playing very clean basketball offensively and applying tremendous pressure defensively. On one Manasquan possession, we defended for over a minute without allowing an open shot attempt or any clean penetration to the basket. Every passing line was tight. Every shot was contested on balance, forcing their shooters off the mark while not giving up a path to the hoop. If there was even the slightest dribble penetration, the help was on time and pushed the action outside. Our rotations were impeccable. Finally, one of the guards for Manasquan threw up a contested, off-balance floater from the foul line that banked in for a goal. That was a win for us. We often talked about how good teams defend for 15 seconds and great teams for 30. We just spent over a minute challenging everything and forcing an awkward, desperation heave from a prolific offensive team. The little things we had been working on and emphasized in our program were starting to take root. It was fun to watch!

We ended the first quarter up five points and survived a slugfest second quarter to go into halftime with a one-point lead. Without one of our best players and our emotional leader, we were very much in a game with one of the best programs in New Jersey. As I headed to the locker room, I gathered my staff at the end of the bleachers and called Pop down from the third row where he had been watching to gather input and insights. We were playing great basketball. However, we had just punched a powerful team in the nose. The third quarter was going to be huge, and we needed to elevate our already strong level of play. Manasquan was known to be a "handsy" team, very physical and aggressive on defense. I fully expected that effort to ramp up and for them to come out swinging.

I wasn't wrong. Every ball handler was straddled with a hand or forearm to the body. Screens were met with shoves and tugs for the defender to clear. They certainly picked up their intensity, and we worked to match it. I believe they were coached to work on the psyche of my team to test our willingness to get into a street fight. The expectation was that my team would wilt under the increased pressure. At first, the theory worked and put us back on our heels. Manasquan opened with a 7-0 run and had shifted momentum to their favor. However, during a timeout, I challenged our mental fortitude and questioned if we were going to continue letting them push us around. I also reminded my senior power forward that she was the best player on the floor and that her teammates needed her to exert that influence. The team answered the call and elevated their toughness. With the increased physicality in the game, the whistle blew more often, mostly in our direction. We weren't doing anything differently than our opponent, but we weren't Manasquan. The free throw attempts in the game were 28 to 8 in their favor, of which they made 18, and we made five. We had a three-person crew that night, but one ref seemed to be making 75% of the calls. That might be a slight exaggeration, but it certainly felt that way, and I let him know it.

All of that aside, the girls showed some moxie and fought their way back into the game. Late in the fourth quarter, we pulled even when my junior shooter nailed a 3-pointer. The atmosphere in the gym was electric. Our sideline was very active, with every girl on the edge of her seat or jumping in the air with enthusiasm and belief. My girls were playing one of their most complete games without one of our best players, but they were able to regroup after losing the lead. The game was there for the taking, and it would have been a significant upset in the Shore Conference, a win that would put us firmly on the map. We had been in some close games early in this young season, albeit not against the same caliber of team. Had we progressed far enough to close out a game like this? Sadly, the answer was no.

We ended up losing the game by five. As we went through the handshake line after the game, I shared an embrace with the head coach and each of her assistants, congratulating them on a hard-fought win. There was a mutual admiration for the quality of play from our girls and how they all competed. I respected the coach and the program she built over the years. In return, it was obvious through their words and actions that we had earned their respect. I took a moment to talk to the freshman from Holmdel who was playing for Manasquan. She had played some good minutes and was contributing to the team. I encouraged her to keep working and wished her luck until our next game with them, which was scheduled for three weeks later.

My girls played incredibly well. The easy thing for them to do would have been to rest on the fact that we didn't have our senior point guard and just mail the game in. They were becoming a different program and chose to dig deep and respond positively to the adversity. My power forward played like she was the best player in the gym, showcasing strength and skills that were hard to match. The sophomore, newly minted as a starter, showcased strong defense and was very active on the boards with 13 rebounds. The junior who was forced into her debut as point guard did a good job of running our offense and commanding the team. Unfortunately, having her in that role took away from her normal scoring contribution, and we struggled to fill that gap. This game taught us more about ourselves and gave us a new platform to build upon.

TWENTY-ONE
THE TIDE RISES, THE TIDE FALLS

EVERY BASKETBALL SEASON has ebbs and flows. The quality of daily practices can be markedly different. Player focus and execution can vary throughout a game. A team's performance can be dramatically different from game to game. Players can be impacted by so many things throughout their day that alter the mindset they bring to the court; relationships with friends, young love, academic stresses, family tensions, not eating right, not sleeping right, partying too much, and a host of other possibilities. As a coach, it can be tricky trying to manage the confluence of life and basketball on individual players and the overall dynamics of the team. At the same time, it is important to be empathetic to the fact that the outside influences are real.

After the Manasquan game, we were flying high and feeling good about the direction of our season. Our next game against Shore Regional was an expected win on paper. My senior point guard was feeling better and came back to the fold. With her at the helm and other players in their normal roles, we played a fluid game to earn the win. The junior scorer was back in her comfort zone, dropping 22 points. Senior co-captain and power forward once again proved formidable, attacking from all angles and leading all scorers with 23 points, rebounding and defending with strength. While we proved to be the better team, there was a star on the rise for Shore. A freshman phenom who made a great choice to stay with her home high school, she demonstrated her potential with a stat line of 17 points, seven rebounds, and seven assists. She was a rare talent and a welcomed reprieve from all of the program hopping that was occurring in high school basketball. Her talents, coupled with a dynamic junior guard, gave Shore Regional a bright future.

Before retreating to the locker room for post-game with the girls, I talked to the opposing coach and said hello to a few parents who were happy with our win and the way the team was playing. After a few handshakes and hugs, I returned to the locker room, where the girls were waiting for me. I noticed the mother of a sophomore player, the 6'1" slender center, sitting in wait for me. As I approached, she stood up, revealing the height she passed on to her daughter. I was expecting another pleasant encounter with a parent after the game, especially from one I considered friendly. To my surprise, my hello was greeted with an angry glare vented by a terse question, "You think my daughter is JV?" I was confused at first since her daughter was a sophomore playing varsity and not spending any time at the JV level. "You think she isn't as good as the other players?"

As a freshman, she played some JV because we needed bodies to complete the roster. Taking advantage of the 5-quarter rule in New Jersey, she was able to support the JV program and pick up some valuable in-game development, then play in the varsity game the same day. As a sophomore, with our growing team numbers, I was able to have her play varsity only on the merits of her skills and desire to be coached, and she was ready for the elevation of effort and competition. However, she struggled with self-confidence and placed so much emphasis on every missed shot, turnover, or any negative play. As player and coach, we had a great relationship and worked together to overcome the doubts and stress she placed on herself. Every day there was progress in practice, but the gains weren't recognized in game action yet. The rising stock of her classmate, who had risen to a starting role, played a part in her mental anguish. She was unfairly comparing herself to her teammate instead of completing her own experience, so the pressure inside of her mounted. I am sure some of that was echoed and shared at home, and those frustrations were now being transferred to me.

Listening to the mother's concerns and trying to assuage her anger to no avail, I told her that this wasn't a good time to talk as I still needed to wrap things up with the team. I offered time to connect the next day, but she refused and stormed off. Trying to balance the conflicting emotions of winning the game with the unfolding parental tension, I congratulated the team on the win, calling out the growth in our team play and indicating a few things we would work on at practice the next day. Seeing the sophomore center packing her bag up as one of the last to leave, I broke one of my rules around the separation of church and state as it applied to my players and their parents. Normally, I would shield my players from those infrequent occurrences of overbearing parents. The last thing I wanted was to create a rift between players and their parents. My coaching philosophy was centered on honor, integrity, and the sanctity of the parent-child relationship. Experiences throughout my coaching career had revealed that the same courtesy was often not extended toward the player-coach relationship. The same banter at the kitchen table that caused the girls to doubt their chances against "better" teams also carried over to who was coaching them, how they were being coached, and decisions being made. Dignity and respect for a coach were often replaced with disdain and dishonor. I didn't want another player disheartened by parental interference or our rising program to be saddled with unnecessary strife and politics. This time, I decided to have a transparent conversation with my player.

I asked my assistant coach to stay with me and waited for the remaining players to leave. Once privacy was assured, I asked the player if she was unhappy or had any concerns she wanted to discuss with me. "Did my mom say something to you?" There was no hesitation or uncertainty in this moment. She was quite confident as to the origin of my question. I let her know that I wasn't upset but rather wanted to make sure that she understood that I was committed to her continued development as a player. We had always enjoyed open, honest discussions toward that end, and I wanted to ensure she felt understood, acknowledged, and valued because she absolutely was—as both a person and a key part of our program's future. She expressed a desire to keep working and earning her opportunities. Once we finished our discussion, she headed out to the gym while my assistant and I cleaned up the locker room. As we headed through the gym to exit, we passed a very frank conversation between mother and daughter, with mom in listen-only mode. We said goodnight and left them to sort things out.

The team was back in preparation mode with a challenging stretch of seven games in fourteen days, four state-ranked teams, and three of those in a row. The string started with a loss to Trinity Hall in a revenge game for them because of the beating they took in our gym the prior year. As much as our previous contest fueled their fire, it saddled us with overconfidence and complacency. Trinity Hall took full advantage of the situation and hung a loss around our necks. With the schedule ahead, this loss could have very easily tipped the scales against us in qualifying for the Shore Conference Tournament. A record of .500 or better was required before the early February cutoff. With the loss, we were now 4-4, with no room for error, given the difficulty of our schedule. We needed to pick up a quality win to help cement our chances.

Two days after Trinity, we played Rumson-Fair Haven in their gym. This was the first in our stretch of games against state-ranked opponents. The tide had shifted back to positive in our play, and we found ourselves with a one-point lead with under a minute to go against a top-20 team in New Jersey. During a time out, I reviewed the game situation with the girls and told them that we didn't want to rush anything, but we still wanted to run our offense and attack the basket, working for a quality shot. Time was our friend. RFH didn't want to foul, as we were in the bonus, and a foul would allow us to increase the lead. They chose to rely on good defense first, trying to force us into bad decisions. We worked the clock beautifully, moving an aggressive defense from side to side and working the ball into an optimal shot opportunity. Having eaten about 30 seconds off the clock, a swing pass found my power forward with the ball about six feet out, staring at an open path to the basket. We couldn't have asked for a better scenario. The girls had executed perfectly to that point. The rest was like watching a slow-motion train wreck, frame by frame. The wide-open layup was passed on by our best player, who decided to make an additional pass, which led to another pass that became a turnover. Rumson converted that turnover to the go-ahead bucket, and we lost by one. The tide receded.

We had just watched a golden opportunity for a statement win slip through our fingers. While I was proud of the girls for putting us in the position to win, I was dumbfounded by how that win evaded us. I applauded the effort and suggested we use the lessons from this game to fuel our efforts in the upcoming challenges. I was really at a loss for words. On the way out to the bus for our return trip home, some fathers approached and challenged, "Why did you put them in a stall offense?" Still stunned by the unfolding of events, I turned to the bleacher coaches and shared that we weren't in a stall and boarded the bus.

TWENTY-TWO
THE SUMMIT IS WHAT DRIVES US, BUT THE CLIMB IS WHAT MATTERS

STILL BATTLING with small periods of inconsistency, we worked through our schedule, beating the teams we should and competing with better teams for a long stretch but falling short in the end. Heading into the gauntlet of three straight games against top teams in the state rankings, we were sitting one game above .500 and working hard to prepare for Red Bank Catholic (No. 12), St. Rose (No. 5), and Saddle River Day (No. 3), an incredibly challenging schedule for any team to play. With some of our recent games, the near misses against Manasquan and Rumson, confidence was growing within our ranks that not only could we compete, but we could win. We just needed to continue sharpening our skills and putting together a complete game. The first game at RBC wasn't competitive. The girls played well but not at the level to match the size, strength, and speed of the Casey's that day.

Moving on to St. Rose in our gym three days later, with a desire to avenge an ass whooping on opening day, we came with a much different mindset and resolve. In typical St. Rose fashion, they came out in an offensive flurry, propelling them to a seven point first-quarter lead. We adjusted and punched back with our own flurry in the second quarter, going into halftime leading by two. The locker room was fired up, and we were rightfully proud of the way we responded to the initial outburst. We had weathered the storm and came back stronger. A good 16 minutes of play. In the third quarter, we played well, but I could see the gas tank getting low. St. Rose had two very physical post players, not tall, but bullish. They also had a junior guard who was lightning quick and ultra-competitive. The more they leaned into the game, exerting pressure on both sides of the ball, the more fatigued we became. Going into the fourth quarter, we were down six, and I was still pushing for us to compete and believe. Looking into their eyes, I could tell the psychology of our team had shifted.

The other coach, a good friend and aunt of my assistant, was phenomenal when it came to sensing blood in the water. She was masterful at coaching the physical execution of the game but even better at manipulating the mental component. Her scout against us, no doubt in my mind, was to challenge the mental endurance of my team. She knew my girls would be fired up and ready to play. She knew we would execute well and demonstrate early belief in our ability to win. What she coached her players to was challenging the endurance of our faith. Play harder, faster, and longer than the opponent is willing. Take their best, then show them that their best isn't good enough. We lost the fourth quarter 27-9 and the game by 24 points. A game we were playing well in ended up looking like a walk in the park for St. Rose.

Two days later, moving up the state ranking ladder, we played Saddle River Day at a showcase event in our gym. A big-time program from northern New Jersey with a great coach, they were the defending state champions for Non-Public B and lost in the finals of the Tournament of Champions. This was the team we faced in our first scrimmage the previous season. They had graduated key senior players, but they also had a very talented returning roster. One of those players was a gifted sophomore guard who would play college ball at UPenn. Saddle River Day only lost three games in the previous year, and to the point of our game this season, it had only been bested once by a prep school in Florida. The wheels had completely fallen off in that last quarter against St. Rose two days prior. I was curious to see how we would respond as a team. If we wanted to reach the peak, we needed to continue the climb. The defensive effort from both teams was incredible to start the game. Each team ran multiple sets, working to find gaps in the defense. Both defenses held strong, and every made basket was a premium. Their superstar guard was handcuffed and frustrated. At halftime, Holmdel was down 24-22 to the number three team in the state. The girls were playing great. . . again. The first three minutes are crucial! 32 minutes of our play, our way! In the third quarter, both offenses started to hit their stride. The defenses were still playing well, but girls were hitting big shots on both ends. We were toe-to-toe in the middle of the ring, exchanging blows with a powerhouse and showing no signs of backing down. At the end of 24 minutes, Saddle River Day was up by four points, and my girls looked fresh and ready for the final round.

Outside of program name and history, the teams were evenly matched. The one big difference was their sophomore guard. We had done a magnificent job minimizing her impact on the game to that point. However, great players tend to elevate their play in crucial moments. Her athleticism and basketball skills began to shine as the fourth quarter played out. Our efforts to contain her put us into a little bit of foul trouble late, causing changes in our approach. As great players do, she took full advantage and exploited opportunities for open 3-pointers, then used her speed to get to the basket against aggressive closeouts. It was an excellent effort by my girls in a 13-point loss. A deeper glimpse into what we were capable of, but also a stark reminder that we weren't there yet.

Following that three-game onslaught, our regular schedule resumed with us going through the division a second time. We won our game against Raritan ahead of our pending rematch with Manasquan. This time, we would go into their gym with a full and healthy roster and the benefit of experience from our recent level of play. The girls wanted another crack, and we had a couple of practices to prepare. My senior captains were great at practice, keeping the team focused and committed. The energy was high, and the competitive nature of practice was intense. At the back end of the last practice, we reviewed some scout out-of-bounds plays, then got up some game shots and free throws. The girls were physically and mentally ready for this game.

Manasquan jumped out to a six-point lead in the first quarter. We weren't moving the ball well and not communicating well defensively. Something was off, but I couldn't put my finger on it. As we continued, the quality of our execution improved dramatically, but there was something still missing. I watched four players on the court moving with great energy and competing, but my senior power forward, the best player on our team, seemed to be dragging and not connected to the rest of the team. Early in the quarter, I subbed her out so that I could get her some rest and coach her up. There was no discernable change. Her senior running mate and co-captain would run by her on the court, pat her on the back and give her words of encouragement. It was like the body trying to operate without a heart. At halftime, I asked my staff if they had picked up on the same thing. They had noticed, and my assistant coach had spent some time on the bench trying to talk her through the apparent struggles. The player didn't seem to care, which wasn't like her. At that point, my assistant suggested that I start someone else in the second half to light a fire under her butt. I struggled with whether that would have the desired outcome and decided to observe her demeanor during our halftime adjustments and the warmup prior to the third quarter.

After watching a continuation of the sluggish behavior, I decided to pull the trigger and insert somebody else to start the second half. I tapped the sophomore center to step in and let the senior captain know of the change. The news hit hard. Death glares through watery eyes, but she found her spot on the bench. As the third quarter started, we were playing well, but we were obviously missing a key piece of our team. I sat next to my team captain and told her the team is much better with her on the court. "Your team needs you, but it needs all of you. Let me know when you are ready to play to your capabilities." This is the first time I benched a player for how they were playing in a game. It was a new feeling for me, and I could only imagine the struggles she was going through. I loved this young lady like one of my own children. It pained me to see her struggling with her emotions from the benching, but it hurt even more watching her not play to her potential. After a couple of minutes, she composed herself and told me that she was ready to go.

Subbing her into the game was like opening the cage of a hungry animal staring at a piece of meat. We were down by 12 at the time she entered the game. She was angry and taking it out on the opponent. Playing to her capabilities elevated the spirit of her teammates, and we were back in action. At one point early in the fourth, we had pulled within six points, and all seemed to be heading in the right direction. That was as close as we would get.

Manasquan always has superstar players who are often the focus of the opposing team's scout. The team is coached extremely well and plays great team ball. So, an opponent can often find success against their best players, but must also account for and understand the capabilities of their role players. Having coached against them multiple times at SJV and at Holmdel, I had a pretty good understanding. They had a sophomore forward on the team who impressed me with her lunch bucket mentality. She worked hard without the ball on offense, often looking to set others up for opportunities. She was tenacious on the boards, especially on the offensive glass. If you didn't box her out, she would work for the board and battle back up, often drawing fouls and going to the line. Worst case, her trip to the line was an "and one." If she wasn't checked, she would end up with about eight points off put-back baskets and create foul issues for opponents. Never made the newspapers the day after a game, but her contributions were key to the success of the program. We scouted her, and she was very much a part of our preparation for the game, but we failed to execute. Her grinding efforts took hold in the fourth quarter and made the difference with 12 points off rebounds and second chances. We suffered another loss to our rival, and I felt we defeated ourselves on this one.

Our post-game was held in a high school classroom that was offered to us as a locker room. As the rest of the team walked to the bus, I spent a few minutes with my senior power forward. We talked about the game, my decision to bench her, the immediate response, and her efforts afterward. She wasn't very talkative, but I let her know that her struggles in the game were noted and that, as her coach, I was there to help. I encouraged her to learn from this and let her know what was expected of her as a senior and a captain. We all needed to be at our best and work every day to get there and reach our potential. I hugged her and walked out into the hallway with her. As we headed in the direction of the bus, I could see members of her family, mom, dad, and brother coming towards us. The father and I were friendly and enjoyed a few conversations about his daughter's potential, talent, and desire to play in college. At a recent pasta party hosted in their home, we covered more commonalities around politics and sports, enjoying some great conversations with our sons as well. Mom was a fantastic person, always kind and engaging. Dad wrapped his arms around his daughter and gave her a big hug, sensing that she was still in anguish. Trailing behind, I tried to lighten the moment by asking her dad if I would get a hug, too. At any other moment, but that wasn't the right time.

After Manasquan, we won two more games we were supposed to win, then suffered another loss to Rumson. The pattern repeated itself. We beat who we were expected to beat, but we never seemed to reach that next elevation of the mountain against the strong teams. In every one of those losses, I could point to one, three minute stretch where we imploded and couldn't recover. After Rumson, two more wins against lesser opponents. One of those wins was against Ocean Township, which elevated our record to 11-10 on the season and guaranteed us at least a .500 record before the Shore Conference Tournament cutoff. We had guaranteed a spot in the post season tourney! We climbed that hill and the team felt great about it. I felt great about my two assistant coaches. Because I was called out of town for business, I couldn't make the game against Ocean. That happened earlier in the season as well during our first game against RBC. I was very confident that my assistant coach and my son as volunteer coach could manage things quite well. We were much better than Ocean, but I encouraged them to take nothing for granted. Play our game, take care of business, and be respectful of our opponents. They accomplished all three, receiving compliments from the opposing team's parents—a proud moment for me.

We had one final regular season game left, our second against RBC, now ranked number 3 in the Shore Conference and now number 9 in the state. The good news for us was that we didn't need a win to make the tournament. RBC had beaten us by 19 points in the first game. They were talented, deep, and a bad matchup for us. A loss to RBC would put us at 11-11 on the season and in the tournament as a lower-seeded team. We could have rested on our moderate success and gone through the motions of the game, but we didn't coach to lose.

Earlier in our season, I had made it a priority to connect with coaches at the lower level in Holmdel. To me, this was a vital part in keeping our girls home to play for Holmdel High School. I had developed a great connection with one of the coaches and invited him to bring his team to our game against RBC. His girls showed up in their basketball uniforms, colors matching ours, and he brought his young son with him who was in kindergarten and attending his first high school game. I asked them to sit behind our bench so they could get a complete view of the game. We had a gym full of people and a fun atmosphere for the big game. Our crowd was better than usual, but the bulk of the fans were from RBC.

Red Bank Catholic always has a strong roster full of players headed to the next level. This team was no different, led by four seniors who were committed to playing at Franklin & Marshall, Amherst, Ithaca, and Lehigh. The opposing coach, a legend in New Jersey girls' basketball, had eclipsed the 600-win mark the week before our game. This was absolutely an amazing accomplishment, and I felt it was appropriate to have our announcer acknowledge that before sharing the starting lineups for the game. We had the Shore's best announcer, someone who loved the role and took great pride in creating a real game atmosphere. He also took great pride in his role as the official scorekeeper for the game. Working on some words that we had put together before the contest, he leaned into making the acknowledgment of the coach's feat very special. After the intro, I hugged the coach and congratulated him. Then, I walked back to our pregame huddle and told the team, "Now, let's go kick their ass!"

We got off to a great start, establishing a quick tempo to minimize the effectiveness of their size. I mixed defenses to keep their offense off balance, pressuring the ball on the perimeter to frustrate entry passes into the post. We led the way after the first quarter to the delight of the home crowd and the little hoopsters behind us. Our bench erupted as if we had won the game, followed by a quick reminder from me that we had won the first eight minutes. Settling them down, we talked about how the sledding was going to get tougher. Our defense was doing a great job of pressuring the ball. I wanted to extend that pressure, but I didn't want to sacrifice our offensive legs in doing so. While we were known for our full-court pressure, this wasn't the time nor the opponent to stretch that far out. Instead, we opened in our 1-1-3 half-court defense. The staggered front allowed us to pester the ball up top while keeping a presence in the passing lane to the high post. We had aggressive jumping movement on the wings to either trap or funnel the ball deeper down the sideline. We aimed to keep their offense on a side third of the court and out of the middle. We had punched them in the nose early, so I warned the girls to brace themselves for the punch back.

Little did I know how prophetic that statement was. RBC started the second quarter with a more aggressive play style. Why wouldn't they? That had been the mantra of some of the other good teams that we caught off guard, trying to bully us into submission. We were still doing a great job of denying post entry, and it was starting to bother the 6' 5" junior center. My slender sophomore, steadily gaining confidence since I subbed her in for the senior during the Manasquan benching, was playing tremendous defense. When the ball was from wing to baseline in our zones, her job was to front the big and force her to move her feet, fighting to reposition. As she moved, my center worked around and fronted again. Using her length and speed, she was winning the battle. With each play, there was more pushing and jockeying for space. In one sequence, the center for RBC lifted to the high post, center of the foul line. With her back to the basket, she caught an entry pass. Met by my senior power forward, playing directly behind her, she cocked her right elbow and smacked my player right in the nose. The whole gym gasped, and Holmdel fans exploded with a call for a foul. Our bench was up in arms, and I was a foot on the court, giving it to the referee for not calling a blatant elbow that could have seriously hurt my player.

I was livid and in full vein-popping mode. In my mind, the refs had lost control of the physical nature of the game and had just allowed the biggest player on the court, frustrated by great defense, to throw an intentional elbow. My senior power forward wasn't hurt; somehow, she took that blow and stayed upright. She was, however, a little stunned. The refs suspended play to calm things down, so I took advantage of that time to get even louder. Allowing some grace, the refs finally had enough and hit me with a technical foul. I called a timeout to check on my player and allow her more time to gather her wits. Thankfully, she was fine. I also took the opportunity to tell my team that if it is a fight RBC wants, then it is a fight they are going to get. Of course, I said it loud enough for the entire gym to hear.

Their second-quarter strategy was effective, giving them a four-point lead going into the half. Still fired up by the perceived dirty play, I reminded our girls that we have been in this situation many times this year, getting the best of a strong opponent only to have them start pushing us around physically to back us down. This was about something other than the first three minutes of the second half. We had to decide right then about how we would play for the next 16 minutes. Were we going to work this hard to melt under a bit of pressure? Were we going to fade away in the crucial points of this game? This was our game, in our house, and we needed to finish.

The third quarter was evenly played, and the lead stayed at four going into the fourth. I was so pleased with our response coming out.

We fought in every sequence, leaving a clear signal that we were there to stay, number 9 in the state or not. RBC opened with a 6-0 run, stretching the lead to 10 points. It would have been easy to consider that the beginning of the end, but all of that sweat equity throughout the season, the rewards of playing an extremely tough schedule came together. We flipped the script on RBC and went on a run of our own, tying the game with about three minutes left. After a quick basket to put RBC back up by two, we had back-to-back possessions with big 3-pointers, pushing us to a four-point lead. We were not just competing, we were winning, with time wheeling away.

Our offense stayed steady, never relinquishing the lead. Our defense remained intense, not giving up any shots. Some free throws were made at their end to get them within two with less than a minute remaining. On our next possession, RBC rebounded a missed shot, and they were out on a break. Our team was in transition, but one of their guards had a clean look at the rim. Miss! The RBC coach dropped to his knees with his hands on his head while we rebounded the ball. After a foul, we made both free throws to put us back up four. RBC called their final timeout after the second make. In our huddle, we discussed game situations and possible scenarios. I stressed that they couldn't make a basket that would hurt us. They had no way to stop the clock at this point unless we fouled them. Our goal was to keep the ball in front of us and keep our hands off. If they made a basket and there were less than five seconds on the clock, don't even inbound it. Stay poised. Finish the game!

When the final buzzer rang, we had defeated RBC in front of a good home crowd. The Shore Conference world was buzzing. Texts and calls were pouring in with congratulatory remarks and celebration emojis. Alumni players and their parents were reaching out. Players and coaches from St. John Vianney, where I previously coached, were chiming in with excitement for beating the archrival Caseys of

RBC. Our girls had accomplished something very special for the Holmdel program and finally realized how good they can be when playing together, when they put themselves last and team first. It was an amazing feeling for our team and our community.

The senior power forward took a literal shot to the nose and used it as motivation to play her best game of the year. Two of my best offensive weapons in the junior class contributed some huge baskets at key moments, but they also combined for 15 rebounds from the wing position against a much bigger team. My sophomore center showcased a physical toughness against a physically dominant player on the way to her best effort of the year. Everybody contributed, and it was time to celebrate. We finally reached the mountain's next elevation in discharging a powerhouse program.

Later that night, I received a text with a video clip from the youth coach who had brought his team to the game. He shared his congratulations and told me that it was the best high school girls' game he had seen. His girls were locked in and audibly rooting us on. I then hit play on the video, which showed the clock winding down with the excited count of the home crowd. As the final horn blew and the scoreboard read Holmdel 63 – RBC 59, he turned the camera to his 5-year-old son, smiling from ear to ear while yelling, "We won! We won!" His first high school game, and he was all in.

The win over RBC was the first ever for Holmdel. We needed to celebrate, and we did, but we also needed to remember that the real season started in less than a week, with the first round of the Shore Conference Tournament, followed by the NJ State Tournament. This win would be huge for us at the seeding meeting for SCT. We gained a higher seed, positioning us with good opportunities to advance. Celebrate that night. Back to work the next day.

TWENTY-THREE
THE ENEMY WE KNOW

THE SHORE CONFERENCE Tournament bracket was out, and we drew a first-round game versus Mater Dei at our gym. Our win against RBC did give us a bump in the seeding and earned us a home game. The winner of that game would be rewarded with the opportunity to advance and play Manasquan in the second round. All those factors checked boxes for me. We were better than Mater Dei and playing at home. The Seraphs were competitive for a good stretch, but our conditioning and experience allowed us to pull away for an 18-point win. Next up was round three against our archrival.

With one day to prepare, there wasn't time to add any new wrinkles. Both teams knew each other well. There were no secrets. Manasquan bested us twice during the regular season, but we matched up well, and it is hard to beat a team three times in one season. We had been playing very well, running off four wins in a row, including the big upset over RBC. Manasquan had split their last six games, with losses to St. Rose and RBC. This was shaping up for another challenging game, and it created a lot of buzz in social media, with some favoring the Hornets.

The game lived up to the billing. Manasquan held a 3-point lead at the end of one. We played each other even in the second quarter. Both defenses were on point and aggressive. The third quarter belonged to us, effectively using some full-court pressure to create easy opportunities on offense. We overcame the halftime deficit to take a two point lead going into the final quarter. Unfortunately, a couple of our old friends came back to bite us. The quality defensive effort was impressive by both teams. We would hold Manasquan to only two made threes, a tremendous effort. They held us to zero makes from behind the arc, which means some of our key scorers weren't having success. Perhaps that was the price to pay for the intense defense. We lost track of the lunch bucket junior again, allowing her to have a big influence on the game with nine rebounds and nine points, seven of those from the free throw line. In the end, our lack of offensive effectiveness in the fourth quarter and lack of output from key players left us on the short end and paved the way for Manasquan to win by 10. Our Shore Conference Tournament experience was over, but we still had the state tournament ahead of us. At this point, the state brackets were already set, and we knew that if we took care of our business, we would see Manasquan for a fourth time in the Central Jersey Group 2 semi-finals.

Our accumulation of power points pushed our position up in state seeding, earning us a home game against South Plainfield. Unfortunately for them, South Plainfield lost their best player to a knee injury in the previous game. During our warmups for the game, I saw the player on crutches, keeping a watchful eye on the preparation of her teammates, so I walked over to say hello. We talked for a little while, and I expressed my condolences for her missing the opportunity to finish her senior year. The game was over at tip-off without her scoring prowess in their lineup. We ran out to a 25-0 first-quarter lead and never looked back. Although not particularly competitive, the game was good for the team. It afforded an opportunity for starters to play less and not have to grind out a win while allowing our bench to get in some quality minutes and gain some additional game experience. Our easy win propelled us into a second-round matchup on the road at Hillside.

I didn't know much about Hillside other than the fact that they were 19-4 to that point in the season and were blessed with a 6' 2" athletic center. Before our first-round game, I asked around for game film from some of the teams they played in anticipation of playing them, and I was able to secure a couple of tapes. We had a day to prepare, so I spent the night after our first-round win watching tape on Hillside. They were not a particularly big or deep team, but they had three very good players: their center, a quick point guard with a good handle, and a good small forward with scoring abilities.

Hillside was the number three seed in Central Group 2, earning them the home game and making us the underdog. My second season at Holmdel brought improvement in the caliber of play and better development of players, and our willingness to play anybody helped define us as a program on the rise. However, our stock wasn't high enough, as a lot of the local sports "experts" predicted we would lose against Hillside. I liked that underdog role anyway. The girls didn't need the added strain of expectation to win. I wanted them to play with a little chip on their shoulder, and that's exactly what they did.

We jumped out to a first-quarter lead and had Hillside frustrated early. Feeling their guard was too quick for our full-court pressure, we opened with our 2-3 zone to minimize top-down penetration. Like we did against RBC, we fronted the low post and made entry passes look unavailable. Those tactics took care of two of the best players, leaving us the scoring forward to deal with. Film indicated that much of her damage was done below the free throw line extended. She was a streaky shooter, and we didn't want her to get a rhythm. My charge to the bottom portion of our zone was simple. If she was on your side, you didn't trap or help down into the post. Play the shooter straight up when she had the ball, stay strong in the passing line with eyes on her and the ball if she was away, and don't over-pursue any shot attempt to maintain position for rebounds. The concept was working well, but we were still allowing too much penetration from the guard. Things were good after one quarter, with the score 13-9 in our favor, but they needed to be better.

I shifted our defense to 1-1-3 for the second quarter. This allowed us to extend pressure on the guard, protecting against penetration with the tandem front. Because the ball was picked up higher, the offense generally lifted to shorten passing lanes. The shift up moved the other players out of their operating zones offensively, which then allowed us to be more aggressive with trapping the other two starters. We picked them apart and completely frustrated their players and coach, sparking some on court squabbling. Their struggles offensively made them desperate on defense, and they came at us with an aggressive man-to-man. My girls maintained their poise and ran our sets very efficiently. We had too much balance in our lineup and great movement on the floor to be impacted. When the first half was complete, we had opened the lead to 29-14.

Hillside moved into a 2-3 zone to start the third quarter. We countered with an odd front 1-3-1 offensive setup. We ran GAPS offense against zones, looking to expose, create, and attack the gaps in the defense. Our players on the perimeter would pass, cut, and fill. Players in the post would flash gaps created by cutters and look for high and low post exchanges based on ball movement. We were moving well against the zone but not getting production early or just settling for the first outside shot. Unlike the bottom of our zone, Hillside stayed relatively flat, even when the ball was above the free throw line, leaving the high post area wide open. I called a timeout and pointed this out to the team. Our sophomore forward had been catching the ball uncontested in the high post, then kicking it out to the wings. I told her to square up to the basket and shoot. If her shot pulled the center up, then attack the lane for a basket or a kick out. With that adjustment, our offense kicked into gear, with our sophomore forward dropping in mid-range jumpers repeatedly. By the end of the third quarter, we had increased our lead to 23 points and put the game out of reach. We pulled off the upset, and the sophomore forward ended the game with 22 points on 10 baskets and two free throws. We were on to the group semi-finals and a fourth dance with Manasquan.

The state playoff schedule was fast and fun. Win a game, get one practice in, go play another game. Every minute of preparation was invaluable. Every second of the game mattered. There couldn't be let down in any situation. My players understood that and were having an amazing practice gearing up for Manasquan. The drills were sharp, the players were focused, and the atmosphere was exciting. We wanted another chance at this rival, the win that had been alluding to us all season long. We wanted another CRACK! I will never forget that sound and the agonizing screams that followed.

We were putting the finishing touches on a fantastic practice by running some scout plays in the half-court. As was a common practice to help elevate competitiveness and better emulate our opponents, my female assistant would play on the scout team. The scout team was running one of Manasquan's sets, and my assistant had the ball. Out of nowhere, my starting guard came flying into the picture defensively and collided head-to-head with my assistant. The screams were coming from my point guard as she was holding her face, rolling on the ground. The assistant coach was also rubbing her head, looking slightly stunned, but seemed alright. The night before the biggest game of our season, my senior point guard was in the emergency room getting treatment for a broken nose.

Throughout the night, I was checking in with her father for status updates. The news was good as far as the injury was not too serious, but early indications were that she wouldn't be playing in the semifinal game. I felt horrible for many reasons, especially since she was a senior, a captain, and a great person all around who always gave her all to the team. Later that evening, I was finally able to talk to the player. She was in much better spirits but still under the impression that she couldn't play. She was going to see her doctor the next morning. Around noon on game day, I received the news that she was going to play, with the aid of a protective mask. She tried to tell me that her nose wasn't broken, but I wasn't buying that prognosis. I believe this was one of those situations where the player and the parents didn't want to miss her last high school game. Having missed the first Manasquan game due to the flu, the player wasn't about to miss this one.

The warmup before the game was a bit comical, watching her try to get comfortable with the mask on. I tried to reassure her that she would get used to it, encouraging her to focus on the drills and getting her vision right. She would go through the line, take her shot, then run over to talk to me again. At one point, she asked me if she had to wear the mask. I told her that was a decision for her parents, not for me. She would get back into the drill, go through her set, and then run back over to me for more dialogue and reassurance. Finally, I suggested that she start the game with the mask on. If she felt the mask negatively impacted her game, remove it. Our compromise seemed to work for her, and she returned to completing a few more reps before the buzzer sounded.

Introductions were made, and we reviewed the final details before the tip. Once we broke the huddle, the team hustled to the court, ready for battle, and my point guard had her mask on. I turned to my assistant coach and asked, "What's the over/under on the mask coming off?" She replied, "About 30 seconds." Twenty-seven seconds later, while running down the sideline by our bench, she ripped off the mask and tossed it to me. I tossed the mask to my assistant for safe storage, and we got a good chuckle out of that sequence of events.

The first 90 seconds of the quarter were no laughing matter. Manasquan hit a 3-pointer in their first opportunity with the ball. They hit another shortly thereafter to go up 6-0. It was very early, and I felt it important for the girls to work through the adjustments needed together on the floor. I contemplated calling a timeout, but I held off and let the girls play. We worked the ball well in our next possession and got off a good shot, but it missed, and Manasquan gathered the rebound. In transition, they reversed the ball very well and kicked it out to a shooter in the low corner right in front of our bench, who knocked down another 3-point basket . . . 9-0. Timeout! To this day, I still don't know if I should have called the timeout after the second 3-pointer. Game-time decisions like that can haunt a coach for a long time. This one was particularly haunting because we were down 9 in the first minute and a half of the first quarter. From that point on, the game's score was 51-51. We played 30 minutes and 30 seconds of fantastic, championship-caliber basketball, but 32 minutes is what we needed.

The final score was 60-51, and our season was over just like that. I loved every bit of this season, all the ups and downs. The program had improved dramatically in our first two seasons, but I was so proud of where we were and excited about where we were heading. My heart was breaking on the way to the locker room, knowing that we would be saying goodbye to exceptional senior players. My regret was that we only got to spend two years together. I was very proud that they would continue their basketball careers at The College of New Jersey and Scranton University. They would leave big shoes to fill, but I had some very talented players rising behind them. Still, it would be great to add some additional talent. I thought about the young lady from Holmdel who had decided to play basketball at Manasquan. She barely played in this game. I couldn't help but think how that was a waste of talent. As I exited the gym heading to the locker room for final words with the team, I passed her father in the hallway. Without hesitation, I pointedly said, "Are you ready to bring her home yet?" Caught off guard by the question, he smiled and said, "We'll talk."

TWENTY-FOUR
THE SHOT NEEDED AROUND THE WORLD

OUR SEMI-FINAL GAME against Manasquan was on March 7, 2020. A week later, the basketball season and state playoffs ended abruptly as the world shut down in response to Covid-19. I felt horrible for the teams who were still alive in the postseason, jockeying for the coveted Tournament of Champions. Basketball would end up being a long list of experiences lost for the graduating class that year. No prom, no graduation, loss of social interaction, loss of family engagements, and nothing but uncertainties ahead of them.

I had been watching eighth grade practices and attending some games during our season, so I was aware of a pretty good incoming freshman class. We were getting a very dynamic athlete, the younger sister to one of my senior players. The blue-collar player who missed all of those free throws in the fourth quarter against Raritan her sophomore year, who was moved from starter to first off the bench early in her junior season, was now a senior captain and starter for our roster. Her baby sister was coming to play for Holmdel, and she could play. Rough around the edges, but talented and hungry. I was very excited to have the prospect of her talents on the team, but equally excited about the opportunity of playing the sisters together at times, knowing the fiercely competitive streak within them.

Unfortunately, one of the other very good players from the grammar school team decided to go to St. John Vianney in pursuit of bigger and better basketball opportunities. She was the daughter of the head coach at SJV, so I knew she wasn't coming to Holmdel. I jokingly offered her a full scholarship to come play for me, but she sheepishly chuckled and said she would play for Mom. Of course, working at a public school, there was no tuition or scholarship, and I was uniquely aware of her desire to play at our neighboring Catholic high school. When I was the assistant coach at SJV, she was a little girl who would follow Mom into many of our practices. During water breaks or when our team was only working in the half-court, she would take advantage of open baskets to work on her skills and dream big of playing as a Lady Lancer someday. *She is what a small girl wants to become and what an elderly woman can remember with great pride that she once was.*

Unfortunately, I also received the news that one of our best teammates would not return to Holmdel High School. My assistant coach brought everything she had in mind, body, and spirit to our team and decided to pursue the head coaching position at Matawan High School. Selfishly, I didn't want her to leave my staff, but I also knew how much she wanted to test her chops as a head coach in high school. She had the mind, the appropriate experience, and the skills. I gave her my blessing, not that she needed it, along with some richly deserved sass. Holmdel and Matawan are in the same division, so I knew we would see them twice during the year. I let her know that even though I loved her very much and the girls were very fond of her, we wouldn't take it easy on her team.

While I didn't get all the freshmen I was hoping for, and my assistant coach was leaving the program, we still had seven really good players coming to join the program, including a 6' junior recruited by her teammates, and my son was in place to take over the role of JV coach and assistant to me at the varsity level. Only one of the incoming freshmen would play varsity, and my new junior had missed a couple of developmental years, but the numbers were meaningful as we continued to show growth for the entire program and build for the future. My son was also a very capable coach and had built a good relationship with the team, so that transition was seamless as well. In addition, Pop had been committing a great deal of volunteer time with our program, so we were in great shape. At the varsity level, we got a big boost when I received the news during the summer that the freshman who left to play at Manasquan last year was returning to the nest. While the rest of the world was lining up for COVID shots, we got a much-needed shot in the arm for our program.

Another significant moment happened during the summer, something that I had never experienced before in my coaching career. The mother, who had been banned from games by her daughter for angrily accusing me of thinking less of her daughter than other players on the team, called me and asked for a meeting to discuss the incident with me. We met at Holmdel Park and sat in one of the picnic areas. She opened the discussion with an apology for her actions, stating that she didn't mean any disrespect toward me. She went on to say that she knew I had her daughter's best interests at heart and that she appreciated the work my staff put into her development, as well as the encouragement we provided. I was truly honored and humbled by the gesture. We had a wonderful conversation, both sharing an enthusiasm for the season to come and the role her daughter would play, now a junior with tremendous varsity experience and improved skills.

Finally, during the summer, the COVID whirlwind would calm down to the point that we could resume some "normal" activities for basketball. We were able to conduct outdoor workouts, but we could not utilize the gym or any indoor facilities. My plans were not impacted as I wanted to try some different ways of conditioning bodies and minds for the upcoming season. We worked through skills and drills on the outdoor courts two days a week. We met as a team at Holmdel Park for 8 AM runs on different parts of the cross-country course. The starting portion of the course was a long, gradual uphill through a grassy open area that transitioned into a steeper uphill section over dirt and gravel. It was a killer start to a 3.2-mile cross-country race for trained runners. The hill must have seemed like climbing Mt. Everest to my girls, who were out of shape and not trained runners—a much different style of running than on a flat basketball court, requiring significantly more mental toughness. At the top of the climb, just as the hill leveled off, there was a small outdoor picnic area, an apparent oasis to the mind and body that had just slugged it out uphill for a quarter of a mile. I thought it was a great place to have them turn around and head immediately downhill, back to the start. We did that three to four times for one of our running workouts.

The other workout was what my cross-country coach called a trail run. I divided the team into two smaller groups, each with a coach in the mix. For this run, we went to the wide-open, flat field that was the site of the finish line for the races held at the park. The two teams lined up in a single file, next to each other, with about six feet between them. On command, the teams would start jogging, with the lead runner setting the pace. The trail runner would then have to sprint to the front of the line, assuming the lead position. Once they reached that spot, the process would repeat itself with the new last person in line trying to get to the front. This run would continue for several laps around the open field. Initially, the girls would try to moderate the pace when they were the lead. I worked to counter that by having a coach on each team, splitting the captains, and having the two teams run side-by-side on the field. The natural competitive juices began to flow, and the runs were intense. Every running day, I would make sure to create new combinations, which helped create tighter bonds throughout the team.

While the girls didn't quite understand why we were running over hill and dale, the dividends were apparent as we took to the outdoor courts for summer league. The running, coupled with the intense skill workouts a couple of days a week, had the team in top physical condition. Our mental toughness, competitive nature, and team focus were also very evident. Even though it was only summer, we had laid a strong foundation for what was going to be somewhat of a sprint season.

As part of the new "normal" coming out of COVID, we learned that our season would be much different than in previous years. We wouldn't start basketball until mid-January instead of the end of November. Our traditional divisions had been replaced by "pods" intended to minimize travel and potentially corral any new outbreaks of variants to the virus. The teams we played were limited to schools that were in geographic proximity, and we would play teams in back-to-back fashion, with a home game on Monday and an away game on Wednesday. We were in Pod five with Colts Neck, Middletown North, Matawan, Raritan, and St. John Vianney. That gave us 10 "divisional" games, and we were afforded two games outside our pod. The season was capped at a maximum of 15 games, inclusive of pod playoffs. Instead of a Shore Conference Tournament, the teams were again divided into eight team pods based on record for smaller group playoffs, finishing with a champion in every pod. There were no state playoffs, which meant no Tournament of Champions—the entire season ended on March 6, with the finals and consolation games for each of the pods. The condensed season made everything a sprint, and we couldn't afford any misses due to illness or mental lapses.

The team was comprised of five seniors, four juniors, two sophomores, and one freshman. We had a wonderful balance of experience and abilities. Losing a lot to the graduation of my dynamic duo, point guard and power forward from the previous campaign, this season was going to be more about balance and depth of talent. The starting lineup showcased seniors at point guard (the junior scorer pressed into duty as a point guard against Manasquan last year), at shooting guard, and at the swing (the blue-collar player who worked hard to improve her game every season and sister to our only freshman on varsity). The two rising stars in the junior ranks completed the starting five. The athletic junior, a gym rat by nature and always getting extra shots up to improve her skills, had taken over the position of being the most complete player in the gym in most competitions. She was suffering through a quadricep strain most of the year, but she would not allow herself to shut down enough to completely heal. She had a stubborn quality, which also made her one of the most focused players, and she didn't want to let her team down. Even at 80%, she was a force to be reckoned with. The lanky junior who was our starting center, the same young lady who banned her mom from games the previous season, had made tremendous strides in her confidence and willingness to exert her skills in game action. Unlike previous years, we also had amazing depth on the bench: a small guard with growing skills (junior), the return of our prodigal player who transferred back from Manasquan (sophomore), an emerging talent in my shooting guard (sophomore), two seniors with game experience, the raw but very athletic junior who had been away from the game for a couple of years, and the freshman who was like catching a tiger by the tail.

We started off the sprint of a season with four straight wins, two against Colts Neck and two against Middletown North. What was great about the makeup of my team this year is that we had multiple offensive threats, making us hard to guard. The balance and depth in our roster could be seen in early box scores, as we had a different high scorer every night, including people coming off the bench to contribute in big ways. The multitude of weapons was visible on both ends of the court as we had our way with early opponents, applying defensive pressure for the length of the court to take souls and create an easy offense. The test was in how we would handle our first challenge of the young season, a back-to-back series with St. John Vianney, the top team in the state.

The first game was at our gym on a Monday night. While we looked competitive after finishing a 13-9 first quarter, the game was over at halftime. SJV outscored us 26-10 in the second, giving them a 20-point lead. They toyed around with us a little in the third, then laid the hammer down in the fourth quarter, closing out a 73-42 victory. As usual, their lineup was stacked with college recruits. The best player was the silent assassin on the court, who would be heading to Princeton to play hoops. Her game was so graceful and fluid that it almost went unnoticed until a look at the stat sheet revealed 30 points, seven rebounds, three steals, and two assists. She was flanked by a 6' 3" center (Holy Cross), a tremendous defensive guard who could score (Central Connecticut), a strong forward at 6' (Richmond), and another do-it-all guard (Fordham), not to mention all the future college players on the bench. We were outclassed by the best and had one practice to get ready for round two.

Wednesday's game, just three miles away in another part of Holmdel, marked my return to SJV for the first time since I was the assistant coach. It was cool to be back in the gym as an opposing coach and seeing my name on one of the Tournament of Champions' banners gracing the gym wall. A flood of wonderful memories hit as I shared a hug and quick conversation with Dawn and a few of my former players, who were freshmen when I left. As was the case throughout COVID, the gym was eerily empty, but it was more noticeable as SJV generally plays before a packed house. Unlike the impromptu adjustment to Triangle-and-2 against Manasquan a couple of years ago, we practiced that with intent to prepare for this game and the quick turnaround. The two best offensive players were Princeton and Richmond. When they were able to attack the opposing defense, the cuts ran long and deep. I had decided we were going to minimize those offensive weapons and see if we could survive a death by 1,000 cuts from the rest of the Lady Lancers.

With warmups completed, the teams went to their respective benches for last-minute words from the coaches and the introductions of the starting lineups. Like our home games, SJV had a long-time announcer who loved to add richness to the game, especially by piling on the hype around the mighty Lady Lancers. Holmdel was introduced first with a ho-hum voice. Then, the pipes shifted as if to introduce Michael Jordan and the Chicago Bulls. In a growling tone filled with excitement, "Now, for your Lady Lancers. Number one in the Shore Conference, number one in New Jersey, number one in the Tri-State, and number five in the country . . ." He went on to introduce their starting five, and the game was ready for tip-off. A very effective psyche job for opposing players and fans, although we were playing in a relatively empty gym, essential personnel only. I turned back into our huddle and repeated, "Yes, they are number one in the Shore Conference, number one in New Jersey, number one in the Tri-State, and number five in the country. I'm not asking you to be all of that. I just want you to be number one in Holmdel tonight. Together on three!" As a coach, the unscripted moments often carry the most punch. My words rang true with the girls, and they were pumped. Hell, my eyes welled up with pride and faith in the unthinkable.

Like our game on Monday, SJV scored 13 points in the first quarter. The difference in this game is that we had matched that effort, tied after the first eight minutes. Our defense was working very well, frustrating the two top scorers as planned. SJV had to get contributions from other players to succeed. Of course, they had several other options, but we had put a wrench in the high-scoring offensive machine they were used to. We switched out of the Triangle-and-2, going man for a different look, but we kept the pressure on the best players by denying them the basketball. Our offensive effort was good, and our balance was on full display as we got contributions from everybody.

The focused team effort continued throughout the second quarter. SJV tried to put together a run by leaning on their traditional full-court pressure. A suffocating flurry of defensive activity often forced opposing teams into bad decisions, which were then converted to easy baskets. The Lady Lancers were always long and quick, giving the impression of being impenetrable. Coaching and watching for my six years with the program was fun. It was heart-wrenching and infuriating to coach against, especially if panic was allowed to set in. However, we spent a reasonable amount of time in practice the day before working on our press break, throwing in six and seven defenders at a time to replicate the chaos. The investment of that time paid off as we broke their press with ease and were able to get right into our offensive sets. With every successful sequence on our part, the frustration mounted with my good friend on the other sideline, and her animated behavior spiked. As time ran off toward the end of the second quarter, we found ourselves down by two points and playing with a lot of intensity. Even after the Princeton recruit banked in a desperation 3-pointer at the buzzer to extend their lead to five, we went into the locker room with a lot of confidence, playing our best basketball against the number five team in the country.

After reviewing and discussing the first-half stats with my coaches, I joined the girls in the locker room. I came pumped and laughing, happy with the outcome but aware that we still needed to climb the mountain before us. The girls asked me why I was laughing, so I shared that I understood how the opponent's locker room worked and the likely events unfolding as we spoke. Based on our performance in the first half, I knew Dawn wasn't happy, and I shared the Red Bank Catholic halftime story from years before. I was trying to keep the mood light while keeping the girls focused on the task at hand. I shared the emphasis that SJV would be putting on the first three minutes and emphasized how we had to be ready to withstand that increased intensity. Then I predicted that the only person in the gym when we go back out will be Dawn, the SJV coach; her halftime speech will have been pointed and brief, most certainly loaded with a few expletives. The SJV girls would then be left to determine how they were going to show up for the second half. As predicted, we jogged out to the court, met by a solo, stewing figure. My girls got into their warmup drills, taking advantage of both baskets being open to get up some game shots. Eventually, the Lady Lancers emerged, calmly walking to their bench.

The second half started similarly to the early stages of the game. We were staying right with SJV, keeping the game within five points late in the third quarter. Better teams have a way of grinding opponents down. We began to experience some foul trouble with a couple of players as the increased focus on their two best players took its toll. While we had the best depth our program had seen in quite a while, there was still a great disparity between the depth in talent. Bench to bench, we might have had some legs to stand on, but our bench against their starters was not a good match-up. Down 12 at the end of the third, the talent and strength of SJV just took over in the fourth. My girls continued to fight valiantly, and we picked up some great experiences, but we lost the game by 27 points. The result was nearly the same as our first game on Monday, and a loss is a loss, but our showing in game two was much more indicative of our abilities as a team. As is always the case, we still had room to grow.

Rebounding from our two losses, we got back on the winning track against Ranney and our first game in the Matawan series at home. It was great to see my former assistant coach now patrolling the sidelines as the head coach at Matawan. She had a great mind for the game and worked wonderfully with the girls, getting the most out of the available talent. Matawan was a tough program to be successful in. Many coaches had tried. However, the Huskies had some early season success under her tutelage, notching three wins before our first game. My pregame comments were very simple to my team. We all love the other coach, and she is a good friend to our program, but we have a job to do. Do not let our emotions get in the way of our execution. We had our way from start to finish, cruising to a 28-point victory. With our early domination, we were able to rotate everybody into the game for good minutes.

Two days later, we traveled to Matawan for the second game of the series. This was one of my least favorite places to play. I don't know why, but it always seemed like my team didn't play well, and somebody would inevitably get hurt. In my first year at Holmdel, my senior captain and sharpshooting guard got hurt in the game, and we had to slug our way to a four-point win. The energy always seemed to get sucked out of us when we walked in, maybe created by the false sense of an easy win. The challenge for successful teams is not to play down to the level of their opponent. The message from my staff was always centered around playing our game to the best of our abilities, regardless of who we play. I tried to create the right expectations by comparing our desire to get up and play SJV. That is exactly what we can expect from Matawan, especially with the very competitive new head coach. Oh, the demons in that gym!

The feelings around pregame and warmup were good, right up to the point where my starting point guard came limping up to the bench, struggling to put any weight on her foot. She couldn't pinpoint what caused the injury, but she was in tears and in obvious pain. We had the trainer look at her, but she was unable to provide any relief. I consoled my player, letting her know that her long-term health was more important and reassuring her that her teammates would pick up the slack. We were not rich in experienced point guards at the time. I chose to go with the sophomore who was playing well but still adjusting to the speed and intensity of the high school game. She was the younger sister of my senior captain, who had been injured at Matawan a couple of years ago, so maybe there was some positive twist that would stem from that experience. There wasn't. The other coach knew her strengths and weaknesses well, shifting her defensive point of emphasis to applying additional pressure to speed up her game. That move drove me to put my junior athletic forward into the point guard position. Still struggling with the quad strain, she wasn't at peak athletic form, but she was doing a great job of avoiding pressure and running our offense. As we started to establish some flow and exert some dominance with our manipulated lineup, my senior shooter took a nosedive, smashing her head on the floor with a very audible thud. I hustled out to the court to attend to her along with the trainer. After a few minutes, we escorted a groggy player to the bench. My sophomore point guard, who had been replaced, was fighting with her own frustration and disappointment, so I worked to keep her confident by getting her to a position of comfort and rolled her to the shooting guard spot. With the rapidly changing landscape of the game, I struggled to find the right rotation to maintain any sort of rhythm. We were in a dogfight against a team that we had beaten by 28 points two days ago, reminiscent of our experience with SJV earlier. Unlike SJV, we had two significant injuries to starters. While we had the depth of talent on the bench to overcome the obstacles we were facing, we lacked the mental fortitude to shake off the loss of two starters and the burden of our cockiness coming into the contest.

As the game came down to the wire, we were tied and still very much in control of our own destiny, with the idea of pulling out an ugly win. We had just made a defensive stop and were now pushing the ball into the front court for offense. I called a timeout to provide a breather to my girls, review our set and approach for the go-ahead basket, and review the game situation. The ball was put in play, kicking off our offensive set. The ball was passed to the right wing into the hands of one of my most reliable players, my blue-collar senior captain. Screening action went to the weak side, bringing multiple options back to the ball. The choice was made to reverse toward the top of the key, which was wide open and a great read. Unfortunately, Matawan's very quick and athletic point guard made a better read defensively and jumped the passing lane to steal the ball. She was off to the races with what became the winning layup. My senior captain, who watched her pass get stolen, the same player who had missed several free throws late in the game against Raritan in her sophomore year, was absolutely devastated. True to her character, she immediately took accountability for the loss, as misplaced as that sentiment was. The loss wasn't hers to own. I let her know that the ownership of the loss was mine, acknowledging all the challenges that her team worked to overcome, putting us in a position to win. We simply fell short. I gave her an encouraging hug. Gave the opposing coach a congratulatory hug. Then, I spent the rest of my night kicking myself for letting this one slip. For the first time in my coaching career, my team lost a game that it shouldn't have. That was on me.

No rest for the weary. We played St. Rose, number nine in the state, the very next day. They were a loaded team who came into the game 7-1, with their only loss coming in the first game of the season against Manasquan, 55-52. St. Rose avenged that loss in the next game, winning 60-53, splitting the series with Manasquan. St. Rose was on a seven game win streak coming into our gym. We were on the opposite end of that spectrum, having just lost in upset fashion to Matawan the night before. There was a palpable hangover feeling among the girls as we came into the gym for stretches and early shoot-around. My senior point guard, who had been kept out of the game the night before due to her foot injury, was suited up and ready to go. I was hesitant to play her for fear of aggravating an injury that could keep her out long-term, but this was St. Rose, and she didn't want to leave her team in a lurch. As a precaution, I had our trainer check her foot out one more time. I also checked in with my senior shooter, who hit her head on the floor in the game against Matawan. She was fired up and ready to play, with no ill effects from her injury the night before. With a thumbs up from both, we found some energy to build from.

In our pre-game talk, I put the loss from the night before on my shoulders, where it belonged. I pointed out the redeeming qualities of this amazing game that we play, how no matter what, there is a next sequence to play, an opportunity to make up for misfortune. This game could provide that redemption and get us back on the right track. We needed to put the torment of the previous night behind us and focus sharply on the monumental task in front of us. We laid out a game plan for beating St. Rose and took the floor in much better spirits than when we entered the gym that morning.

The first quarter was a track meet, ending in an 18-15 lead for St. Rose. Led by a hard-charging, lightning-quick senior point guard and Lafayette recruit, St. Rose was showing all the signs of their number nine ranking. Not a very tall team, St. Rose relied on speed, pressure, and precise execution. Although we were losing at the end of one, St. Rose had suffered a greater loss when one of their starters, a senior leader heading to Stonehill College, suffered an ankle injury in front of our bench. She was out for the game. A coach never wants to see an injury, especially in a big game where it can present both challenges and opportunities. The question is always about which team can adjust the quickest in adversity.

This was my 29th game as head coach against St. Rose. One of the things I always admired about their program was the depth of their bench and how the quality of play never dipped throughout substitutes. Great programs often have that trait, where wave after wave of good players continue to apply consistent pressure, wearing down their opponents. With the injury to one of their starters, another player stepped in, and the team didn't miss a beat. In the early minutes of the second quarter, the Purple Roses built their lead to 13 points and were pulling away from us in all phases of the game. We needed a time out and an opportunity to regroup. Moments like this are big in the game, and I expected us to gather our poise and get back into the contest. The girls responded well, pushing back with a late run of our own, closing to within six points by halftime. We could stick around through most of the third quarter, but St. Rose elevated their game to a level that we couldn't match that day, closing out the game on a 35-15 run. We played well in moments but were still showing inconsistencies that needed to be resolved to get to where we wanted to be as a program.

St. Rose was at a different level, as demonstrated by the way they managed early adversity in the game and their consistency of effort. They were quick but never rushed. They were intense but never frantic. The girls embodied the spirit of their head coach, one of the best in the business, and one of the most fiercely competitive people I know. She was also the aunt of my old assistant, who had beaten us the night before in Matawan. A rough 48 hours for my team and for me personally. Something that comes up anytime we compete on the tennis courts or when we are out socially.

With the Covid-shortened season moving quickly, we had two games to get right before we entered the post-season structure of that year. Fortunately, our next two games were against Raritan, which provided us with that opportunity. Our practices and our execution in the Raritan games weren't focused on beating them, which we did, but channeled towards improving our chemistry and building resolve for the final run of three games, the Shore Conference Tournament for Pod B. We now had a week to prepare for the three games in five days, a flurry that would mark the end of the season.

Analyzing the teams in our tournament pod, we had a great opportunity to claim the title of Pod B champions. This would have been a crowning moment in a strange season, riddled with all the complexities that the world was experiencing as we all tried to emerge from COVID. We were the third seed in our pod of eight teams and opened at home against Central Regional. Our balance was back with clean offensive execution and intense defense, propelling us to a 26-point win. With that victory and an upset in the two versus seven matchup, our next game would be at home against Freehold Township. They were a senior-laden team with talent at the point guard and center positions. If we played with the same effort and focus that was on display against Central, I liked our chances.

Inconsistencies continued to plague our team. Freehold Township, coming off a big, emotional win over Howell, was playing spirited basketball. Their five senior starters were hungry and determined. It showed in the first half, as they led by seven points going into the locker rooms. My team adjusted and flexed in the third quarter, returning us to even as we headed into the final frame. Eight minutes of quality basketball would put us in the championship game.

We had turned the tide. The question was, could we build on that momentum to win the game? In the game's final minutes, their best was better than ours, and they finished the game with a 48-42 win. Their upset run in the tournament continued while we were faced with playing for third place against a very good Neptune team. With the disappointment of the loss to Freehold Township and no carrot of a championship out in front of them, I was curious as to how my team would respond for one more game. No matter what, I wanted to continue our growth as a program and send our seniors off with a win in the last game of their high school careers. We had one practice left to ready ourselves, and I believed in our resilience.

My faith was rewarded as we put on a basketball clinic against Neptune. We jumped on them early with a 17-5 first quarter. Never looking back, our lead was 20 points at halftime, and we would maintain that separation for a 21-point win to close out the season. I was proud of the complete effort, especially from my seniors, who accounted for 41 of the 62 points. They led the way to victory, celebrated with a group hug at the bench. With all the concerns still floating around COVID, we knew this would be our last moment together. By this time in the season, the rules had bent just enough to allow two family members for each player to attend the game. We spent the next hour in the gym talking with the families, sharing the moment with our seniors, and saying goodbye for the season.

While we still had ups and downs to deal with, this season was a big step to the next level for our program. We would be losing some key talent and leadership in our graduating seniors. However, we had a great pool of talent in the balance of our roster. Our JV team had put together a great season, losing only one game, and some of those players spent time with Varsity in our season's final weeks. I had invested time observing the eighth grade team and saw some very good talent rising. Of course, we would lose two more players to SJV, but there were some great prospects for our program staying home. We also connected our high school program to the grammar school programs for younger girls, including having some of my girls assist the coaches of those teams in practices and being at games to support the teams. We had spent the last three seasons building a program and integrating with the broader Holmdel community. Year four was where I thought it would all come together, and I was looking forward to continuing a very productive and rewarding journey.

TWENTY-FIVE
TROJAN HORSE

AS I THINK IS typical for most basketball coaches, I began to evaluate talent in April, already looking forward to the next season. Before we would lace them up for the high school season in December, we had work to do in the summer and fall. We lost three starters who accounted for about 30 points per game. I wasn't overly concerned about our ability to replace the scoring, as we had a talented core returning with three seniors, two juniors, and one sophomore. The question I needed to answer centered around where the depth of our roster would come from. We had two additional seniors who had been perennial JV players. There was another junior at the JV level and five sophomores who all had the potential to make the varsity roster, or at least swing, getting time at both levels. From what I had seen of the soon-to-be freshman class, we would also have options for contributors.

Watching them as eighth graders, we would have some nice players coming up. There was a 6'1" center who was raw but talented. She had a nice outside shot and could score in the paint. Her post-play was lacking diversity and finesse, and she needed help with footwork at the block. At this point in her life, she relied a lot on being very tall for her age. I enjoyed watching a pesky point guard who was a soccer player first. Soccer players were some of my favorites to coach because they had excellent vision, understood angles of play, had great endurance, and were generally very coachable. The power forward for the eighth grade team caught my eye early. Her basketball-specific skill sets were developing, but she had a strong competitive nature and a great work ethic in the games and practices I observed. She had the heart and hustle to go along with a disciplined nature and a real grit about her. She received coaching well, which meant we could work on the skills. There was a fourth player who would come in off the bench. She wasn't the quickest player but always seemed to lumber through with good effort. She would often bury herself in the left corner outside the arc, but she could knock down the three when the ball got to her. I had watched her practice several times and saw some developing skills on display. Over time, another ball of clay could be carved into a key part of the program. I was genuinely excited about the opportunity to succeed in the coming season and continuing to build our program's pipeline. All these girls would need work to play at the varsity level as freshmen, but there would be opportunities depending on how well they integrated into our style of play and how well they blended with their other teammates. Even if they didn't play up, we were getting at least four good additions to the program, adding to what continued to be a bright future for Holmdel.

In early June, while the school year was wrapping up, I heard that one of the eighth graders had decided to enroll in St. Rose. We had already lost two players to SJV, but this was one I didn't expect. This was the player who was a little slow in movement but could bury the long ball when left open. Even with that, I didn't think St. Rose was a great fit for her skills. As well documented in early chapters, the Purple Roses were a fast, aggressive team that lived on intensity on both ends of the court. Her lack of foot speed would need to be an early area of improvement, as well as her desire to play defense. St. Rose also played a tough schedule. On the other hand, I thought she would be a great fit for our program. While we were also a team dedicated to intense defense and a fluid, unselfish offense, we were often more dependent on the youth in our program due to smaller numbers. I wrote the player an e-mail sharing my disappointment in hearing the news that she would not be at Holmdel in the fall and congratulating her on playing for St. Rose, acknowledging that they are a good program with a great coach. I shared my observations of her game, encouraging her to put in the time and energy needed to continue improving, to keep a positive mindset, and to love the game. I also let her know that if things didn't work out at St. Rose, we would love to have her back at Holmdel.

A couple of days later, I received a phone call from her father. He thanked me for taking the time to write the e-mail, stated how much he appreciated the kind, encouraging words, and shared with me some of the rationale behind their decision to send her to a different school. He shared stories about bullying from teammates, talked about how they would shun her on the court by not passing the ball, and stressed how they felt a fresh start would be good for his daughter. Empathetic to what I was being told, I told him that I was sorry to hear of such negative experiences, sharing how we have worked hard to create an environment of teamwork, trust and learning from each other. I also acknowledged that teenagers can be hard on each other, which I had experienced in my first season at Holmdel. Teenagers and drama seemed to go hand-in-hand. I shared with him how we worked together to iron out wrinkles in relationships on the court. While girls may not ultimately like each other or hang out off the court, they can certainly learn to respect each other and how to function well as a team. This was one of those lessons that went beyond sports into the real world, in work and family. We had a pleasant conversation and wished each other luck in the coming season.

Once the team was permitted to start summer workouts, we put together a schedule of skills development, conditioning, and signed up for league play. When they reported for the first practice, the returning girls, several of whom played AAU in the spring, looked fantastic. They were in great physical shape and came with fresh, eager attitudes. The returning players were excited about the prospect of the season ahead, and it was infectious. I had designated two seniors as our captains, the two tall freshmen who had grown tremendously as players since. They embraced the leadership role and got to work pulling the team together. I was proud of them and their commitment to Holmdel basketball. Unfortunately, we were lighter than hoped when it came to the freshman class, losing the young lady mentioned above and the pesky point guard who had decided to focus on soccer. Nonetheless, we had an energized, eager group of players who wanted to get better.

One of the things I did to maximize our time and experience during the summer was to put together a team camp. This was a four-day schedule of two games a day against some of the best teams in the area, including St. John Vianney, Trinity Hall, Manasquan, Rutgers Prep, Rumson-Fair Haven, Shore, and St. Rose. The object was to give the girls some early competitive experiences, providing the players with the opportunity to see how they stacked up against other talented teams in New Jersey. It gave me a test environment to see how some of the younger players adapted to high school basketball's style and pace. The camp carried none of the regular season stresses of having to win games, so coaches were able to try different combinations, run new plays, try different defenses, and ultimately have fun in a low-key but competitive environment. The team camp also served as a fundraiser for our program, which would help us with new uniforms and shooting shirts for the season.

Holmdel High School has two gyms, so we had games running in both with officials. The Covid restrictions were finally over, so we could also have parents and fans in attendance. It was refreshing to be in the company of our extended basketball family and back to normal. Several of our parents had volunteered to keep the clock and scorebook at the games, sell concessions, and help with the cleanup afterward. When we weren't playing, my girls would also assist in the effort, and I would mill about making sure both gyms were being run safely and on time. I would take the opportunity to watch the different teams play.

During the first day of games, I took time to watch St. Rose play, curious as to how the Holmdel transfer was fitting in. St. Rose was younger than they had been in previous years, so this could have been a good opportunity for her to showcase her skills and work to earn time on the court. She played a little in the first game, looking a little uncomfortable and frequently positioning herself in the bottom corner beyond the three-point arc for offense. To me, it made sense. She wasn't familiar with any of the plays that St. Rose runs, having only been with the team for a few days. Instinctively, she would fall into habits from eighth grade, finding her comfort zone on the court. If the ball swung around, she would shoot it—typical freshman in summer play. The same was true for some of the freshmen on our team in their first summer games. When they got in, they relied mostly on what they brought with them from grammar school— muscle memory. I didn't think much of it, keeping everything in perspective.

After the game, I took a moment to say hello to the player, now a part of the St. Rose program. I encouraged her to relax on the court, not to put pressure on herself, and to let the game come to her. As we were talking, her father came over, shook my hand, and we engaged in some small talk. He made a snarky comment about the lack of playing time. I reassured him that St. Rose is a great program and that his daughter will learn a lot, following up with the suggestion that he trust the coaches and the maturation process. Shocked to hear such words of discouragement from the father of a freshman barely into her high school basketball experience, I offered a few more words of encouragement and left to prepare for our first game in the other gym.

We played very well. The returning varsity players looked like they were in mid-season form, very fluid offensively and aggressive on defense. The sophomores from last year's JV team and the incoming freshman all had bright moments, picking right up on the defensive tenacity required in our program and demonstrating some early signs of picking up the offenses. The team chemistry was very good, reflecting how my two captains were running the show. Across the court, many spectators were watching our game, including a young lady in a St. Rose game jersey and her father.

Later that day, I had the opportunity to watch another St. Rose game. They are such a good program and enjoyable to watch. Even without the head coach present, who was away on summer vacation, the staff and team had a great rhythm in their game. There were many young players on the roster, but several of them already showed that they fit into the system, except one. Her playing time was scattered in the second game, her movements slow and unsure, and she continued to bury herself in the left baseline corner on offense. Every time the ball came to her, she shot it, often without success. In two camp games, it was obvious that her frustrations were mounting and her confidence waning. Her dad quickly found me after that game to express his discontent and get my input. Again, I reassured him of the quality of the program and the patience required to integrate into a new style of play. I even suggested that the absence of the head coach could impact rotations and decisions. He muttered, "I think I mistakenly sent her there." I encouraged him to stay positive, offering the perspective that it was only summer.

There would be plenty of opportunities to learn, grow, and earn her way into the rotation.

Day two of camp was more of the same theme. My team continued to work together impressively. I was starting to see the foundation of the three previous years really start to take shape, which ramped up my enthusiasm for the season to come. With only two summer camp games from the day before under their belt, our younger players showed marked improvement during the second day. The lone sophomore returning from the varsity lineup last season played more maturely. She was still somewhat of a raging bull but learned how to harness her energy and aggressiveness better. Her basketball skills were improving. I continued to see great promise in her abilities. In addition to her emergence as a force to be reckoned with, I began to see solid contributions from two of the freshmen. Decisions for the season are not made during the summer, but the potential varsity roster was beginning to take form.

The other part of the theme was the growing disgruntled behavior of the player and father on the St. Rose side. The games on day two did not bring any satisfaction. Playing time was even less, confidence and enthusiasm were shot, maybe a little bit of the chicken or the egg theory. Nonetheless, the player and her father were noticeably unhappy. As I was walking to the adjacent gym after our game, the father stood in wait in an open area next to the bleachers. When I got closer, he approached me with hand extended, asking if I had a minute to talk. Always willing to engage with others, we stepped out into the hallway between the gyms. Without hesitation, he launched into stories of girls "icing" his daughter on the court, the coach not getting her any playing time, and just how uncomfortable and unhappy his daughter was with the program. After a brief stint with St. Rose, the list of reasons why they wanted to leave was long and had a familiar ring to it. I again encouraged him to have this discussion with the head coach of St. Rose. Out of respect, she should be afforded the opportunity to hear his concerns and maybe offer insights and solutions. He said he would have that conversation but then went on to ask me about the transfer process back to Holmdel. I let him know that I don't get involved with transfers, suggesting that if they really wanted to pursue this, they should reach out to the principal. The principal was formerly the athletic director at Holmdel and was promoted to his new role toward the end of the previous school year. I certainly didn't want to do anything that could be perceived as unethical behavior by me or anything that would put him in a tough spot as a relatively new, inexperienced senior leader in the school. I didn't know what the transfer protocol was, so I directed the father to the "professionals" in the school administration.

Several of the Holmdel parents passed us in the hallway on their way to the other gym to watch some of the other teams. Once my conversation with the disgruntled father was over, I continued to the other gym to check on the game as well, a good matchup between two teams that we were scheduled to play the next day. Another great day in team camp ended with a genuine buzz of energy from our team and from the coaches as they enjoyed the high-level competition and the quality of the experience. Lending some support to the final cleanup for the day and preparation for another round of games, a father for one of my freshman players approached me. We started talking about how our team was playing and how well his daughter was integrating into my program. He was very complimentary of the older teammates, their style of play, and all they were doing to make the younger girls feel at home. Another proud moment for me as Coach. Then came the warning. "I saw you talking to (that father) earlier. Be careful. The mother and father caused a lot of trouble in middle school. They are dangerous people."

I was already made aware of some of the negative history that festered in the middle school program. I am not one for rewriting history, but I prefer to offer fresh perspectives and new beginnings. I thanked him for sharing his concerns and told him nothing had happened yet to raise any concern. While I couldn't erase any sour feelings, if the family were to return to Holmdel, the team would work on welcoming their daughter with open arms and build a better, brighter future together. I noted the concern, thanked him for the overall conversation, and walked back to the locker room area to make sure it was clean and ready for the next day. My mind was focused on all the good that came out of the second day at camp.

Before day three of camp was over, the frustrated father found me and let me know that they had made the decision to transfer back to Holmdel. They had started the process with the school administration. He expressed gratitude to me for listening to their challenges and for my positive treatment of his daughter, both in the e-mail I wrote to her after graduating eighth grade and the discussions I had with her after the camp games. He wrapped up the conversation with, "Thank you for saving us $14,000 (yearly tuition for St. Rose)!"

I was excited about the prospect of the freshman's return to our program. Having watched her in games and practices as an eighth grader, I noticed raw talent and ability. In my years as a coach, I always enjoyed working with all the players, especially those with "undeveloped talents" who wanted to be coached and work on improving their game. I saw this young lady as one of those players. Once I received the formal news, I shared it with the team. Pulling my two captains aside, I encouraged them to embrace our new teammate and work together to get her integrated as quickly as possible. When day four of team camp rolled around, she was in the stands watching our games. She was no longer a member of St. Rose, eyes locked on our team and how we worked. After our last game of the day, I talked to the new player and her father, welcoming them to our program and letting them know that we would get right to work on getting her up to speed. The entire team, varsity, and JV, work together during the summer, so there would be plenty of opportunities to work, learn, and grow within our program.

With everybody gone and a successful team camp complete, in the quiet of an empty gym, I reflected privately on the promise of the season to come. We were in a great place.

TWENTY-SIX
FALL – GATHER AND BE GRATEFUL

AS SUMMER WORKOUTS END, New Jersey rules prohibit coaches on staff from working with their teams out of season. So, as fall sports officially began, I would be out of the picture, but basketball would continue for Holmdel as it did for every other program in the state. There were informal workouts and fall leagues run throughout New Jersey. Hoping to build on our summer momentum, I didn't want to wear the girls out, but I did want them to have opportunities to work together as a team, deepening and strengthening the bonds that had developed. We had a few more sessions for the summer, so I worked with the girls and set the table for our fall activities. We were also ending our summer league with just a few more games on the schedule. Everybody was committed to finishing the summer strong. My newly acquired freshman was banged up, having tweaked a knee during personal training. She gave it a go but was really hobbled, which hampered her practice and game experiences. Not wanting to make matters worse, I pulled her from game action and full court drills at workouts, allowing her to shoot at the side baskets. Being competitive in spirit, she was frustrated, but I reminded her that we had a busy fall in front of us and that her health was important.

Pop took over coaching duties during the fall league. As I had previously, I sought a father to help on the bench. The girls knew what we wanted to work on, and my senior captains ran the show, but Pop managed game flow and substitutions. From previous observations, I knew the father of the freshman who transferred back to Holmdel recorded every one of his daughter's games. Thinking it might help with the integration into the program, I asked him if he would record the fall games for us, and I gave him access to Hudl, our video library, so he could post those games for players to review later. It also allowed me to watch game action and player progress. He did a good job with the recordings, and the inclusive effort seemed to work out well. I enjoyed watching the team's progress on the court.

Later in the fall, Pop and I visited The College of New Jersey, where my former point guard was going into her sophomore year. I contacted her and asked her to seek permission from the coach for us to observe one of their practices. She was so excited about the prospect of our visit. The coach was kind enough to grant us access to the practice and even bragged about how our player had recently won the "She-Hulk" award for the team, a weekly acknowledgment of hard work and hustle. We had a similar recognition on our team, the championship belt, which my son had created to recognize players weekly. He did a great job with the design, mimicking a WWE championship belt made in school colors and adorned with Hornet insignia. It looked great and the girls warmed up to the idea, posting pictures on social media, showcasing the honor.

While at the TCNJ practice, I took copious notes on the team's secondary break action. I loved the continuity from the primary break and believed it would be a very natural transition into our offenses. The coach was kind enough to share the breakdown with me, which I studied during the off-season. After practice, Pop and I spent some time with our former player, who I had visited a couple of times prior, taking her out to lunch and checking in on her college life and her progress with basketball. My job had me traveling throughout the state of New Jersey, so when my schedule allowed, I would connect with some of my former players in the towns where they were attending college. I thought it might bring them a little taste of home by seeing a familiar face and allow them to get off campus and enjoy a nice meal. A couple of years earlier, I visited one of my players who had been cut from the college basketball team. She was confused, hurt, and full of doubt. She shared these feelings with me during our visit, which allowed me to encourage her that there is life beyond basketball. We talked about how much she liked the school, her academic successes, and her decision to play volleyball. Our brief time together left her optimistic and restored some of the joy often present in her smile.

This most recent visit to the campus of TCNJ was a similar experience as my former point guard was struggling due to headaches associated with concussions. This was the same player who broke her nose the day before our state semi-final game with Manasquan two years prior. Apparently, she was still leading with her head as she continued to play with unbridled energy. The physical toll from a few more collisions in college caused her to realize that basketball may not be in her future for much longer. Passionate about the game and only a sophomore in college, that prospect was taxing her mentally and emotionally. I am grateful that we had the opportunity to talk through the experience and hopeful that any sentiments shared served as some measure of guidance and hope for a new direction in life, a new passion to pursue.

Our trip to TCNJ was fruitful in so many ways. I was already stoked about the potential for the program. We had been building for three years and were looking to have the biggest number of players and the deepest talent pool we had seen, both of which would provide full rosters at the JV and varsity level. After our observation of a college practice, we also picked up some new drills and a secondary break that I couldn't wait to introduce. Post-Covid basketball would have us back into normal divisional format, which meant we would see Manasquan and Red Bank Catholic twice, along with a strong out-of-conference schedule I had requested.

During this trip, Pop gave me a copy of Jay Wright's book *Attitude*. Coach Wright led Villanova to two NCAA National Championships, creating a tremendous program for the Wildcats and an enduring legacy. In those pages, I found the treasure that would become our motto for the season, "Stay connected to the vine." It is a simple parable that speaks to the power of unity and teamwork, a realization that we are all part of something bigger than ourselves. Armed with some new wrinkles and excellent core talent, I couldn't wait for the season to arrive. The challenge in front of us, one I eagerly embraced, was building and defining our bench to provide depth and support for a very solid core.

Tryouts began the Monday before Thanksgiving. We had three days to evaluate talent and set rosters for the initial part of the season to determine who would begin on varsity and who would begin on JV. I always looked forward to tryouts. Because our program was still relatively small in numbers, we generally didn't have to make any cuts. However, early in the summer, I thought there might be a chance that some decisions would have to be made because I was looking at the prospect of seven returning seniors. Outside of the three who were full time varsity the year before, the others were still learning the game and developing their skills. I was content with the idea of keeping all of them and carrying a bigger bench. The struggle would be around keeping practices competitive, getting the developing players quality reps, and ultimately carving out some playing time for them. Younger players were better, and their upside was much greater. I was worried about having some frustrated upper class who could then upset the mechanics of our season. Moreover, I was concerned about those parents who would become angered to see their daughters deep on the bench with sophomores and potentially freshmen playing in front of them. I ran through a multitude of scenarios, deciding to wait and see who came to tryouts.

Six seniors showed up, with one deciding to concentrate on volleyball, a new sport, and one for which she had already shown great potential. She was tall, athletic and very easy to coach. An absolute joy to have on the basketball team, she played JV primarily in her sophomore and junior years, with the entire coaching staff working with her to help develop skills and confidence. She worked hard, but things didn't always click for her during the games. On the volleyball team, she found a more natural fit in a game that allowed her to take advantage of her raw athletic abilities. Her decision paid off as she went on to play volleyball in college at Johnson & Wales.

Because we never had to cut anybody, I always liked to run tryouts as close as possible to actual practice. We did a lot of full-court work on our fast break technique. We mixed in a lot of shooting drills, making them as game-like and competitive as possible. I never liked static drills, so I would mix conditioning with ball handling, defensive movements, rebounding, passing, or any other skills, sometimes creating a sequence that would combine all the above and have the girls running the length of the court. The girls would jump rope to build footwork and coordination. We had them doing pushups, crunches, and fun runs like 17's or suicides. I would take the opportunity to reacquaint the returning girls with one or two of our base offenses while introducing sets to the new players. Once we had the basics down, we would get a run in with mixed lineups to see how well the girls were picking up the plays and help them integrate with each other on the court. We would mix in free throw shooting after periods of running to test tired legs and frazzled minds. Just about every practice would end with a timed full-court shooting drill with a goal to hit. The intense three days gave us a focused lens for evaluating our talent.

Weighing all options with my coaches after the third tryout, we decided to keep everybody. The only thing we needed to decide was what level, stressing that six spots on varsity were going to be held by seniors. We shared our evaluation of each of the players, outlining a varsity roster with six seniors, two juniors, three sophomores, and two freshmen. Two of the sophomores and both freshmen were designated swing players, given the opportunity to see game time at both levels. Knowing that three of the seniors were going to be challenged to see playing time, I wanted to make sure I talked to them individually to level set expectations. They were very much a part of our family, but I wanted to make sure they understood that every playing opportunity would be earned through the competitive lens of practice and efforts shown in gameplay. I also wanted them to understand this was a mental and physical commitment they were making, ensuring buy-in for the length of the season. The conversations went very well, and each of the girls brought a wonderful perspective. Two of the three wanted to stay on as players.

The third senior asked me if she could stay on as our manager, even though she had been with the team since she was a freshman when I asked her older sister to encourage her to be a part of our program. This young lady always came ready to give her all at every practice and in every game situation. She more than made up for what she lacked in skill with heart and commitment to give her best. She played JV through her junior year, showing improvement every step of the way. At the JV level, she was counted on for good minutes and a variety of contributions, whether in the game or on the bench. As a senior, she would have to play varsity. While she no doubt would continue giving her all to every sequence, I believe she was keenly aware that her best wasn't as good as her teammates and that playing time would be hard to come by. As hard as she worked on the court, she also worked a lot off the court in after-school jobs. Her thought process led her to a decision where she could still be a part of the basketball family and achieve some of her other ambitions. I was very proud of her and grateful that she continued to lend her talents to our team as a very good manager.

Outside of the emotional gymnastics of figuring out how to manage my senior class, tryouts ran very smoothly. We picked up another freshman, a tall soccer player, who decided to get back into basketball. She was a very good athlete, raw in basketball skills, but possessed a boundless energy to go along with a desire to learn. At first assessment, she would be a JV player for the season, but there was a lot of varsity-level playing time in her future. The coaching staff marveled at our surprise addition to the roster.

The last key element to our preparation for the season was to add another coach. As much as I liked to work on developing players, I loved working with young people who were interested in becoming a coach. Since we were limited in the number of paid positions, I was looking to add a volunteer coach who could develop into a paid position on my staff or prepare themselves for another opportunity. My first thought was to add an alumnus of Holmdel. I had reached out to one of my seniors from the first year with the program. Unfortunately, there was a minimum requirement for college credits to work in a coaching capacity for high school. As a junior in college, she was light of the number needed and ineligible to assist.

With that option no longer available, I looked toward some of my former players from SJV. Granted, Holmdel wasn't their old basketball team, but several players from SJV loved the game and knew it well. More importantly, they knew the level of competition required in every practice to achieve greatness in the program. The first person I reached out to had recently graduated from Gardner-Webb, where she played forward for the Bulldogs. During our time at SJV, we worked very well together in developing skill sets and growing confidence in her abilities. She parlayed her brilliant high school career into a scholarship with LIU Brooklyn as a freshman, then transferred to Gardner-Webb. I thought she would be a perfect addition to our staff and incredibly helpful with the talent we had on the roster. Who better to help elevate our program than a Tournament of Champions winner? She gladly accepted the position, devoting her available time to us while pursuing her post-graduate work to become a physician's assistant. We were lucky to have her amazing example as a player and as a young professional.

With a great core group, some emerging young talent, and a gifted group of assistant coaches, I looked ahead to the coming season with great anticipation and enthusiasm. Reflecting on the previous three seasons, I was drawn to the words of Robert Louis Stevenson, "Don't judge each day by the harvest you reap but by the seeds you plant."

TWENTY-SEVEN
LOOKING FORWARD TO HARVEST

WE STARTED official practices on Monday, November 29, 2021. I had scheduled four scrimmages, including a final run against Manasquan. With a change in structure to the Shore Conference, Manasquan was no longer in our division, so scrimmaging them wasn't a problem. However, there was still a chance we would face them at least once during the season, either in the Shore Conference Tournament or in the state playoffs. I knew they would be great preparation for the initial stretch of the season. I also knew, although a scrimmage, there would be a level of intensity in the competition, given the nature of our rivalry. I wasn't disappointed, as the two teams battled as if we were playing for a championship at that moment. After the scrimmage, I worked my way through the handshake line, ending up with a hug from the head coach, her two assistants, and one of the players whose older sister I had coached in AAU. The exchanges were very pleasant, with both coaches being satisfied with a well-played, cleanly executed scrimmage. Both teams were ready for regular season play.

Our first scheduled varsity game was December 18, at home, versus Archbishop Carroll from Pennsylvania, a very good basketball team, in a She Got Game showcase. They had a three-game advantage on us as the season in Pennsylvania starts sooner than in New Jersey, but we were playing at home as one of the host teams for the showcase event. This would be a good early test for us.

Archbishop Carroll got off to a great start, outpacing us 16-5 in the first quarter. Our first game jitters were on full display, which surprised me, given the older group of core players. The returning players were plagued with indecision and sluggish play early. My very young and inexperienced bench struggled to be productive in game action. This team looked nothing like the team that had just executed so smoothly in the scrimmage against Manasquan. Perhaps the moment was too big for the makeup of our team at that point in the season. The first real game on the big stage of a college showcase, with a gym full of parents, fans, and college coaches.

I utilized halftime to calm the girls down. We needed to drown out the noise of the exterior influences, staying connected to the vine. We acknowledged that this was our first game, but I reminded the players that our group was special and building toward bigger things. We just needed to trust in each other and play our game. Down 33-18 at half, there weren't any 15-point baskets that were going to close the gap magically. We needed to work one sequence at a time.

We lost by 11, but I was proud of how the girls bounced back from a choppy and inefficient first half. The team played much better, winning the second half and showing a display of resolve in the fourth quarter that showed us the promise of things to come. We would return to work at our next practice and begin preparing for the holiday tournament in West Orange, which would begin after the Christmas break. That time would give us about a week of practice to adjust and continue preparing for our season.

She Got Game was a three-day event, with games hosted in our gym Friday through Sunday. Our game was on Saturday. Since the girls were going to be in the gym most of the day helping work the remaining games, we decided to have a light shoot-around on Sunday morning, prior to the start of the first games. We briefly reviewed a couple of areas for improvement based on gameplay from the day before but spent most of the time just putting up game shots and letting the girls work independently. It was a fun practice, and the girls were in a great mood.

Later that evening, I received notice from the moms of JV players that their daughters were sick and tested positive for COVID. There were four players in total, three of which were swing players to varsity. I was concerned but not panicked by the news. Our improved numbers in the program allowed us to practice separately. The swing players would come to varsity practice after the end of JV and spend some additional time with us. We were a year removed from the heart of the COVID pandemic and the hysteria that came with it. Generally, COVID was being treated more like the flu at this time, and the quarantine time had been reduced to five days. As a precaution, I canceled JV practices for the week before Christmas. Their first game was January 4, so they would have time to heal and get some practice before playing. We proceeded with varsity-only practices prior to the tournament.

On December 23, we had gone three days without any other signs of illness on the team. The girls who had tested positive were home resting and working toward being symptom-free. However, with the two swing players out, I needed to decide to temporarily bring two of the JV players up to fill bench spots and provide depth until we had everybody back and healthy. I checked with my two assistant coaches about who they felt deserved the opportunity. Their initial choice was a sophomore guard. I was quick to accept. She was a good player and a hard worker, and she was somebody I thought could benefit from the potential exposure at the varsity level. I chose the second player, the freshman transfer from St. Rose, who had been hobbled with a leg injury through the summer and fall.

She had been practicing well and appeared to be finally healed. I wasn't sure that she would get any playing time in the tournament, but I felt the experience would be good for her and encouragement to keep working. I knew she wanted to be on varsity, especially since two of her classmates from JV were swing players. The simple truth of the matter was that she wasn't ready to play at that level. Her game was too one-dimensional, always spotting up for a 3-point shot and minimizing the movement of the offense. Defensively, she was slow and often out of position. These weren't bad things. They were very typical of most freshmen and aspects of the game that can be coached and developed over time. I thought a court-side seat to see how the game is played at the next level would serve as inspiration for her to stay committed to the work ahead.

I told both JV players about the decision and the caveat that this was a temporary fix until our varsity team was whole again. I reiterated that we would continue to evaluate them for future opportunities to move up to a swing player later in the season. They were both very happy with the opportunity, and I was excited to see how they would perform in any tournament action they received. With a plan in place for our game on December 27 against West Orange, the team broke the huddle with holiday wishes. They would have Christmas Eve and Christmas Day off, and we would resume practice on December 26. On December 24, I tested positive for COVID. I would have to quarantine and hand the reins over to my son for the tournament's first two games.

We started the tournament off with a bang, defeating the host team, West Orange, ranked number 20 in the state at the time. They had the best player on the floor, a Yale-bound senior, who poured in 31 points. We had the better team, showcasing a balanced effort with four double-figure players. The senior captains sparked the effort, each with a double-double in points and rebounds, while our junior guard led the scoring effort with 15 points. My son chalked up his first varsity win and came home with great reports about the team effort. He relied heavily on the starters early, who rewarded his confidence in them with a 20-8 second quarter, giving the team a 14-point lead. In the second half, he was able to use the bench in spot minutes to afford key relief for the starters. The bench did a good job in making the most of the light minutes and picking up some game experience. I watched the game on film later that day and was very pleased with the overall performance. This was a big win and a good step forward from our struggles in the first game.

The second tournament game was the following day against Union City, another good team with a firebrand coach. He was extremely loud and vocal, often shouting negative things at players and riding officials throughout the game. He was prone to technical fouls for his behavior. From what I heard of him and observed on game film, I was shocked that he was allowed to coach in high school. I warned my son of the opposing coach's antics, encouraging him not to be distracted but to focus on our team. Our team rang the victory bell again with another solid effort. Again, the offense was very balanced, but in a display of the depth of our talent, our junior forward, the transfer from Manasquan a year ago, racked up a double-double with 17 points and 17 rebounds. The depth of talent in our starting five was obvious. We needed to continue working on our depth to have long-term success on the season. With a day off before our next game, we would have the opportunity to work on our depth in practice and benefit from the return of our sick teammates, including me. We had one day to prepare for our next tournament game against a very good opponent.

New Providence, a perennial Group 1 powerhouse who had just elevated to a Group 2 school, would be a great test for us. Not only were they consistently playing for state championships in Group 1, but they had played in the Tournament of Champions just two years before. If we wanted to win a Group 2 title and play in the TOC at the end of the season, we would most likely have to go through New Providence, Manasquan, or both to get there. I felt this was a good gauge as to where we were at that point in the season.

It was good to be back on the sideline with the team, our full roster, and the two call-up JV players. Knowing that we still had players recovering, I felt the added depth would be helpful. New Providence was talented but young without a senior in the lineup. Our maturity, balanced offensive attack, and defensive pressure would be an advantage on paper. It didn't pan out that way. New Providence jumped out to a 28-10 halftime lead. We couldn't put the ball in the ocean. Our defensive effort was porous at best. We played well below our capabilities. At one point in the second quarter, one of my seniors jogged by the bench in transition to offense with a panicked look, flailing arms, and complaining that nothing was working. She wasn't wrong in her observation, but the lapse of leadership from her was my biggest concern. With my starters looking gassed, disjointed, and mentally checked out, I pulled a hockey substitution with a complete line change. I put the last five in the rotation on the floor, including my two JV call up players. They played with enthusiasm and spirit, allowing us to stem the tide for the moment. I knew my bench's success wasn't sustainable, but I wanted to give the starters an opportunity for reflection.

We regrouped in the locker room at half and played better in the second, but we were still well off the mark for where we should be and how we had been playing. No disrespect intended toward New Providence. They finished 26-3 that season, with their final game being a loss in the Group 2 finals against Manasquan. As was always the case, my focus was on us. We did not play well on the big stage, like our first game against Archbishop Carroll. If we were to recognize our potential of being a great team, ranked high in the Shore Conference and the state of New Jersey, we needed to be better in all phases. We needed to be more consistent in effort and focus. We needed to stand together in moments of adversity. All those attributes were absent in the New Providence game.

After the game, I firmly shared my disappointment and dissatisfaction with our collective performance in the locker room. I told the girls everything was up for grabs at our next practice. Starting spots, playing time, who should be on varsity, and who needs more time at JV were all going to be evaluated. I also spoke directly to my senior captains about the lapse in leadership, with nobody stepping up to pull the team together, allowing doubt and selfish play to creep into our game. It was a difficult conversation that needed to occur, but I didn't want to leave on a sour note. I had been toying with the idea of adding a captain. In previous years, I would have senior leadership and a junior to provide an opportunity for peer-to-peer experience and allow for smooth transition into the next season. The junior forward who returned to us from Manasquan stood out with her positive attitude and strong efforts in practices and games. I took this opportunity to elevate her to a team captain position. We left the locker room for a two-day break around the New Year celebration. At 2-2 on the season, we would return to regular season play with some tough games in the Shore Conference and in our division. The real season was about to begin.

TWENTY-EIGHT
HAPPY NEW YEAR?

WE HAD three games in five days after the holiday season. Our first practices out of the break were focused on rebuilding a positive mindset and getting us back into the groove of good basketball. We stumbled hard against New Providence. I needed to remind everybody that we were still early in the season, implementing new sets, figuring out our depth, and identifying roles on the team. Bad games are going to happen, but they are only bad if we let them linger. As I had often encouraged the team, we needed to focus on the next sequence, on learning from our struggles to become stronger as a team. We went to work preparing for the stretch ahead.

The first test was against Trinity Hall in their gym. The last time we played in their gym was a couple of years prior when Trinity Hall got the better of us in a tight competition. They were an emerging program with a good coach and two very good guards, a senior and sophomore combination, that could cause opponents fits. The senior was a gifted athlete. A lacrosse player first, she brought speed and grit to the basketball court. She would later take her talents to Princeton University for lacrosse. The sophomore was a rising star in the Shore Conference, who played with a confidence above her age and possessed a mean crossover that would often catch opponents leaning in the wrong direction. She eventually would take her talents to Harvard.

We were the more complete and balanced team. At this point in the season, both of my senior captains knew where they would be taking their talents next, one to Colgate and one to Emory. We had two great practices leading to this game. Our strength was our starting five, but we still had questions about depth and role players off the bench. Over the last few games, one of my seniors, Champ, had started to string together some quality minutes. She was smaller in stature but never let that get in her way. Because of her quickness and tenacity, she became one of my most reliable defenders, especially at the top of our 1-1-3 zone. Her ability to clog lines of penetration and drive opposing guards toward trap zones was very effective. She understood the offensive sets well and would often find her spots when the other team was paying too much attention to our key players. She would direct a teardrop basket in over the reaching arms of much taller players or stick a big three when left alone in the corners. Her emergence was very welcomed and allowed me to work her in early and often. I was still figuring out where my sophomore and freshmen players fit into the overall scheme. The two freshmen swing players had been playing very well early, showing signs of promise. We were still carrying the two temporary swing players as well. After discussions with my coaching staff following the previous practice, I had decided that they would be heading back to JV, but I didn't want to make that announcement until after the Trinity Hall game.

We held a 9-6 lead after a tight first quarter. I liked our pace and decisions with the ball, but I felt we needed to elevate the intensity of our defensive effort. We needed to disrupt the rhythm of their guards, take away passing lanes and driving lines, and speed up their decision process. The girls responded, opening a solid lead in the second quarter. Through our defense, we were dictating the pace of the game. Trinity Hall couldn't handle our balanced offense when playing man defense, so they shifted to their 1-3-1 zone. It slowed us down for a bit, and we held on to a 9-point lead with less than a minute to go in the quarter. Observing their zone, I noticed that the left baseline corner was exposed due to the overshifting of their players. Lacking eye discipline, the weak side of the zone would follow the ball and lose sight of players in their zone. During a timeout, I reached deep down the bench to the freshman, who was one of the temporary swing players. At that point in the game, with momentum favoring my team, I thought we could put a dagger in our opponent prior to halftime. As she was checking into the game, my son reminded me that she was only eligible for one quarter, as she had played the entire JV game earlier. I went with my gut and let the decision roll. We came out with the possession.

As the ball entered the front court, we began to probe the 1-3-1 zone. My freshman sub skirted the left side of the court and buried herself in the corner, a trait she had developed during grammar school. We were working with her on diversifying her game, but in this moment, that tendency was going to be used as a strength. The ball worked from the left wing into high post, then out to right corner. The defense shifted accordingly, overplaying the right side. From there, the ball lifted to right wing, then quickly to the left wing. The exaggerated defensive shift to the right side had them scrambling to recover with ball movement. As the defense adjusted to the quick movement from right wing to left wing, my freshman was sitting all by herself in the left corner. Receiving a quick pass to her waiting hands, she didn't hesitate to nail a corner three. Dagger delivered. We took momentum and a 12-point lead into halftime.

We finished the game with a 13-point win, never letting Trinity get settled into their style of play. My newly appointed junior captain led the way with another double-double, 15 points and 10 rebounds. The Emory-bound senior added eight points and eight rebounds but really showcased her defensive prowess with seven blocked shots. The team effort on defense showed out with 13 steals and 10 blocks. It was a good game day. The girls were playing well and chalking up wins for both levels. The positive vibes were all around and something we would need to build on for our next opponent, Toms River North.

After the Trinity Hall game, I texted the two temporary swing players, letting them know that they would return to full-time JV. I noted their contributions over the four game stretch during our struggles with COVID and thanked them for their willingness to put in the extra time and effort. I would have preferred to tell them in person, but my only opportunity would have been before the next day's practice. I didn't feel like that would be fair to them, giving them only minutes to process the information and mentally prepare for practice. I opted for the text, which both girls responded graciously. The next day at practice, I took the time to speak to them individually and share my gratitude. I also told them to hang on to the varsity uniforms because I was confident they could work their way back to swing spots. During our conversation, I also offered them suggestions on what to focus on improving in their individual game to help them get back to varsity sooner. The sophomore player had the physical attributes needed to play at the next level, but she lacked confidence and often seemed unsure of where to be and what to do on offense. Both are things that can be worked on through competitive repetition at practice and by putting them into play during games. While we want to win the games we play, JV is a great lab for testing new skills and trying to improve gameplay.

The freshman had some good skills but seemed to put all her emphasis on shooting the three. While that can be of value, it made her a very predictable player and easy to guard. The habit of burying herself in the baseline corner and waiting for the chance to shoot minimized the reality of her potential and stagnated the team's offensive flow. She was also slow-moving in transition and on defense. Some of that was due to her recovery from the earlier leg injury, but I believe she struggled with her quickness due to her running style. She ran straight-legged and didn't really bend her knees for drive and power. We talked through both things. I encouraged her and later spoke to her father about seeking out SPARQ training (speed, power, agility, reaction, and quickness). I offered to connect them to a good friend of mine who was a trainer and who would probably help for little to nothing. He just loved working with young athletes; his reward was their improvement and success.

As for her offense, I encouraged her to move with more purpose. Our offenses were predicated on motion, so if she didn't get the ball, work away to screen for a teammate and bring them back to the ball. As she screens away, the ball will be working back to her direction, allowing her to set off the screen for a shot or basket cut for an opportunity to attack the lane. I also encouraged her to read the defense as they close out to her shot position. If they are high and out of control, shot fake and go by. Those simple movements would help her be more productive, open opportunities for her teammates, and give her a chance to attack the basket, potentially getting her to the free-throw line as well. I also encouraged her to use her size and strength to be more active on the boards and more of a presence defensively. She took all my words to heart, working on them in practice that day.

Going into the season, Toms River North was ranked in the top 10 in the Shore Conference. They also played a competitive early schedule, and we were both entering the game at 3-2. As the basketball season goes, we had one day to implement our scout and prepare for the game. JV played first, so I sat in the bleachers to watch the game. I enjoyed watching the lower-level girls; evaluating their skills, how they play as a team, and how well they receive coaching. I was inquisitive about how well the four swing players not only played at the JV level but also interested in how present they were as leaders on the floor.

The swing players performed very well. The two freshmen swing were showing great improvement, so they had been limited to two-quarters of play at JV, giving me three-quarters at the varsity level. The sophomore swing players were allowed three quarters at JV, leaving two for varsity. Everybody on JV was playing well, and the coach had a very productive rotation going on. While I was watching, the freshman I spoke to the day before about improving her game stood out. She would still favor the left lane in transition, heading down to her favorite spot, but she didn't settle there. Instead, if the shot didn't present itself, she moved off to set a down screen to the post. She was moving with purpose and looking to assist in the flow of the offense. Because of her movement, she found herself open and drained some 3-point shots. A couple of times, I even saw a shot fake utilized to get by an over-aggressive defender, leading to a drive to the basket. She had a great game and looked to be finally settling in. JV went on to win in big fashion. As the varsity team took the court for warmups, I went over to the JV girls to congratulate them on a well-played game. I took a moment to sit with the freshman, expressing how proud I was of the quality effort she displayed. I encouraged her to continue adding diversity to her game. I left her with a big high-five and a smile.

During our last pre-game huddle for the varsity, I encouraged the team to feed off the JV team's energy, holding them up as an example of great teamwork. Toms River North was a well-coached, senior-laden team, with a strong post player who was headed to the United States Naval Academy. As an alum of Navy, I was very interested in the prospect for the Midshipmen. As the coach of

Holmdel, I wanted to make sure my team did everything possible to throw her game off. I thought we could control the game if we could minimize her effectiveness and force others to shoulder the load.

My girls stayed true to the scout, controlling the game's tempo from the tip. We went to halftime with a 3-point lead, which we increased to nine by the end of the third quarter. For the last eight minutes of the game, my girls put on a clinic, winning all phases of the game and closing out with a 21-12 quarter. My Colgate-bound senior led the way with 19 points, ten rebounds, four assists, and three blocks. For the first time in a long while, she looked to be fully healthy and embraced her role as a leader on the team. From my perspective, the best statistic of the day was our defense's effectiveness in holding the future Navy player to three points. Our defense moved well, pressured the ball, maintained eye discipline away from the ball, and was on the mark with help and rotations off the ball. As we moved through the handshake line, I took a moment to talk with the senior from Toms River North heading to Navy. I congratulated her on her appointment, wished her the best of luck, and let her know that she could always call me if she ever needed to talk to someone about the challenges and opportunities ahead. Her coach had my phone number, so I offered an assist when needed. We left Toms River as a proud program with both levels playing well and our chemistry growing every day.

A noticeable trend in our team was the multitude of weapons we had on both sides of the court. We were long and quick as a defense, with tenacious on-ball defenders and rim protectors. The girls communicated well and moved well to defend as a team. On the offensive side, we had three established weapons in my three captains and had some emerging talent in our junior and sophomore guards. Their contributions were coming with more regularity. Our bench was starting to take shape with Champ, the small senior guard, and the two freshmen swing players, who were getting stronger and more confident. I was starting to consider moving the two of them to full-time varsity. Our next game versus Shore Regional would be another point of observation for me. While we had separated ourselves from Shore at this point as far as the level of team play in the division, they were still a respected opponent.

With a great coach at the helm, a top player in the conference with their junior forward, and the addition of a young gun freshman, Shore was not a team to be taken lightly. Our point of focus was the junior. She was the heart and soul of the team, averaging 22.8 points and just under 10 rebounds per game. She was a dominant force on the floor. Shore didn't have a lot of surrounding talent at the time, but her leadership and unselfish play helped elevate her teammates' play. She was a wonderful young lady and a joy to watch, except for when she played against us. Minimizing her impact on the game would be the key to our success.

We wasted no time in demonstrating that we were the better team, jumping out to a 10-point lead at the end of the first and building that to a 35-21 advantage at halftime. We continued our dominance in the second half, securing a 72-49 victory. The spread is a little misleading, as there was never a time when we could afford to take our foot off the pedal. Shore's star player had to earn every bit of her 17 points, but she was a force to be reckoned with throughout the game. Our focus on slowing her down paid off, but it left their freshman guard open often, and she took advantage of every opportunity, scoring 17 points, her career best to that point. Our winning effort was paced by another amazing performance from our junior captain, leading the way with 21 points, including four long balls. My Colgate-bound senior captain notched another strong game with 12 points, 10 rebounds, four assists, and two steals, making her presence felt in all aspects of the game. Our bench provided quality minutes, allowing me to substitute regularly without missing a beat. We had interchangeable parts that gave us great freedom in rotating people and changing assignments. The girls sensed how well they were playing as a team. They were truly beginning to understand that we had opportunities to reach new heights for the program. We were clicking on all cylinders as we headed into the biggest game of the season, Red Bank Catholic at home. Euphoria ran through our program, and it felt great!

TWENTY-NINE
BOMBSHELLS AND SNIPERS

I WAS BEAMING and full of pride as I exited the locker room, having just lost a tough, hard-fought game against Red Bank Catholic on January 11, 2022. Coaches rarely feel good after losses. The emphasis on winning in competitive sports leaves little room for moral victories. At least, that is the environment that conventional wisdom has created in the sporting world. After our loss to RBC, our locker room and team energy were very positive. The driving force behind that euphoria was the recognition that we were starting to see the results of hard work and dedication in the growth of our program and the nuanced changes made to our game approach during the summer and fall. We came into the summer with a good core group of players but uncertainties around bench play and depth. We introduced new offensive concepts. High emphasis was placed on conditioning and endurance to support our desire for a quicker pace of play and defensive intensity. We got off to a shaky start with the COVID interruption, culminating in a bad showing against New Providence. The coaches challenged our team to be better, build stronger chemistry, lead self and lead laterally to drive success on the court. As evident in how we played coming out of the

265

break and in the tremendous effort against Red Bank Catholic, the girls understood and embraced our collective potential. We were ready to launch. I was very proud of our progress and on an emotional high on the morning of January 12, 2022. I couldn't wait to outline practice for that evening and continue the path to excellence for the Holmdel Hornets.

When my cell phone rang, and the caller ID showed the name of the principal of Holmdel High School, I was quick to answer the phone. As I said before, I had a good relationship with the principal, who was the Athletic Director for Holmdel before his promotion. We worked together to elevate the level of athletics at Holmdel for a couple of years. I had also coached against his teams when he was a boy in seventh and eighth grade. His father and I were friendly through those early coaching days against each other. Years later, his father and I would always see each other at high school games, making a point of connecting and spending a few minutes together checking in with each other. I knew his wife, the coach of Manasquan, having competed against her teams many times at SJV and Holmdel. As written earlier, we had many spirited games against each other, always with mutual respect and appreciation. The principal and I often talked about the program challenges he faced in the school and shared our interests in professional sports, especially the NFL and March Madness. When I saw his name on the phone, I thought we would be celebrating the progress of the team and the great effort of the night before.

Instead, I received the devastating news that a horrid accusation of inappropriate touching had been leveled against me. At first, given our friendliness, I thought this was a misplaced attempt at humor. I asked the principal if he was joking, to which he solemnly assured me that he wouldn't joke around about such a matter. I struggled with the thought that any of my players would accuse me of such rancid behavior. I asked for the identity of my accuser. "I can't tell you." I asked for the specific accusation. "I can't tell you." I asked to know the evidence that was submitted in support. "I can't show you that, but they have pictures." I asked for an explanation around the "pictures" and was met with another, "I can't tell you. The only thing I can share with you is that you are suspended indefinitely until all of this is reviewed." I asked about the protocol and timeline. "I don't know. It is in the Board's hands now."

The bomb had been dropped. Somebody had accused me of inappropriately touching my players, an insinuation that anybody who knows me would be dismissed out of hand as categorically false, but somehow it was taken as gospel truth. I was suspended for something I didn't do and left completely helpless. There was no presumption of innocence or indication of due process. No answers were provided. No support was offered. No direction from leadership as to process and timing. Just a boundless suspension and an undefined process.

Although this was an attack on my character and integrity, my thoughts shifted to the girls. My assumption was that the assistant coach, my son, would assume responsibility for the team during my suspension. "He is suspended too," was the retort I received. I sought clarity to his suspension. Did he do something wrong? Was he accused of something as well? The answer I received was heartless and cruel. "He was not accused of anything but has your last name." So, I was not only suspended for a baseless accusation and presumed guilty without any investigation or inquiry, but my son was also guilty by association for the sin of having my last name. I couldn't find the words as I struggled with the rush of emotions. Angry, frustrated, confused, disappointed, dejected, tearful, concerned, betrayed . . . all floating in my head as I was trying to process what was being said. In addition to my son, my two volunteer assistants were also shunned, as if we were the masterminds behind some child abuse ring. This no longer sounded professional but very personal for some reason. This appeared to be more of a coup de tat, something you would read about in seedy political maneuverings—shots fired from hidden enemies.

The principal told me he would coach the team during my absence. Before hanging up, I implored him to take care of my girls. With our conversation over, my head was swimming. I ran through questions and scenarios in my now tortured mind. I couldn't piece together any words or actions on my part that may have caused offense to someone, let alone one of my players. I replayed the night before in my head, desperately searching for any action that could be misconstrued as "inappropriate touching." My emotions continued to plummet as I tried to imagine who was behind this slander. Even more, I tried to figure out why somebody would attack my morals and character in such a way, especially someone from inside my basketball family. I ran through the list of varsity players in my head and was striking out in my attempt to identify potential accusers. None of the varsity girls nor any of their parents would do this to me. What was I missing?

My son scoured film from the RBC game the night before. He showed me four clips of engagements I had with players: a simple high five, a hand on the top of a player's head, my arm around one of my seniors in a side hug coming off the court, and a moment where I used my clipboard to tap the back of one of my starters when breaking huddle. Nothing rose to the occasion of inappropriate, demeaning, unwanted, or sexual in nature. Every motion was an act of encouragement or a moment of celebration for a job well done and reciprocated by the players. This was the nature of my coaching and the way I lead today, summarized in John Gordon's book *The Power of Positive Leadership*:

> *Positive leaders and communicators rely on nonverbal communication. They encourage through nods, facial expressions,*

*high-fives, handshakes, pats on the back, fist bumps, and even hugs when appropriate. Positive communication isn't just verbal. It's also physical. We must remember that it is a way we humans communicate naturally and is very powerful and beneficial when done **appropriately and with good intention**.*

All that said, the phone call I received was the only suspension notification from the school. I wasn't provided with written notice or any other sort of formal documentation outlining the parameters of the suspension. Nobody else on my staff received any notification or correspondence from the school. Although not part of the accusation, no professional courtesy was offered to my staff, paid or volunteer. On a subsequent call with the principal that I initiated, still confused by the allegations and left alone to figure out the protocol, I had asked for the opportunity to speak with the girls to at least assure them that everything would be alright and to encourage them to stay connected to the vine, the faith and confidence in each other, in our team. I was told that wouldn't be a good idea and that I was to avoid any contact with the girls. I reassured the principal that I had done nothing wrong. The accusation was an egregious assault on my character, and I had the right to know who the accuser was and what the actual allegations were. I asked to meet with him, the AD, and the person who filed the complaint to flush out the real situation. I offered that this was some sort of tragic misunderstanding and that it could all be worked out in an hour. No harm, no foul. After pleading my case and stating the importance of my rights being protected, the principal simply said that he couldn't argue with me on anything I noted. "I don't need you to argue with me. I need you to argue for me."

The two calls and the subsequent whirlwind of emotions transpired on the morning of January 12th. Immediately after the second call with the principal, my phone began to blow up with texts from coaches and athletic directors from throughout the state. The first two I received were from high-profile coaches from the Shore Conference who knew me well and had written letters of recommendation when I applied for the job at Holmdel. I had competed against one of them the night before. After the first dozen texts from coaches, I reached back out to the principal to find out how this sudden, shocking news had become public. Again, stressing the preservation of my rights as well as the accusers, I asked why I was receiving text messages from people who had nothing to do with the administration of Holmdel High School inquiring about the vile and false accusations levied against me. Of course, I let him know that every single text was an endorsement of my honor and integrity, an acknowledgment that the accusations were baseless, and a desire to see me on the sidelines again very soon. I was told the administration can't control what people say or do. Yet, some of the things I was being asked about were things that only the administration should know at that time.

After that call, the wave of text messages grew to a tsunami, then turned into phone calls from parents within my program. They shared their horror that this was happening and offered absolute support for me, each expressing concern about the well-being of their daughters. Stories were shared of girls crying and emotionally distressed over the suspension and the disruption to our season and our family. I was appreciative of the parental backing, but I felt distraught and helpless. The parents had begun to piece together what had transpired, sharing various details with me. I shot a text to the principal, letting him know that I was receiving a flood of texts and calls from parents. If they knew something was amiss, why wasn't the administration taking any action to resolve the problem? Who was leading the effort and accountable for due process?

In the early afternoon, I received a text from a gentleman who is a large fan of girls' basketball. He would often travel to all parts of the state to watch games at all levels, predominantly high school and AAU. His observation of players, teams, and coaches would find its way to social media to showcase various individuals. He would often share videos of conversations with players, highlighting their accomplishments, ambitions, and a few fun facts about themselves. The bits were fun to watch, giving many girls a spotlight they would never have otherwise and sharing news about teams and players that may never get ink in the local papers. Along his travels, he would share his opinion of eateries throughout the state. This was a hobby, not a paid position. There was no glory or limelight, only an opportunity to showcase young student-athletes. It was a crusade of sorts by somebody who just enjoyed the game and the community of girls' basketball in New Jersey. Out of kindness, he reached out to me to express his disbelief and to offer his support. It was a very kind gesture but also one that heightened my level of concern. While not the press, this was a person who had the eyes and ears of many throughout the basketball world in our area. While I trusted him implicitly, I began to wonder who else was getting this information and how it was being shared or interpreted. I was encouraged by the overwhelming support, but I was equally concerned that my rights and privacy were not being preserved.

Within 30 minutes of that text, I received a call from a sportswriter for NJ.com asking me for comment. I knew the writer well; he had often covered our games and many others in the state. He was always very good at presenting a balanced perspective in his games reviews, often sharing the successes of players from both teams. It wasn't just about final scores and statistics. We had interviewed on several occasions, so I wasn't surprised to see his name on my phone.

He was doing his job in reaching out. I told him I had just learned of my suspension that morning, assuring him there was no merit to what was being suggested. He wanted to know the story, but I had nothing else to offer because I wasn't even sure what had happened to trigger this event. I asked him not to publish anything for fear of greater distraction and harm to the girls, telling him that I would be happy to talk to him when the time was right.

The final straw of frustration for me came with an e-mail I had received at work from a customer who knew I was a high school basketball coach. We had become friendly over the years when I was coaching at Saint John Vianney, and his daughter was playing for Raritan. He worked for a local college I called on to win business, and we were both members of an association for higher education. His e-mail very simply stated that he knew what he had heard was trash, offering his phone number so I could call him if I needed to talk. In a matter of a few hours, a false accusation prompted an unnecessary suspension, which triggered a flood of texts and calls, including the media and a customer. I was mortified.

Again, I reached out to the principal to voice my concern over how easily the news was flying around, questioning how the administration was managing the process. I was searching for some modicum of direction and support from leadership but only got vague responses and uncertainty about the next steps.

Throughout the day, texts turned into phone calls. One was from my opponent the night before, who reached out to offer me encouragement. As an Athletic Director and varsity head coach for many years in the Shore Conference, his words rang true, "If they are willing to do this to a man of your integrity and reputation, who do they expect to get to coach at the school." Dawn Karpell also called to offer her support. She provided an interesting perspective as she used to be the head coach at Holmdel early in her career. She was not as shocked that the administration would act so harshly, as she shared stories of internal politics and self-serving people in positions of power. She offered her unabashed support at any time, in any way needed. I began to hear directly from more of my players' parents, both past and present at Holmdel, and from other programs I have coached. They were paralyzed with disbelief, sharing their support and looking to help in any way they could. Several mothers called me to tell me how distraught their daughters were, crying and confused, knowing that the accusations were without merit. JV players and parents were texting my son with similar comments and thoughts of quitting the program. Our message of staying connected to the vine was consistent. Fathers called me to thank me for the positive influence I had on their daughters beyond the game of basketball. This all had an eerie feeling of permanence, like the condolences offered at a funeral service.

Later in the day, I received this text from the father of one of my senior captains:

Hi, Darren. . . I wanted to commend you on the game last night. That was one of the best high school games I have seen. It was played well by both sides.

I understand that some of the parents have an issue about your interactions with the girls. It was mentioned that you patted (daughter's name) on the behind last night and I actually saw that and thought there was nothing remotely inappropriate about that. I am truly sorry that someone has questioned your integrity and reputation. I am not happy that (daughter's name) was used in that way.

I never really got a chance to speak to you 1:1. I always felt that (daughter's name) needed to build her own relationship with you as her coach without me interfering. Please know that I am happy (daughter's name) played for you as you always treated her respectfully, which is what you promised when you spoke to the parents your first season.

I am sure you are proud of Nick (assistant coach). I think he is a very good coach. When you were out during the West Orange tournament, he did really well, very calm and controlled. (Daughter's name) speaks very highly of Nick, and I have seen him trying to help (his daughter's name) on the bench and between the halves. He has really helped to develop (daughter's name) and increase her confidence, which is her biggest battle.

Just wanted to send this note and thank you again for your leadership over the last 4 years. I also sent a note to the school board in your support.

I found out a few days later that the same father had written an e-mail to all the parents in the basketball program, admonishing individuals who thought it was ok to use his daughter's name to "further their own personal agenda" and stressing that his daughter "was not touched inappropriately in the game Tuesday night and anybody who viewed that interaction as sexual is misguided." He went on to rebuke individuals for circulating videos of his daughter to support "unfounded accusations," all without his permission or support. He wrote in summary, "It is very disappointing that the accuser(s) didn't have the courage or respect to come to me directly to express their concern about my daughter's well-being because if they did, the message would have been to speak on behalf of your own kid. What an embarrassment to this township and our high school that a good man and the team is being dragged through the mud."

The father's text to me and his e-mail shared by another parent began to provide some context, but there were still gaps to fill. Another call from the mother of one of my freshman varsity players added some additional color to the situation. She shared information about a single accuser, a freshman not playing varsity, with the support of her "crazy" parents submitting a written complaint to the principal, using game footage of interactions with two other players to support their allegation. She identified the senior captain, which I was already aware of, and told me the other was my sophomore sensation, whose older sister was one of my former players. My heart sunk to my stomach. Once the two "victims" were identified, I knew the complaints didn't come from the players or their families. How could somebody use two other players, two unwilling participants, to present false accusations against a coach? Even more confusing was how an administration would accept such accusations as valid and leap into blind actions, harmful to a coach and a program full of wonderful young players and good people who are equally in the administration's charge of serving and protecting.

I had no explanation for what was going on, the next steps, or the timeline. The only decisive action taken by the school was to suspend me, an innocent man, without any formal process other than a phone call. Every indication I had from the multitude of calls that came within hours of the news pointed to a sham of an accusation perpetrated by a frustrated family. If I knew the truth, and everybody else knew the truth, why wasn't school leadership stepping into action and providing guidance? A supposed victim didn't initiate the malicious accusation raised against me. Instead, it was recklessly issued by a third party, cowardly actions of one set of parents, using their daughter as a shield from potential litigation for defamation of character, all the while using two other minors, without the permission of their parents, as weapons to attack my honor and the integrity of my coaching staff. I was furious at the callous, uncaring demeanor of the administration, which shifted to autopilot in covering their collective asses, blinding them to the truth of a slanderous ruse played by parents who had unrealistic expectations for their daughter in terms of what level she should play. This could have been resolved in a day . . . an exonerated coach back on the sidelines, a team returned to normal, and a program restored. Instead of conversing with the coaching staff and trying to find a constructive path forward, the parents acted like selfish, petulant children. Unfortunately, thanks to the inaction of the administration and the BOE, that family got their way. In the process, a magnificent team was stolen from their coaching staff, an extremely promising season hijacked, and the progress of ongoing program development for Holmdel High School Girls Basketball was tarnished. This was only the beginning of a story centered on a flailing administration and failed leadership.

THIRTY
THE IMPERFECT STORM

OVER THE NEXT TWO DAYS, I began to take the initiative to uncover and fully understand what I was up against. On January 14, I sent a letter to the Acting Superintendent for the Board of Education, introducing myself and sharing the news of the allegations made against me. I stressed my concern about the multitude of texts and calls I had received and shared the e-mail I received from my senior captain's father. I continued with:

In my 33 years of coaching (21 as a girls coach in the Shore Conference, and in my 4th year at Holmdel), I have always taken extreme measures to protect the players in my charge, cultivate positive player-coach relationships, and create programs based on honor and integrity. In that time, there has never been a complaint like this, not even a whisper. The fact that this stems from a third party and not the supposed "victim" or her parents is concerning. Furthermore, my immediate removal gives the appearance of an assumption of guilt and leaves the girl's program in a state of flux unnecessarily, especially since my assistant coach is not allowed to continue with the girls until the process flushes out. This is patently unfair to me and my rights as an accused, and detrimental to the faith and confidence of my team.

How and why is news of baseless allegations being allowed to circulate outside of the school? How long until something ends up on social media or in print? Is the school board taking steps to make sure my rights are being preserved and protected throughout the "process"? I respect that there are laws like Title 9 to defend and protect student-athletes, but those same laws have protections for coaches as well.

Why is it that some random person gets to question my integrity and degrade my honor, getting full protection from the school, while I am left on the sidelines flapping in the breeze?

I would like to know what the process is pertaining to this matter. What is the timeline for review of any "evidence" and a discussion with the accused? The suspension is not warranted as it stands and I would like to discuss this further in the appropriate setting with the right people, in a timely fashion.

Later that day, I received a response from the Acting Superintendent sharing that the board was "obligated to thoroughly investigate any complaint" and are "required to notify the appropriate authorities and receive clearance from them before we can proceed." He also stated the standard process in these circumstances is "to suspend the coaching staff pending the investigation."

Not hearing anything further from any person in authority at the school, I sent a follow-up message on January 19:

It has been a week since my suspension, and I have yet to be contacted by the school or the board with any further insight, direction, or timeline regarding my role in this process and the reinstatement of my staff. I truly appreciate the desire to "thoroughly investigate" the circumstances around this misguided accusation, but I don't understand how that can be done without talking to the alleged victim, or the parents of the alleged victim who have already offered unsolicited testimony contradicting any sense of wrongdoing. Furthermore, I question how any investigation can be considered thorough when I haven't been interviewed or spoken with directly about the merits behind any questions around integrity of my basketball program at Holmdel High School. The assumption of guilt and the lack of protection for the rights of coaches at the school, in this case me and my staff, is deeply concerning. We could have resolved all of this last week at a meeting with the Principal, the Athletic Director, the accusing parties, and the parents of the alleged victim.

I am reaching out to you again seeking that engagement, the opportunity to flush out the truth in all of this. The lack of transparency in process and the absence of urgency in resolving this matter in fairness to all parties is disturbing and frustrating. Caught up in all of this is a team of innocent girls who do not deserve the angst brought about by a frustrated and misguided parent. I have been loyal to the growth and development of the Holmdel Girls Basketball program, with honor and integrity. For that to be unfairly questioned, and to have the false accusations supported by the directions and measures taken by the board, is beyond just.

Crickets! I never heard directly from the BOE or the school administration again. My disappointment grew. As the saying goes, "The only thing necessary for the triumph of evil is for good men to do nothing." This was more evident in the void of ownership and the lack of action witnessed throughout my suspension. Maybe the imperfect storm of an Athletic Director in his second week, a first-year non-tenured Principal, and an "acting" Superintendent led to such a broad display of malfeasance. I do believe that all three parts of the administration had good people in the positions. Still, they failed in the lack of process, the reluctance of ownership, fragmented and misleading communication, and poor leadership. They succeeded in self-preservation and cowardice. In the end, a loyal team of employees, albeit Schedule B (part-time, non-union), were left without any protection and support, which is absolutely a key element in the function of any school administration.

I continued to receive regular calls and texts from concerned parents to kindly check in on me. It was there that I learned that my girls were all being called into the police department to give their testimony. Police? How did we get to this stage? If the girls were being called in, I guessed that I wouldn't be far behind. It was a shocking and demoralizing revelation that drove me to hire an attorney, something I couldn't afford but had to do as a measure of self-preservation. Knowing I was my best advocate, I also began digging into the published school policies for disciplinary action against employees. The first one that jumped off the page at me came from section 3150 regarding discipline for teachers and staff, stating:

> In the event disciplinary action is contemplated, notice will be given to the employee in ordinary and concise language of the specific acts and omissions upon which the disciplinary action is based; the text of the statute, policy, rule, or regulation that the employee is alleged to have violated; a date when the employee may be heard and the administrator who will hear the matter, and the penalty that may be imposed.

This policy was ignored entirely. I received a phone call from the principal indicating that I had been suspended for "inappropriate touching" in the game versus Red Bank Catholic the night before. When I asked for clarity, none was offered. When I asked for a time frame, none was defined. When I asked about my assistant coach taking over the team, I was told he was suspended for having my last name. To this point, I had struggled through a week of misdirection and vague information until I finally took it upon myself to reach out to the board directly, hoping to gain insight and clarity. I received a response from an acting superintendent with vague information. I was adrift on a rudderless ship.

What was revealed to me was that the administration, without conducting a basic internal review, quickly punted this case to the Holmdel police. The school policy reads:

> *The Assistant Superintendent for Curriculum and Instruction will begin a prompt, thorough, and impartial investigation. The preliminary investigation will be completed no more than ten working days after the Assistant Superintendent for Curriculum and Instruction received the report.*

I was already eight days into a suspension that fell well short of being "prompt, thorough, and impartial," with no end in sight.

On January 20, my girls were scheduled to play at Matawan Regional High School, where my former assistant coach was in her second year as head coach. This was a game I marked on the calendar, only to exercise the demons of losing to them the year before. As much as I loved my former assistant, there was no way I was going to let the previous season go unchecked. With my suspension, the only thing I could do was consider whether to attend the game. I ran the idea by my attorney, who shared that there was no legal reason why I couldn't attend. Holmdel had failed to outline any conditions of my suspension. They had no jurisdiction over a game at Matawan High School, and I was well within my rights to go. With an all-clear from a legal perspective, I still didn't feel right about going. The last thing I wanted to do was be the cause of distraction for my girls. My assistant coach, my son, having never been notified of any formal suspension, decided to attend the game. He wanted to support the girls and be there for his friend, the head coach at Matawan.

My son was met with a warm welcome from his JV players, who were warming up for their game, the varsity players who were shooting around and passing the time, and those parents who could attend. Other players waived excitedly at the sight of my son, happy to see him and encouraged by his presence. The overall feeling was warm and comforting until a voice shouted out from across the gym, "What are you doing here?" The principal, now the coach of my team, had decided to very publicly admonish a staff member by yelling from across the gym, showing no respect or professional courtesy. The look of joy on the girls' faces was replaced with shock and disbelief, some with mouths agape. My son took the high road and suggested that if the principal wanted to talk to him, he should come talk to him privately, not shout across the gym. Continuing with his highly questionable approach as the principal of a high school, he told my son to "Shut the fuck up and leave."

Many people—players, parents, and the opposing coach at Matawan —witnessed this episode. In fact, later that evening, on one of the many continued calls from parents, I began to share what happened with one of the fathers, who stopped me partway through my retelling to let me know that he had witnessed the entire thing unfold and was shocked by the actions of the principal.

Fired up by the public verbal assault and embarrassing actions taken by the principal, my son wrote a letter of complaint to the school board, admonishing the behavior. His concerns were legitimate and supported by witnesses to the event, as indicated by a supporting letter from Matawan's coach. Worried that a formal complaint against the principal would only create unnecessary tension and further delay in our return to the sidelines, I cautioned against writing the letter. Yes, at this point, I was still very optimistic about that possibility, knowing the truth and holding on to faith in the "leadership" of the school to act with prudence and expedience. My son honored my request, but I should have let him lodge the formal complaint.

Friday, January 21, I took the arduous five mile journey to the Holmdel Police Department for a scheduled interview with two detectives, one of which worked for the prosecutor's office, and my attorney, to be interviewed as part of the investigation into any criminality surrounding the allegation that caused my suspension. *Criminality!* I know the Holmdel Police Department was doing their job, but the thought that a bullshit accusation had elevated to this point only infuriated and confused me further. Why wasn't the administration doing their job? Where was the "leadership" of Holmdel High School, and why were they letting this baseless nonsense drag out so far? Because of these petulant actions by a singular, callous family, catering to the rantings of a spoiled child, I was now sitting in the police department, under investigation, and had to hire an attorney at a significant personal cost, further adding to the stress on my family. The only other occasion where I spent time at a police station was when I was five years old. Somehow, I had been separated from my mother and wandered off. I had made my way down some side streets and crossed over the railroad tracks. A police officer pulled his car over to the side of the road and came out to check on me. Discovering I was lost and separated from my mother, he took me back to the police station. I don't remember much else, but I do remember the police officers being very nice, offering me toys to play with and a chocolate bar to snack on.

Although this was a much different circumstance, the police officers at Holmdel were still very nice, many of them making their way out into the hallway to shake my hand and say hello. In my time with the high school basketball program, I had the opportunity to meet several of the officers as they always staffed our home games or served security at the school. During non-game days, the police officer on duty at the school would often come into the gym to observe our practices. We had many conversations about school, the basketball season, and general topics. As I traversed the halls of the police department, on my way to the interrogation room, a few senior officers popped out of their offices to say hello and provide moral support. Some criminal!

I spent about 45 minutes with the two detectives in general conversation about the accusation against me. The detective for the prosecutor's office was more aggressive in probing and asking questions. I didn't shy away from anything she asked, speaking plainly and truthfully. I had nothing to hide. There was no evidence shown to me, which made me think they didn't have anything worthy of showing, and I still didn't know any specifics about the accusation. When they finished their inquiry, I was asked if I had anything else to add. I thanked them for their time, professionalism during our interview, and service to our community. I encouraged them to see this for what it was: a freshman girl and her parents casting dispersions at me because they think she should be playing basketball at the varsity level, capitalizing on highly charged political times centered on the #metoo movement. The detectives told me they would have their findings sent to the school as soon as possible. Given the time-sensitive nature of the situation, I asked if they could expedite the process as a courtesy.

A report of **non-criminality** was issued to the acting superintendent on Monday, January 24. In an inexplicable display of insensitivity to my staff and a complete lack of urgency for an active sport season, the administration sat on the information for four days. The Board of Education held its monthly meeting on the evening of Wednesday, January 26. The administration and the BOE were recipients of public outcry through calls, e-mails, and letters from parents, players, students not affiliated with basketball, alumni, and even people outside of the Holmdel community, all in support of me and my staff. At the board meeting, in an incredible display of solidarity, parents from the girls' basketball program verbalized their support. The parents in attendance all stood as the mother to one of my senior captains, read a letter on behalf of the group expressing "unwavering support" and noting the "respectful and professional manner" in which their daughters were treated in our program.

> *He has created a culture of positivity whereby the girls sincerely support one another. The team chemistry has been a pleasure to witness.*
>
> *In summary, we unequivocally support Coach Ault and would like to see his name and reputation restored, not only as a coach but as a man of outstanding character within our community.*

The players offered a second letter, read by the mother of one of the alleged "victims." Mother to my other senior captain, this person was banned from games by her daughter a couple of years earlier. The letter presented on behalf of 18 out of the 19 players in the program stated:

> *We would like to express our support for Coach Ault as well as the rest of the coaching staff. Our safety and comfort with Coach Ault were never questioned, as he always treated us respectfully. His love and passion for the game shined through in everything he did for us. He treated us like family and was a person that our team*

looked up to. We hope our undeniable support will help to close this process and restore the reputation of a good man, coach, and mentor.

My wife and daughter attended the meeting out of curiosity. They wanted to see who would attend and how the meeting was conducted. I wept as they shared how the letters were presented to the board and how so many people had shown up in my honor. Much of my emotion was connected to how humbled and appreciative I felt. My basketball family's show of strength and representation restored my hope of getting back to the team. With all the families except one showing devotion to me and my staff, offering tremendous support and a plea for our return, as well as a report of non-criminality from the police, I thought the board had all they needed to close the matter. The board responded curtly, "Thank you for your input."

I waited for a phone call, a text, or some sort of correspondence from the school. Nothing came for me, but on Monday, January 31, a letter arrived for my son. It was the first formal correspondence of any kind received on this matter from the school. The letter was from the acting superintendent indicating that the principal made him aware of an "incident" that occurred on Thursday, January 20, at the Matawan game. The letter was dated January 26 but wasn't received until January 31. In that gap, my son attended another Holmdel game at Rumson-Fair Haven High School, where he was warmly received by parents, players, and opposing coaches, all asking about me and my state of being offering encouragement.

As you know, you have been placed on temporary leave from your assistant coach position pending an investigation of a complaint involving the coaching staff. During the period of your leave, I am directing you to not attend any District athletic or other events or practices, and you are not to have any communication with District students or their parents.

Failure to comply with this directive will constitute insubordination resulting in discipline, up to and possibly including termination of your position.

Until then, the school administration had not issued any formal accusations, directives, or notice of suspension to me or my son. Again, I was the one accused of wrongdoing. My son and my other coaches were all victims of circumstance, and the administration notified none of them. The only correspondence from the administration was the reply to an e-mail of inquiry I initiated 17 days prior. Now, because of a situation initiated by the principal, a public display of disrespect and unprofessionalism toward a staff member, the administration decided to formally document a suspension of my assistant coach that was without cause. Remember, from the principal's words, my son was suspended because he had my last name.

Again, my son had a letter ready to fire back to the administration, admonishing the inaccurate details they received and offering a formal complaint against the principal for his childish antics and lack of professionalism at the Matawan game. We talked for a while. This time, I asked him to think hard before sending the letter. By this point of the season, the JV schedule was complete, but the varsity would have a couple of tune-up games, and the Shore Conference Tournament and the state playoffs were still ahead. Plenty of time for us to get back and capture momentum to continue what started as a magical season. Blinded by my desire to get back to the girls and put this entire sorted mess in the rearview mirror, I still clung to the possibility of returning to the court. My son chose not to send the letter out of respect for me.

Frustrations continued to mount, and the waiting game continued. At this point, it was abundantly clear what was happening to anybody and everybody who had a remote connection to the story. On Friday, February 4, after already being suspended for 24 days, I was finally scheduled to meet with members from the Board of Education and their attorney on Wednesday, February 9.

THIRTY-ONE
FAILURE TO ACT IS OFTEN THE BIGGEST FAILURE OF ALL —COACH JOHN WOODEN

I MET my attorney in the lobby at the Holmdel Board of Education office. After a brief wait, we were escorted to a conference room, where three board members and the board attorney were waiting. We exchanged pleasantries and made formal introductions. The board attorney opened with a review of the fact that I was suspended for an accusation of "inappropriate touching." Still, to this point, 29 days after my suspension began, not one single shred of evidence was presented to me, nor was a formal accusation ever presented to me. As the accused, I was not allowed to see the suggested evidence or discuss the circumstances with administration representatives for over four weeks. According to the school's policies, this should have been deliberated within 10 working days. While the board representatives tried to defend their process, I outlined their policies for them, emphasizing that this should never have been allowed to drag on for so long.

Under statutes 4150 (Support) and 3150 (Teachers) for discipline against staff:

In the event disciplinary action is contemplated, notice will be given to the employee in ordinary and concise language of the specific acts and omissions upon which the disciplinary action is based; the text of the statute, policy, rule, or regulation that the employee is alleged to have violated; a date when the employee is alleged to have violated; a date when the employee may be heard and the administrator who will hear the matter, and the penalty that may be imposed.

That policy was not followed, and at no point was any of the above executed. The attorney tried to tell me the paragraph referred to the policy application to students. I offered him chapter and verse for "support" and "teachers."

I then questioned them about why letters to the board from all the families and players, except one, were dismissed. When I asked why, without any attempt at internal investigation and review as stipulated in their own by-laws, this was turned over to the police, furthering the anguish and pain for me, my family, and my basketball family. The attorney offered that complaints of this nature automatically get submitted to the police. With that dismissive answer, I offered a reading from statute 3281 of the Holmdel Board of Education by-laws as it pertains to Inappropriate Staff Conduct:

The Assistant Superintendent for Curriculum and Instruction will investigate all reports with a final report to the Superintendent of schools. The Assistant Superintendent for Curriculum and Instruction may, at any time after receiving a report, take such appropriate action as necessary and as provided by law. This may include but is not limited to, notifying law enforcement.

I pointed out the fact that the position of Assistant Superintendent for Curriculum and Instruction was vacant and asked who was responsible for the process and execution of disciplinary actions. I stressed the word "may" and argued that nothing was mandating the pass-the-buck actions taken by the board. Even after the police came back with a declaration of non-criminality, the board simply failed to act, dragging out a process that could have been resolved in a day because they lacked the testicular fortitude to tell a single family out of 19 families in the basketball program that their claim was unsubstantiated and unsupported. My points were countered with a weak effort at applying the broader umbrella of sexual harassment, another leadership paralytic in what had become a culture of "me too." Just the mere twisted implication of some vague wrongdoing was enough to hang an innocent man.

I shared statute 5751 of their by-laws, centered on sexual harassment:

> Hostile environment sexual harassment is sexually harassing conduct (which can include unwelcomed sexual advances, requests for sexual favors, or other favors, or other verbal, nonverbal, or physical conduct of a sexual nature) by an employee, by another pupil, or by a third party that is sufficiently severe, persistent, or pervasive to limit a pupil's ability to participate in or benefit from an educational program or activity, or to create a hostile or abusive educational environment.
>
> Nonsexual touching or other nonsexual conduct does not constitute sexual harassment.

I could tell that I wasn't making friends with the members of the board and their attorney. There wasn't any shouting or angry retort from me, just a calm rebuke on the lack of execution of the process, spelled out thoroughly in the district by-laws created to guide their collective actions. Statute 4281 addressed inappropriate staff conduct, outlining the procedures and details of a "Prompt, thorough, and impartial investigation," further stating that, "The investigation will be completed no more than 10 working days" after receipt of the report. Here we were 29 days after the initial accusation, 17 days after the police had issued a declaration of non-criminality, and this was the first time the board engaged me. The same statute went on to say, "The preliminary investigation report indicating inappropriate conduct did not exist will be in writing and will be provided to the staff members and to the parents if requested."

A representative from the board, in what appeared to be an attempt at a "gotcha" moment, asked if I would like to see the evidence. This would be the first time details were revealed to me, and I was very curious to see what actions I took in the RBC game, as the principal described as the root of my suspension. I had scoured that game and came up with nothing harassing, sexual in nature, or inappropriate in any way. I was eager to see what was supporting the suspension and subsequent punishment of a longstanding high school coach with an impeccable reputation. Three icons for clips and images on the big screen represent the so-called evidence. With an air of confidence, the first video was played. To my surprise, it was a very brief clip, not from the RBC game as indicated by the principal in his phone call notice of my suspension, but from a scrimmage against Manasquan played five weeks earlier. The only people with access to this film were my staff, the principal, the principal's wife (coach of Manasquan), and the accusing father I had given access to help integrate their family into my program. The clip showed one of my senior captains coming out of the game after a substitution, being greeted by me with a high five and a pat on the back. After watching a five-second clip showing a congratulatory exchange between coach and player, I looked back to the board members, who all seemed to have a look of admonishment. "Can you explain that?"

I chuckled and replied with, "What do you need me to explain? I am obviously congratulating the player for a job well done. I don't see anything worthy of the accusation and my suspension. What else do you have?"

The second icon was clicked, which was a replay of the same moment, which I quickly pointed out to them. Embarrassed by the realization that they had two identical clips, which indicated to me that the board didn't really pay attention to what was presented, they quickly moved on to the third, which wasn't a clip but a still taken from a video showing another moment in the same scrimmage where I am going to pat the player on the back. The still is conveniently frozen at a fraction of the second where it looks like my hand was either making contact or about to contact the butt of my sophomore sensation. I was leaning awkwardly because I had a medical boot on my right foot due to a recent ankle surgery. Again, I felt a sense of vindication from the board as they looked as though they had presented me with the proverbial smoking gun.

That was it! The video clip and a still image were all the board had after 29 days of anguish, frustration, embarrassment, agony, and suffering. Those grainy clips represented the mountain of compelling evidence that was too difficult for the school administration to litigate and enough to launch a police investigation, which resulted in a finding of non-criminality. After having my team stolen from me, a rising program hijacked, my coaching staff cast away like yesterday's garbage. My integrity and reputation were questioned; the administration hung their hat on this despite the numerous e-mails and letters written speaking of my character, the calls made endorsing me, and the letters presented to the board in their January meeting. This is why I had to take time out of work to be interviewed by the police and more time to sit in front of these stalwarts of justice and keepers of failed policies as they decided my fate. My family and I had to suffer through the humiliation of the leaks and speculation all centered around a lie. I was livid.

"How can you defend that?" I was asked. It took a lot to maintain my composure. "Defend what? You have provided me with two video clips of the same sequence and a still image from a video taken out of context as evidence, from a camera angle directly behind that would imply the same whether my hand was three feet away, three inches away, or touching the player's butt. The two clips involved two different players, neither of whom accused me of any wrongdoing. They and their parents have been very outspoken supporters of me and my entire coaching staff. There is nothing to defend."

I later reviewed the entire video sequence around the still shot presented to me in the meeting. If the board members, the principal, the AD, or anyone remotely involved had taken two minutes to watch the entire sequence, it would have been obvious that I was encouraging a player, working on building her confidence, and helping her recognize her true potential. That is a coach's job and something I worked on daily with my players for the 33 years I coached. This was the hard-core evidence presented to the board and ultimately used to derail our season and cripple what had been a very good relationship between coach and administration. If time was properly spent watching the events unfold, the next frame clearly showed that I did not brush the player's bottom as accused, but her lower back, as demonstrated by the ruffled shirt above the waistline as the player was walking away from me.

Even if my actions shown in the video were considered borderline or a point of concern for anybody associated with the team and our extended basketball family, why not set up an opportunity for a dialogue to help mitigate the concerns and determine positive steps to move forward? As I did with the police, I encouraged the board members to recognize the true intent of the accusation. To identify it for the cowardly attempt it was, using other innocent children as weapons against me without the permission or support of their parents. This was a disgruntled player who didn't want to put in the time or effort to earn their stripes, being endorsed by mommy and daddy, who found it easier to blame somebody else rather than hold their daughter and themselves to account. I shared my frustration as leadership continued to ignore the facts and the expressed desires of the basketball community and placate the bad actors, lacking the ability to discern right from wrong.

My attorney, sensing my disgust and rising anger, jumped in to offer that my "indignance" stemmed from the frustrations around the false accusations and the pain affiliated with this long, drawn-out process. He pushed for a public apology letter and an immediate reinstatement of me and my coaching staff. After a few more exchanges, the board thanked us for our time and told us they would notify me of their decision through my attorney.

Ten days later, on February 19, 2022, I received a call from my attorney that he received a letter from the board indicating that they were going to uphold my suspension for the remainder of the season, pay me and my son our full coaching stipends, and allow me to apply for the position next year after completing some undescribed sensitivity training. In essence, I was done as the coach of Holmdel High School. The payment of my stipend and the "grace" afforded to let me apply again for the position were all attempts to cover the collective asses of the administration, attempting to shelter themselves from any future litigation.

THIRTY-TWO
NOT CLOWNING AROUND

WITH THE NEWS of the letter and its misguided results, I decided I no longer needed to be sidelined by the "authority" of the administration at Holmdel. The lack of competence that rippled through the leaders, from the principal to the Board of Education, drove me to the realization that I would never return to Holmdel basketball. I would have done anything to coach my girls again, but why would I continue to be a faithful supporter of an administration that didn't reciprocate that loyalty and was disinterested in fairness and justice in the execution of their duties? They had no power over me and my decisions, nor did they deserve my commitment and allegiance. There was no way I was going to "bend the knee" to an organization that lacked leadership and common sense.

The quarterfinals of the Shore Conference Tournament were played that night at Middletown South High School. Four games with the best teams left standing in the annual event, one of which was a rematch of Manasquan and my girls from Holmdel, a showcase of great talent. All four matchups were intriguing, but none more enticing than the opportunity to finally get to see my girls in person.

Pop, my son, and I decided to spend some time together, taking in all the quarterfinal games. I enjoyed being immersed in the high school girls' basketball atmosphere again. Throughout the event, I ran into many people offering a public display of support and saying how glad they were to see me back in the gym. Reporters, podcasters, coaches and players from other teams, referees, athletic directors, players and parents from Holmdel, and my extended basketball family from St. John Vianney, all with positive greetings and embraces of friendship.

After we found our seats opposite the team benches and scorer's table, we settled in for a great night of basketball. I sat a row up from Pop and my son to provide some space in what was going to be a packed house and to allow myself the ability to stretch my legs out on occasion. The parade of people saying hello and offering support continued intermittently throughout the night. One interaction was rather memorable. At a lull in the early games, the movement of one man in the gym caught my eye. He wasn't hard to spot as he stood about 6' 9", a big man with many tattoos, moving with confidence. I first noticed him in the corner of the gym, diagonally opposite where we were sitting. He walked in front of the home bench, then the press table, then the visitor's bench, and along the baseline behind the basket. I did not recognize the man, but for some reason, I was locked in on his movement. As he made his way to the sideline bleachers, it dawned on me that he was headed in my direction, which was confirmed as he started ascending the bleachers directly toward me, not using the steps but walking through the gaps between people in attendance. As he drew near, I realized just how big he really was, and I became curious as to the intent of his lap around the gym. Only a few feet away at this point, he stretched his arm out and offered a hand for introduction. As I shook his hand, he said very plainly, "I just wanted to come over to say hello and say that everybody knows what you are going through is bullshit." While I thanked him for his words, I was still trying to place him. He then said, "Thank you for talking to my daughter earlier in the year about the Naval Academy. Your willingness to do that says a lot about your character." He was the father of the senior player from Toms River North, to whom I had offered my assistance after our game earlier in the season. The experience went from harrowing as I contemplated the size of this man to a wonderful acknowledgment of unity and support.

During a break in the action before the Holmdel game, I ventured out to find the bathroom and to grab some concessions for the gang. My timing was great as I briefly engaged with two of my seniors and one of my freshman players, who were returning to the gym. Their faces lit up as this was the first time I had seen them since January 12. I did not want to distract them, so I offered a high five and encouraged them to beat Manasquan. I returned to my spot in the bleachers with some drinks and snacks, where the three of us waited for the beginning of the game.

The girls played an incredible game against Manasquan, with no bigger cheerleaders than the three of us. Momentum was on Holmdel's side early as they went into the locker room with a four-point lead at halftime. Throughout the first half, I got texts from excited parents sitting across the gym, proud of how their daughters were playing. I was equally proud, not only of their play but their resilience throughout this entire ordeal. They were clearly staying connected to the vine and relying on each other to pull through. My hope for them is that they would continue that way in the second half and secure the victory. We had been there several times before, playing well for long stretches, working to put together 32 minutes of Hornet basketball. This was a Shore Conference Tournament quarter-final game against Manasquan. They weren't going to shrivel at the presence of a halftime deficit. A historic coach, a strong staff of assistants, and a winning program would come out ready for battle.

The third quarter was a monumental struggle, ending with Holmdel expanding their lead to five. Everybody was playing well, but the bench was being used minimally, if at all. Young players who I had been working hard to develop seemed to be buried on the bench, emerging skills and talents wasting, while the six players utilized had to scratch and claw with every ounce of energy they had. I began to wonder how fatigue would impact play and decision-making. The situation was complicated because my sophomore sensation was experiencing foul trouble, forcing her to the bench and changing the game's dynamic. Without her on the floor, Manasquan's experience and defensive pressure proved enough to help them to a 17-9 fourth-quarter performance and pull out a 62-59 win. Regardless of the outcome, I was so proud of the girls and the way they played. I missed the opportunity to be in battle with them, urging them to dig deeper and realize their potential together.

Being in the gym that night, watching the quarterfinals, and cheering my girls on in a hotly contested game gave me great relief, knowing that my ordeal was over. It didn't end the way I wanted it to or should have ended, but it was over. I could now begin the healing process.

Heading home, with my son driving, I sent out a text to the principal of Holmdel and his wife, the opposing coaches in the game we just watched, to offer them sincere congratulations on a great game. I told them they both had much to be proud of in how the girls played. No reply from the principal, which didn't surprise me. I did get a return text from his wife, "Don't ever contact me again!"

I was stunned by the hateful reaction. We had been friendly and respectful opponents for years. I wondered what could have irritated her so greatly that she would respond with such venom. Later that evening, I received a call from the mother of one of my senior captains, the same woman who read the letter on behalf of the players at the board meeting. She was angry and asked me why my son would post something mean-spirited about the principal, who, in her eyes, had stepped in to help keep things as "normal" as possible for the girls during my absence. I had no idea what she was referring to, but I assured her I would look into the matter. As soon as I hung up from one call, I received another from the coach at Rumson-Fair Haven, a good man who I consider a friend. He was calling me to give me a heads-up that several people were upset about "the shirt." Still clueless about what was happening, I asked him what he was talking about. He then went on to tell me about a shirt that my son was wearing during the Holmdel game, depicting the principal's face as that of a clown. Again, I was unaware of any such shirt or action my son took. Offering my appreciation for bringing this to my attention, I ended the call and went to find my son.

Later that evening, I checked in with my son and asked him to tell me about what was posted on the internet and about the shirt. He had a wry smile as he explained what had happened. In his frustration with the entire situation, and as a protest statement against the administration, which he aptly equated to a circus, he made a replica of the Barstool clown-style t-shirt, representing the commissioner of the NFL as a clown, substituting the face of the principal for the face of the commissioner. During the game against Manasquan, he decided to remove his sweatshirt and reveal the T-shirt directly across from the team benches while seated in front of me. I listened as he described his rationale and defended his actions, but he could see the anguish on my face. I told him to immediately remove the post and burn the fucking shirt.

Any steps towards my healing process were paused at that moment. I now understood the fiery text received from the Manasquan coach earlier in the evening. I had no defense to offer for my son's actions, but they weren't mine to defend. I certainly did not condone or agree with the protest and let my son know about it. While I appreciated his anger and frustration, I felt it was done in poor taste and didn't consider how his statement would affect others, reminding him that despite any feelings about the principal and the board, they all had loved ones and supporters of their own.

After our discussion, I went to my room to reflect in private. While I was looking for an opportunity to heal, forgive, and move on, I wasn't giving much thought to my son's journey through all of this. After all, he was a good, young, passionate coach who had also invested a lot of time into the Holmdel program. Not only were his emotions connected to watching what I was going through during the entire suspension process, but he was directly impacted just for having my last name. He was unfairly suspended along with me, then verbally assaulted by the man who was supposed to be leading us through the circumstances and ensuring the well-being of our girls while the suspension got sorted out. This was the man who told my son to "shut the fuck up and leave the gym" at Matawan, then had the balls to cry foul to the Superintendent, filing a formal complaint to cover his ass and make himself out to be the offended. Meanwhile, I was coaching my son to be the better man and not file his complaint concerning the principal's actions for fear of aggravating our situation. While I began to understand his angst, I still didn't agree with his actions.

The next morning, I called the principal's cell phone. He didn't answer. I didn't expect him to pick up my call even without the shirt. When the beep came at the end of his voicemail response, I left him a brief message of apology for my son's actions the night before, letting him know that I was unaware of the shirt and that I didn't agree with the decision to make a public display of it. I summed the entire thing up as an inappropriate response to countless frustrations around this entire circumstance.

THIRTY-THREE
MEET THE PRESS

HOLMDEL'S BASKETBALL season ended on March 4 in the state playoff semi-final round for Central Jersey, Group 2. Another hotly contested game against Manasquan, this time losing by four points. I couldn't help but feel that things would have been different in those games had I still been at the helm. Nonetheless, the season was over, and I was hopeful about accelerating the closing of this chapter in my life. Closure doesn't always come easy, especially with open wounds and items left open.

First on my list was formally responding to the Board of Education and their decisions around honoring my suspension. I wrote an eight page letter to the newly appointed Superintendent for Holmdel schools and the rest of the board, outlining the administration's failures throughout this process. Many of those sentiments have been shared in this book. I used the still clip that they shared with me as evidence, then began to outline the importance of human touch in sports, as mentioned in the previous chapter. I explained that, "Touch between coaches and players in sports is quite common, and a meaningful tool of expression to show togetherness, compassion, understanding, and encouragement. Touch between players and coach, contact between coaches, and even between opposing players and coaches are all positive expressions of sportsmanship and togetherness within a greater community," supported by images of me hugging the male assistant coaches after that fateful scrimmage with Manasquan, the female head coach (principal's wife), and receiving a big bear hug from the daughter of one assistant, whose older sister I had coached in AAU.

I continued by pointing out that these actions were not unique to me but are tactics used by most coaches in all sports to maintain that connection and to foster a mutual understanding of togetherness. I showed images of the coaches that replaced my staff hugging players, patting them on the shoulder, exchanging high fives, and even one showing the head coach (principal) with his hand on the lower back of a player just above the waistline, as he leaned in to talk to her. I offered my feeling that, "There is nothing wrong with any of the images shown above. The wrong is found in the way the high school administration and BOE cowered from the effort to uncover the truth and protect the basic principles of innocence, making absolutely no effort to support the basketball coaching staff. A paralyzed administration enabled the woeful actions of a misguided child."

The next section of the letter read:

> *Unfortunately, this is the way of the world today. This entire fiasco could have been resolved in less than 40 minutes with effective leadership and a focused effort toward equal protection. Instead, the coaching staff was treated like a disposable entity. No formal procedures were followed or documented. I was told in a phone conversation that I was suspended but never given any details or descriptions of what that entailed.*

Furthermore, my assistant coach was also suspended for the grand offense of "having the same last name." At the beginning of the season, the volunteer coach brought on my staff, a former St. John Vianney standout, TOC champion, and D1 player, was completely discarded and ignored. A senior volunteer and personal consultant who supported our program, devoting his personal time to the girls and our extended basketball family, was also treated poorly. All of the coaches were horribly disrespected and were not afforded simple professional courtesies . . .

This entire process, or lack thereof, was a shameful display of a dysfunctional, leaderless organization. A board that can be so easily manipulated into shunning a very loyal coaching staff due to an abusive interpretation of HIB laws and a cancel culture mentality expressed by one bitter family that left Holmdel once, and now appears to be on their way out again. Something that, under the guidance of constructive, accountable leadership, could have been resolved in a day, affording a harmonious path to move forward. Instead, this mess dragged on for a torturous 40 days, with the rightful coaching staff on the sidelines and the accuser getting to continue her season like nothing happened, playing at the JV level . . .

. . . I enjoyed working with my Holmdel girls, coaching them through the various aspects of playing basketball, the nuances of teamwork —sacrificing singular mentality for something greater than self, and developing an extended family within the greater Holmdel community.

After sharing all my thoughts and feelings around their collective ineptitude, I closed with the following:

More immediately, I implore you to review the missteps throughout this entire process. This was not about the board protecting a student. This was not about the board protecting a staff member. Any effort that was made by the board was only about protecting the board. Not a posture often desired from people in a position of leadership or elected officials. Your teachers, coaches, and all staff members deserve protection and due process. Basic legal concepts of innocence until proven guilty should not be dismissed out of hand. Students and parents should not be allowed to weaponize laws intended to ensure an even playing field, to ensure the safety and protection for those who truly need it. Students need to be held accountable as much as they need to be protected. Part of that protection is helping them understand that their words and actions have consequences. Part of our job as educators and coaches is to prepare young people for the next level of education or athletics, to position them for the best chance to be successful in their life ambitions. Instead, they are emboldened by feckless leadership and the lack of ownership as displayed by the Holmdel BOE. Injurious behavior is enabled by a governing body afraid to lead. Please look back at this mishandled situation and poorly executed suspension and learn from it. If you choose not to, you choose to fail twice. No coach or teacher should ever have to go through this experience again.

I sent this letter to the Board of Education, knowing it was an exercise in futility. There was a new Superintendent with a strong background, but I'm sure he had his hands full with all the gaps in the administration. Once I sent that letter out and the stipend checks had been cashed, I felt it was time to have a conversation with the sports reporter who had reached out to me on the first day of my suspension. I wanted to set the record straight and expose the farse promoted by the administration at Holmdel High School.

We met for lunch to discuss what had transpired over the last several months. Before we talked, I gave him a copy of my letter to the board for his review. The one stipulation was that he could not use or reference any of the images shown, as I wanted to protect the players that were shown. We ordered our lunches, and then he went to work reading through my letter. Once he finished and was afforded the opportunity to process all the details, we spent the rest of our time together in an extensive question-and-answer session. There were no restrictions placed on questions and plenty of follow-up opportunities. With a writing pad full of notes, the reporter went to work writing an article that was posted on NJ.com on May 2, 2022.

The response was amazing, with people from all walks of life offering support through all forms of media. In addition to the article, I was asked to participate in a local podcast with two gentlemen who committed a lot of time to covering girls' basketball, often interviewing players and coaches to share their stories. The views on that podcast more than doubled previous programs. People wanted to hear the truth, and I was compelled to provide it. While I struggled with the emotions and frustrations around the suspension, I was careful to maintain dignity and respect for everyone involved.

The last interaction I had with the Holmdel Board of Education was later in the year, on college signing day when a former player invited Pop to witness her special day as she prepared to commit to Johnson & Wales for volleyball. The suspension and all the unfortunate circumstances were in the rearview mirror. The young lady and her family invited Pop as their friend. I was so happy for him to receive a player's acknowledgment of his positive impact on her life. He got dressed in his Sunday best and went to Holmdel High School. The security guard at the front door let him in, and he was promptly greeted with joyful hugs by several of the basketball players in attendance. Shortly after, the principal approached him with a demand that he leave the premises. Telling Pop he "should know better than to be here" and that he had to leave. Another classless act perpetrated by failing leadership.

The call from Pop came as I was on the Garden State Parkway, working my way home from a business trip. I couldn't believe my ears, and my heart thumped with anger as he detailed the pettiness of the principal's actions. As soon as I got home, I wrote an e-mail to the Superintendent about the situation, asking how a person in a position of authority could continue behaving in such an unprofessional manner. Pop, a 72-year-old gentleman who was never accused of anything yet treated so unfairly by the school, was invited by the player and her family to participate in a very special moment. Without discretion, offering no dignity whatsoever, the principal of the school executed another horrid public display. I reminded the Superintendent that I was the person suspended and that these disgraceful, dictatorial acts will not continue to be tolerated. I demanded an apology be issued to Pop. The Superintendent acknowledged that Pop should have been allowed to attend and asked me for Pop's phone number so he could talk to him and offer an apology. With new leadership in the Superintendent position, I was hopeful that some sense of honor in action was restored to the school district. Pop never received a phone call.

THIRTY-FOUR
TIME HEALS ALL WOUNDS

IN ALL TRANSPARENCY, it took the better part of two years for me to move beyond the suffering of my suspension. I couldn't get past the reckless, selfish nature with which the accusing family acted. Every day, sometimes multiple times, I would have a period of reminiscing on the events of my suspension. Inevitably, those thoughts would be followed by guilt and regret for not being there for what was supposed to be our year. I couldn't shake thoughts of not being present for the little things that come with the relationships with players, seeing those moments of personal growth and the positive impacts on the team dynamic. I was unable to participate in senior day, missing the opportunity to honor the six seniors who had been a large part of our growth, especially my two college-bound seniors who spent all four years playing varsity. I wasn't going to have the experience of watching my younger players mature and develop as they made their way through our program. Oddly enough, I regretted the missed opportunity to help the young lady who issued the complaint. She could have been a very good player, an important cog in the wheel for the continued success of a dynamic program.

I had been offered a couple of coaching positions in high school, other youth programs, and an assistant coach position at a college in New Jersey. One of the high school jobs would have had me matched up with my accuser again, as an assistant to a young coach I had worked with at St. John Vianney. I knew I could forgive and forget, but I didn't want to bring the strain of unwanted drama to her program. The college job would have been a lot of fun and something that drew my interest, but I couldn't commit the time required to be an effective coaching staff member. The head coach told me to come when I can, but that isn't my style. Making practices would have been manageable, but the game schedule, along with travel through the conference, would have been a stretch given the demands of my job and the importance of a quality family life.

I went from being an absolute basketball junkie to fulfilling the role of a casual fan. Of course, my focus was still on the Holmdel girls, hoping for the continued development and success of the program I left behind. The roster was depleted by several girls who quit based on the experience from the year of my suspension. However, my core varsity girls were still there, and I wanted to see how they were progressing. I sent periodic texts to my girls in college, checking in on their progress in school and on the court. The opportunity sometimes presented itself through business travel to visit a couple of my former players in their respective college towns. I enjoyed taking them out to lunch and catching up on their experiences. With basketball very much in my heart, I would go to the occasional high school game of interest, including away games for Holmdel. If I couldn't make games, I always checked the box scores of my former players, including the one who caused all the trouble.

She had transferred to a new school to start her sophomore year. As the season progressed, I kept pace with low minutes and an average of about two to three points per game. The same was true for her junior year, where she started the year at the same school but then transferred partway through the season to another school, where the same trend continued. By the end of her junior year in high school, she had enrolled in or attended four different high schools. Watching this unfold only made me more frustrated. If her parents had stayed out of the way and allowed their daughter to mature and develop at her pace, she would have had a more pleasant high school experience. The program we had in place at Holmdel would have afforded her the opportunity to enhance and improve her skill sets, putting her in a position to enjoy much more success. She would have elevated to varsity in her sophomore year and would have been an integral part of the team by her junior year. Knowing what she was capable of, she could have easily been the type of player who averages 10 or more points and grabs 10 rebounds a game. To this day, I cannot reconcile how badly her parents ruined the experience for her and so many others. Occasionally, I would see her on the AAU courts, still burying herself in the left corner waiting for the ball to come to her.

I never saw the parents again, but I often thought about how that interaction would go. If that were to occur, I hope that the better angels of my nature would allow me to forgive them for their transgressions. The struggle in my heart is that I am not sure they feel they did anything wrong, and given the same circumstances, they would be as heartless and cruel as ever. An indication of their sinister nature is when the father saw my son at an AAU event. My son had just had shoulder surgery, so his arm was in a sling. The father took that as his opportunity to blurt out that he was glad somebody finally did what he should have done a long time ago. Big man! There is no explaining the idiocy of some people.

One of the benefits of not coaching was the focus of those efforts and energies on other parts of my life. I knew how much time I devoted to basketball over the years, but never gave much thought to the imbalance in my life. When I coached my children through various stages of their basketball experiences, I always appreciated the father/child time and watching them develop differently than at home. I always enjoyed having unique connections with my players, wonderful relationships that are still honored today. The relationships created when they were players have forged bonds that have survived the years, even decades.

Signs of those bonds have played out in real time over the years. The gentleman I coached with at the Naval Academy Prep School recently celebrated his 60th birthday. We were able to reunite after not having seen each other for a while. One of the players from our first team at NAPS could attend the birthday celebration, rounding out the reunion. The player and I always shared a unique connection. Like so many things in life, time and distance got in the way of staying connected, but we picked up as if we had just seen each other the day before. A few laughs, some great memories, and a few cold ones left me smiling ear to ear on the four hour road trip home.

Another wonderful stroll down memory lane came when my son had arranged a gathering of former players from the Holy Family undefeated teams of 1997-98 and 2000-2001. My son and I co-host a sports podcast, *Outside the Coaches Box*, that he was inspired to create. He had worked behind the scenes to schedule a remote podcast, surprising me with about 10 players from those two teams. Of course, the remote location was inside a basketball gym. It was quite the production, sitting there with those young men, some pushing late 30s or early 40s, listening to them share stories of when they were playing for me in seventh and eighth grade. To learn of the impact and positive influence my assistant coach and I were able to have on them during the early stage of their lives, with some of those lessons carrying through their adulthood, helping shape and mold them, was an extremely positive experience for me. The timing couldn't have been better as I was finally in a position mentally and spiritually to let go of basketball.

ABOUT THE AUTHOR

Darren Ault coached various levels of basketball for 33 years, from township ball to college prep, with the majority of that time as a head coach for high school girls varsity in the New Jersey Shore Conference. What started off as a hobby quickly developed into a love for coaching centered on helping young men and women realize the potential within, understand the power of teamwork, and learn to not only think the game, but to play the game with passion.

This passion began for Darren when, as a young Ensign in the Navy, he was assigned to duty at the Naval Academy Preparatory School (NAPS) in Newport, Rhode Island. As a graduate from the United States Naval Academy, Darren spent 4 years of service at NAPS as an English instructor and as the assistant coach for the men's basketball program. Grounded in the Naval Academy's mission "To develop Midshipmen morally, mentally and physically and to imbue them with the highest ideals of duty, honor and loyalty," Darren set about bringing those principals to every level coached. Through 22 years of coaching girls high school basketball in New Jersey, Darren earned a reputation for developing winning programs and building enduring relationships with players, parents, and coaches throughout the state.

Darren has been married to his lovely wife, Anne, for 35 years. They have three wonderful adult children – Victoria, Nicholas, and Caitlin. Darren was fortunate to have the pleasure of not only being their father, but of having the opportunity to coach all three in the great game of basketball.